D0760892

MADE TO MEASURE

MADE TO
MEASURE

A HISTORY OF LAND SURVEYING IN BRITISH COLUMBIA

KATHERINE GORDON

sononis
PRESS

WINLAW, BRITISH COLUMBIA

Copyright © 2006 by Katherine Gordon

Library and Archives Canada Cataloguing in Publication
Gordon, Katherine, 1963-
    Made to measure : a history of land surveying in British
Columbia / Katherine Gordon.

Includes bibliographical references and index.

ISBN 1-55039-153-4

1. Surveying—British Columbia—History. 2. Surveyors—British
Columbia—Biography. 3. British Columbia—Surveys—History. I.
Title.

TA523.B7G67 2006   526.9'09711   C2006-900687-3

Sono Nis Press most gratefully acknowledges the support for our
publishing program provided by the Government of Canada through
the Book Publishing Industry Development Program (BPIDP), the
Canada Council for the Arts, and the British Columbia Arts Council.

Edited by John Eerkes-Medrano
Copy edited by Dawn Loewen
Cover and interior design by Jim Brennan
Maps by Eric Leinberger

Published by
Sono Nis Press
Box 160
Winlaw, BC V0G 2J0
1-800-370-5228
books@sononis.com
www.sononis.com

Printed and bound in Canada by Friesens Printing.

The Canada Council | Le Conseil des Arts
for the Arts | du Canada

For my sister, Caroline

*Surveyors...forged...out of the wilderness the structure
on which the fabric of development in this Province
has been hung. These are the men by who their loyalty
and perseverance have made British Columbia what
it is today. They have scaled its peaks, forded its rivers,
followed its valleys, tramped its muskegs, and flown its
skies, sometimes in appalling conditions but always with
the determination to conquer its rough terrain and lay
bare its secrets. They have helped fight its wars, guard
its coast, form its laws, and execute them in performing
their surveys. They have set high standards and maintained them in their work.*

Some have been famous; all have done their part.

To be listed among them is a great honour.

**P.J. "Paddy" Brennan, BCLS 396,
March 1979** (THE LINK, VOL. 2, NO. 4)

CONTENTS

ACKNOWLEDGEMENTS

The Guys on the Side of the Road

Only 150 years ago, the land that was to become the future province of British Columbia was almost exclusively occupied by peoples whose society had no need to create maps, townsites, resource tenures, and legal property boundaries. Within the space of a few years that would change forever, as men with instructions from London and Victoria slowly but surely made their way along the trails and up the waterways of the land, observing the stars, setting their compasses, and drawing the lines that would become roads and railways, international and provincial boundaries, towns and cities, farms and homes. By 1905, these land surveyors had joined forces in what was then called the Corporation of Land Surveyors of the Province of British Columbia (shortened in this book to the Corporation of British Columbia Land Surveyors, or more simply, the "Corporation"). In 2005 a sturdy membership of men and women continuing to do more or less the same work as their predecessors, albeit with different tools, voted to shorten the Corporation's name to the Association of British Columbia Land Surveyors. With respect to matters post-January 2005, I refer to the Association.

Despite the importance of their work, to many, the land surveyor remains "that guy by the side of the road," holding up traffic. British Columbia Land Surveyor (BCLS) 425, Gord Thomson, said in 2005: "It was, and I think still is, a secret, a relatively unknown career and, by the general public, so accustomed only to rodmen images on highway construction, misunderstood."

In the spirit of greater understanding of their remarkable contribution to British Columbia's story, I would like to thank all the members, past, present, and future, of both the Corporation and the Association and their unincorporated predecessors. You are, indeed, far more than just the "guys by the side of the road."

The financial support of the Foundation of British Columbia Land Surveyors made it possible to engage the brilliant services of researcher Heather West (see page 373) and to devote most of 2005 to the writing of this book. I will always be grateful to the Foundation and its supporters for the opportunity to tell this remarkable story. I have also been delighted to be able to work with Heather. Her wealth of experience in provincial surveying, combined with her research skills and attention to detail—and both her support and her ability to go with my "creative" flow—have been priceless. My thanks also go to Robert Allen, BCLS 487, whose help in reading and commenting on drafts of the manuscript have been greatly appreciated.

My thanks as always to some other great people: Diane Morriss, a publisher who always goes above and beyond in supporting her authors; John Eerkes-Medrano and Dawn Loewen, both editors who are a pleasure to work with; and Jim Brennan, as thoughtful as always in his design. Janice Henshaw, Loraine Wake, Debbie Robertson, and Rebecca Burton at the Association of British Columbia Land Surveyors in Victoria presented smiling faces, helpful advice, and practical assistance whenever I wandered into their office, as often as not unannounced. Thank you! And last but certainly not least, to family and friends who have given me unqualified love, support, and encouragement, my eternal appreciation.

Gord Thomson, BCLS 425, carving a reference post on a timber berth survey, Upper Stave Lake, 1964. GORD THOMSON

Without land surveyors, there would be no organized land settlement. Land and other real property are an important part of economic wealth in a free society. —*Russell Shortt, BCLS 454*

Without land surveyors, there would be chaos in the determination of property boundaries. Ownership could not be relied upon in the manner that it is relied upon today. You only have to be involved in a dispute settlement of a survey that has hopelessly been surveyed incorrectly and you would see the chaos that reigns without surveyors. Just look at the problems in third world countries where land ownership is not based upon a strong survey fabric. It becomes much more difficult for countries to develop economically without that survey framework.

—*Chuck Salmon, BCLS 535*

Without land surveyors, there would be no widespread prosperity.

—*Rick Hargraves, BCLS 537*

Without land surveyors, there would be no breweries.

—*Peter Thomson, BCLS 472*

Surveyor General Rick Hargraves (right) with Brian Brown, BCLS 623, at the 2005 annual general meeting, which was also the centennial of the incorporation of land surveyors in British Columbia in 1905. Traditions continue to run strong within this group of professionals: Brown had just been elected "Sergeant-at-Arms," with responsibility for assessing and collecting fines from members for such infractions as forgetting to use the word "Association" instead of the now-defunct "Corporation." B. JERRITT

A NOTE ON MEASUREMENTS

A book on land surveying that wasn't full of measurement terminology would be a contradiction in terms. But the sheer number of different types of measurement, and the frequency with which they have changed over the years, can be confusing. In 1890, land was measured in

B. JERRITT

acres; by 1990, it was hectares. Ditto for miles and kilometres. But in my view, attempting to provide metric equivalents in the text adds to the confusion. Accordingly, in this book I have adopted the practice of simply referring to the appropriate measurement for the period or context under discussion rather than cluttering the text with conversions.

For those readers who want to understand the metric or imperial equivalent of any particular land measurement, here is a general guide:

One chain is 66 feet. One foot is about 30 centimetres. One metre is 3¼ feet. One chain is therefore just over 20 metres.

One mile is 1,760 yards, or 5,280 feet. One yard is three feet, or just under one metre. Sixteen hundred metres makes one mile, or 1.6 kilometres.

One acre is 10 square chains. Ten square chains are 43,560 square feet, or 4,047 square metres. That would be, by the way, 0.4 of a hectare. So of course, as you've already no doubt worked out, a hectare is close to 2.5 acres, or about 25 square chains, approximately 108,000 square feet, or exactly 10,000 square metres.

For readers who would like to know more, I somehow feel certain that any land surveyor in the province, retired or otherwise, would be pleased to assist.

Working for the Land

In January 2005, British Columbia land surveyors celebrated their one-hundredth year as a professional association. Having changed the name of what had been the Corporation of Land Surveyors of the Province of British Columbia to the Association of British Columbia Land Surveyors, they admitted Kenneth Schuurman as BCLS 800 to the current practising list of about three hundred registered surveyors. They also admitted Shauna Goertzen as BCLS 798, the third woman to join their ranks. The first were Teresa Myrfield, BCLS 773, and Julia MacRory, BCLS 775, in 1999. The fourth, Shannon Onderwater, was sworn in as BCLS 802 on May 8, 2005.

The total number of qualified provincial land surveyors who have worked in British Columbia to date, since the first official land survey was undertaken in Victoria in 1851, comes to just over one thousand. These mere thousand men—and four women—have been ultimately responsible for all the land surveys and mapping of the province's 95 million hectares. Since before Confederation, their work has been fundamental to the unique manner of settlement of this rough and beautiful child of imperial ambition, different from that of any other province or territory in Canada. Land surveyors from this province have done extraordinary things and seen extraordinary changes occur. Those one thousand people have walked, paddled, ridden, driven through, and flown over British Columbia, measured its mountains, and drawn its boundary lines. The story of their work is awe-inspiring.

It was surveyors who witnessed at first hand the erosion of culture, rights, territory, and well-being of aboriginal people in British Columbia. It is they who have, more recently, been instrumental in re-establishing those territorial rights.

It was a surveyor who found Alexander Mackenzie's famous stone near Bella Coola, inscribed: "From Canada, by Land." But while Mackenzie's name is on every Canadian schoolchild's lips, the surveyor's name is unknown to most.

It was a British Columbia surveyor who led the military team that surveyed the D-Day beaches at Normandy in the Second World War. His work in determining water depth and tidal changes contributed to the element of surprise in the Allied landings that helped win the battle.

British Columbia led the world development of aerial surveying technology and techniques. The first helicopter-supported survey in Canada took place in Chilliwack in 1948, and the helicopter company that supplied the machine is now one of the largest in the world.

In the early 1950s, during the initial surveying and construction phase of the Kitimat–Kemano power project, barrel loads of lampblack and diesel oil were sprayed from a small airplane over the ice on the lake near Kemano. The idea was to break the ice up faster so that much-needed supplies could be brought in by barge. No one thought it a bad idea at the time. A similar technique was used in 1955 to spray DDT over a base camp in the Peace River district. The mosquitoes were no problem that summer.

In 1968, pens were still being dipped into inkwells to draught plans on linen in some government offices. The linen used for plans was always of very good quality and an enormously high thread count. (During the Great Depression, the draughtsmen would take the old plans home for their wives to boil white, then make into fine linen shirts for them to wear.) But if anything at all was spilled on the linen—even moisture from an inadvertent sneeze—years of work could be utterly ruined. A practical joke misfired terribly when the staff of one firm rigged a fake stain on a railway plan that had taken the draughtsman four painstaking years to complete. Before they could stop him, the draughtsman--howling in despair—cut the plan that he supposed was ruined into dozens of tiny pieces.

By 2005, plans would become entirely electronic. That was a challenge for some, but a relief for others. You can't sneeze on an electronic plan.

What exactly is land surveying? In the simplest of technical terms, and as referred to by land surveyors, it is the definition of the *cadastre*: the legal boundary lines that mark each surveyed property from the next. Land surveyors can of course do much more than legal boundary surveying—

Mount Logan
(5959m)
Mount Elias
(5489m)

Alaska Highway · Whitehorse

Klondike

Atlin
Lake

Palmer Lake

CASSIAR

YUKON TERRITORY

Liard
River

Fort
Nelson

ALASKA

COAST

MOUNTAINS

ROCKY

MOUNTAINS

Dease River

Stewart-Cassiar Highway

Stikine River

Alaska Highway

Finlay River

Mesalinka River

Graham River

Alaska Panhandle

M
O
U
N
T
A
I
N
S

Bell-Irving
River

Mount
Bell-Irving

Stewart

Nass River

River

Tweedsmuir-Omineca

Region

Bulkley River

WAC
Benne
Dam

Pi

Parsnip R

Dixon Entrance

Hazelton

Prince Rupert
Metlakatla

Skeena

Grand Trunk Pacific

McLeod Lake

Fort
St. James

Haida Gwaii
(Queen
Charlotte
Islands)

Kitkatla

Kitimat

Tahtsa
Lake

INTERIOR

River

Cumshewa Inlet

Kemano

C
O
A
S
T

Nechako

Prince George

Kenny
Dam

Tweedsmuir
Park

PLATEAU

Quesnel

Ocean
Falls

Dean Channel

Bella
Coola

Cariboo

Williams Lake

Bentinck
Arm

M
O
U
N
T
A
I
N
S

Tiedemann
Glacier

Homathko R

Fraser

River

Bridge

Mt Waddington
(4015m)

Lilloo

Knight Inlet

Bute Inlet

Orford Bay

Duffey Lake

Whistler

BCR

Doug

Zeballos

VANCOUVER
ISLAND

Desolation
Sound

Sechelt

Nootka
Sound

Port
Alberni

Strait of Georgia

Vancouver

PACIFIC   OCEAN

Nanaimo

Long Beach

San Jua
Islands

Victoria

Juan de Fuca Strait

E&N

ALASKA

Dawson
City

YUKON

Whitehorse

CANADA

BRITISH
COLUMBIA

ALBERTA

Fraser R

Columbia R

49th Parallel

PACIFIC
OCEAN

Vancouver

Seattle

Fort Colville

WASHINGTON

Fort Astoria

UNITED STATES

OREGON

IDAHO

mapping, engineering surveys, and measuring competitive sports tracks for the purpose of comparing international speed records, for example. But they swear that their first duty is to the cadastre, above all other considerations—even those of a client who would prefer the property line to be somewhere else.

The cadastre is more important than most people realize. When asked what the world would be like without land surveyors, the response from surveyors is almost always the same: "There would be no orderly settlement." Our property boundaries are what we rely on to raise a mortgage, fend off trespassers, make an income, and feel secure in what we call ownership. Without recognized boundaries, there would be no political and economic stability. Compare the province's relatively stable land ownership system with that of Cambodia, for example, where land surveyors from British Columbia have been training Cambodians to conduct legal property boundary surveys through landmine-infested territory. The finished surveys are now lending economic stability to that devastated country, allowing individual property owners to use their land as collateral for its development and improvements. The chaos, say the survey crews, appears to be slowly dissipating.

Stan Nickel, BCLS 665, describes the role that land surveying plays in our society this way:

> A plumb-bob stone...enabled the construction of pyramids as well as the annual post-flooding reallocation of vast tracts of fertile farmland along the Nile River valley. Two millennia later, modern computerized measuring devices [also] enable incredible construction projects.
>
> [But] in that time, considerable human conflict has occurred due to our passion for land...History teaches us about the negative consequences which have evolved from such feelings. Part of the solution to the problems...is found in the development of an acceptable system of rights to land...[That's] called land surveying. Understanding the history of land surveying is to recognize a portion of the solution to problems which otherwise hinder peaceful human co-existence.

Surveying, of course, isn't a matter of simply looking through an instrument and writing down measurements. Land surveyors have always had to be physically fit and capable, have had to be mountaineers, diplomats, expedition managers, cultural ambassadors, technicians, astronomers, mechanics, teachers, archaeologists, navigators, and lawyers. It is hard to think of other professions requiring proficiency in such a broad range of disciplines. It is unsurprising that among their numbers have been many lieutenant-governors, mayors and politicians at all levels, teachers and historians, engineers and entrepreneurs.

In the early years of the province, without the benefit of alpine experience or sophisticated climbing equipment, let alone helicopters, surveyors had to carry their heavy equipment up peaks thousands of metres high, tolerate freezing cold and extreme heat, paddle up wild rivers and endure thousands of mosquito bites—some so severe that men had to be hospitalized. The season could last several months, without any way to communicate with friends and families, without access to fresh food supplies, with no sense of what was happening in the outside world. More than a few emerged from the bush to find out that a world war was raging, and had been for weeks, even months. Radio communication, when it finally came, was a blessing beyond measure. Using the most basic of tools and equipment, surveyors endured uncomplainingly.

The earliest surveyors were simply carrying out the corporate objectives of the early fur-trading companies and pursuing the political and economic aspirations of London, England: searching for resource potential, locating suitable agricultural land for settlement, placing markers in the ground to fend off the province's ambitious neighbour to the south. With their understanding of geography and topography, surveyors were uniquely placed to be the first European explorers to assess the potential of this new land. For the better part of a century, they were required to write detailed annual reports to government commenting on the country they had explored. Their instructions required them to "make the reports as interesting as possible." In 1936, Surveyor General Frank Green wrote this to his deputy minister, in a bid to obtain better funding for mapping purposes:

Altitude and slope place definite limits to our agricultural areas; geological formations govern the occurrence of the various minerals; watershed areas and the drop therefrom limit power; while the potentialities of our forests are closely bound up with latitude, altitude, slopes, and drainage.

Altitude and slope have a far more important bearing on economic development here than in any other Province of Canada; hence the necessity for contour-lines. With contour maps and a soil examination it can with full confidence be determined whether an area should be reserved for forest, grazing, or other purposes, or whether there is a sufficient area of suitable land to make a successful community possible, and to warrant the consequent provision of roads, schools, etc.

This association with bureaucracy, of course, has its downsides. "I've always thought of surveyors," said a friend when he learned of this book, "as rather a dour and humourless lot. A bit like accountants."

But "dour" and "humourless" are two adjectives impossible to apply to any of the surveyors I met or read about in the course of my research. "Self-deprecating," perhaps; "passionate," definitely; and, without a shadow of a doubt, often wickedly funny. Former surveyor general Gerry Andrews, for instance, liked to relate the story of Douglas MacDougal, an assistant of his during the 1936 field season. Teased by some of the old-timers that his little .22 pistol would not be much help against a grizzly bear, MacDougal retorted that it certainly would be. "If we meet a grizzly," he affirmed straight-faced, "we can shoot ourselves with it." Doug Meredith, BCLS 368, on the other hand, didn't shoot the bear he and his colleagues unintentionally chased up a tree one day in the early 1950s, not far from the Kitimat–Kemano worksite. He climbed up after it on a dare, only to receive a bladder full of bear urine in the face at close range—fifteen metres up and with no possible escape from his acrid dousing.

Despite swearing solemnly in their student articles to maintain a state of respectable sobriety at all times, stories are also legion of festive occasions on which many bottles of the hard stuff featured heavily. Gerry Andrews recalled that a van and driver used to be hired in Victoria

John Elliott, BCLS 7. The date and location are uncertain but likely to be 1909, the year of his marriage, in Vancouver. ELLIOTT CLARKSON COLLECTION

after parties, to take prone gentlemen home. Not knowing which of the slumbering partygoers belonged where, the driver would ask the long-suffering wives at each house to come out and identify which husband they would like him to bring into the house. Even in the heart of the Great Depression, laughter was possible. With a sly dig at the tendency of the Corporation of British Columbia Land Surveyors to form a committee to deal with any situation, John Elliott reported in the 1932 proceedings of the annual general meeting that the "Professional Engineers Contact Committee" was one that worked "on the principle of the fewer meetings it has the more successful it is. On that basis," said Elliott, "we have had a most successful year."

A comprehensive account of every aspect of land surveying in the province's history that included the work of every surveyor and the details of every exploration, every development, every regulation and reorganization of government public works departments, and every plan submitted or townsite created would, of course, not only fill dozens of volumes; it would quickly dull the reader's senses. One book alone could be devoted simply to the instruments and technology developed to survey the kind of terrain that British Columbia boasts. While that might be of interest to a select group, it is hard to imagine the armchair reader of popular history remaining engrossed.

Accordingly, what I have attempted to do instead is bring out the richness of the story in general, to provide a sense of the incredible stories and the vitality of the role that land surveyors in the province have played in its history and development. All the same, the hardest part was deciding what to leave out—for every story in this book, for every taste of the flavour of the history of land surveying in British Columbia, there are easily a thousand more that could be added. There is, however, a bibliography on page 359 that will set readers on their way to a more detailed understanding of any particular aspect that engages their interest. I encourage the reading of the historic government reports and the annual reports of the Corporation over the years: each one alone is a fascinating account of the era in which it was written and an unparalleled window into the early years of the province.

Some of the younger surveyors I met looked puzzled when they were informed that the story of British Columbian land surveyors was being told. They didn't know what all the fuss was about. But the ones who've been around for a while do. Here is their story.

Doug Meredith, BCLS 368, at seventy-five: still enjoying an adventurous life. DOUG MEREDITH

▼ Shauna Goertzen, BCLS 798, received her commission in 2005, only the third woman in the province to do so. SHAUNA GOERTZEN

▲ Frederick Clements, PLS 53, was instructed by Surveyor General F.C. Green in the spring of 1930 to undertake triangulation work around Kootenay Lake. Clements was in the habit of taking many photographs and cataloguing them carefully. On August 11, 1930, this image was taken at Station Meachen looking west toward Station Hall. OFFICE OF THE SURVEYOR GENERAL

▼ Modern technology has gone a long way to help surveyors get where they want to go, and four-wheelers have proved immensely useful. This photo was taken in 2001, in an area north of Fort Nelson that Wayne Brown, BCLS 758, said is known as "Maxhamish." WAYNE BROWN

▲ Tommy Gurr in front of the Bell helicopter used in the 1955 season on the Fort Nelson surveys to bring supplies and men to tower sites. STIRLING KNUDSEN

◀ Men on W.S. Drewry's crew cutting a "tie line" in the snow, 1912 or 1913. It was sometimes necessary—such as in the muskeg country of northern British Columbia, where frozen ground was much easier to navigate—to work in the winter as well. MRS. JOANNE DREWRY

The Traverse of History

Canoes were standard surveyors' transportation for decades, and were sometimes hired, together with guiding services, from the local First Nation. These canoes were employed on the Skeena River circa 1912 by John Elliott, BCLS 7, and Mervyn Hewett, BCLS 66. CHAPMAN LAND SURVEYING

The figure standing in the rain at the side of the highway just outside Victoria, wearing a fluorescent orange vest, is looking through a total station, a sophisticated piece of surveying equipment that is recording data in a tiny but massively capable computer. He is determining the correct location of the road allowance for the city, which has plans to widen the highway. His cellphone rings: can he work on an accident scene reconstruction that needs to be completed before a court case scheduled at the end of the month? He reaches into his briefcase to check his electronic diary. He'll have to fit it in between the subdivision survey for the new golf resort and retirement village, he says to the caller, but he thinks he can manage.

In the midst of the clinging and semi-frozen mud of the muskeg northeast of Fort St. John, several hours' travel from the northern city by four-wheel-drive vehicle, BCLS 798 is wrestling her snowmobile out of a snowbank so she can complete the oil well location that she is working on. She is carrying heavy electronic surveying equipment and several spare batteries. She's also packing a heavy axe, lots of flagging tape, and extra gas. It's a long drive back to Fort St. John for more supplies.

A few hundred kilometres to the west, on a sun-warmed hillside overlooking the Nass Valley, BCLS 727 is enjoying the unexpectedly mild afternoon sunshine while his GPS unit hums silently in the background, collecting data. He and his partner are working on the newly agreed southern boundary of Nisga'a Nation lands under their final land claims agreement with the governments of Canada and British Columbia. Carefully negotiated protocols have been determined as to how the survey must be conducted. But the large black bear that has come in search of the surveyor's salmon sandwich isn't interested in protocols, and the bear spray that BCLS 727 brought with him is in his jacket, on the other side of the clearing. He mutters a few words into his radio headset, and within moments the helicopter that is already en route to collect the two men clears the steep ridge. The bear vanishes, running pell-mell down the hillside to safety.

Surveyors in the twenty-first century are using satellite technology and electronic equipment and working on projects that would have been difficult to conceive of in British Columbia 150 years ago. They are measuring three-dimensional airspace to determine flight paths into and over airports. They are locating sites for cellphone transmitter stations. They are determining the exact spot on centre ice to drop the puck at new hockey stadiums, and the precise camber of a cycling track or length of a swimming pool for international sports competitions.

All the same, they are walking on a path of ancient knowledge and techniques that have been in use for thousands of years, since mankind's earliest efforts to measure the planet and make sense of its surface. The relationships of stars, gravity, time, and space vary only according to their own rules, not to those of mankind. While the tools may have changed, the fundamental concepts and principles of longitude and latitude, meridians and parallels, have therefore remained constant. For millennia, human beings have been studying those things in order to pursue the scientific measurement of land and the best means of demarcating boundaries—whether for commercial gain, the administration of the rule of law and the acquisition of property rights, or the sheer passion for science and love of adventure.

In the dry vocabulary of science, surveying is readily defined in straightforward terms. It is, simply put, the measurement of dimensional relationships on the earth's surface for use in locating property boundaries and mapmaking. The *Columbia Encyclopedia* elaborates:

> [Surveying is the] method of determining accurately points and lines of direction (bearings) on the earth's surface and preparing from them maps or plans. Boundaries, areas, elevations, construction lines, and geographical or artificial features are determined by the measurement of horizontal and vertical distances and angles and by computations based on geometry and trigonometry.

But the use of apparently simple terms to attempt to describe the science of surveying is a risky business, and not only because the factors involved are complex and the mathematical genius required to understand the computations of angles, azimuths, astronomy, and algebra—to name just a few of the matters involved—is not particularly common to ordinary mortals. It is also risky because such simplification may fail to recognize that the measurement of the earth has captured the hearts and minds and imagination of human beings since they first studied the stars. Geodesy—the study of the shape and size of the earth—and the accuracy of surveying measurements are fundamental to social, political, economic, and cultural structures the world over. They have been so through the course of many civilizations, past and present.

These are the fields of study that geodesy and surveying are related to: altimetry, atmospherics, bathymetry, biometrics, cadastration, cartography, chorography, cosmical geology, dynamic geology, geognosy, geography, geology, geomorphology, goniometry, gravimetry, hydrogeology, hypsometry, mensuration, mineralogy, oceanography, paleontology, planimetry, soil mechanics, stratigraphics, thermometry, and topography. It's a litany of scientific disciplines, a veritable poem: measured not in stanzas but in the very way in which human beings define their respective places on the earth.

The answer to the apocryphal question "How long is a piece of string?" is "It depends where it starts and ends." The same is true of a surveyed line. Its measurement on the ground is only as good as its related reference to everything else—and that's not as easy as it might sound. To begin with, the earth isn't flat. In one sense, then, there is no such thing as a straight line over the surface of the planet, only a curved one. Nor is the earth immobile, or its geographic features unchanging, or its atmosphere and temperature constant. All these factors affect the measurement of its surface, but some of them are only relatively recent discoveries in the spectrum of scientific history—the movement of tectonic plates, for example, or the magnetic impact of mountain ranges and the poles. Even sea level, the reference point for altitudinal measurement, has only been defined as a mean point, not an absolute. And, finally, the earth isn't even a perfect sphere. A straight line drawn between the North and South Poles, if that were physically possible, would be shorter than a similar line drawn between two opposite points on the equator.

None of this makes things any easier for surveyors required to measure not only distance but elevation, and to do so in reference to universally accepted constants. On the other hand, working out how to deal with these difficulties has occupied the minds of mathematicians and scientists, especially the Greeks, for a very long time. The ancient Greeks figured out the spherical nature of the earth fairly early on, on the basis that the shadow it cast during a lunar eclipse had a circular edge. Greek sailors supported the theory, noting the apparent "rising" of the land to meet them as they sailed toward port. Furthermore, topography, the study of the physical characteristics of the earth's surface—elevation, slope, and orientation—derives from a Greek word meaning "the writing of places."

In fact the Greeks pretty much scooped the pool on earth measurement at the time. Eratosthenes (unforgettably pronounced "Era Tossed the Knees," according to the instructions of the Geodetic Survey Division of Natural Resources Canada), a mathematician living in Egypt around 240 BC, calculated the circumference of the earth at the equator as 40,234 kilometres by using a couple of sticks placed a considerable distance apart in the sand and measuring the length of their respective shadows. Quite remarkably, given such primitive technology, he was a mere 160 kilometres out—an error of only 0.04 percent. While he was at it, he also measured the tilt of the earth and its size and distance from both the sun and the moon.

Eratosthenes was a busy fellow, but by no means the only one working on these ideas. Well before his time, the Egyptians had mastered the art of accurate surveys. The great pyramid at Giza, for example, built around 2560 BC, is almost perfectly square at its base and oriented accurately to the cardinal points of the compass. The Egyptians also had a more practical application of the science: after each annual flooding of the Nile, surveyors were sent out to re-establish farm boundaries that had been washed away. At around the same time in Babylon, carved boundary stones or markers recording property information were already in use. Even the Bible talks about surveying: in the Book of Numbers, chapter 35, the Lord "spake unto Moses in the plains of Moab by Jordan near Jericho," telling him he had to give the suburbs of the cities to the Levites, measuring "from the wall of the city and outward a thousand cubits round about." Furthermore, instructed the Lord, "Ye shall measure from without the city on the east side two thousand cubits, and on the south side two thousand cubits, and on the west side two thousand cubits, and on the north side two thousand cubits; and the city shall be in the midst: this shall be to them the suburbs of the cities."

Once it was generally accepted that the earth is ellipsoidal in shape, a logical system of reference points was required to determine the location of any point on the planet. Latitude and longitude are the familiar and long-accepted tools of that measurement. Latitude was relatively easy to define—a series of parallel horizontal lines around the earth measured in ever-decreasing size from the central—and largest—circular line around the middle of the earth, the equator. There are ninety degrees of latitude, called parallels, from the equator to each pole. The 49th parallel, for example, familiar to all British Columbians as the international border with the United States of America, is simply the forty-ninth degree of north latitude. The popular television show *North of Sixty* is set above the 60th parallel, which also happens to be the boundary between British Columbia and the Yukon and Northwest Territories.

Longitude, on the other hand, poses a few more problems. Unlike lines of latitude, longitudinal lines, called meridians—all 360 degrees' worth drawn vertically around the globe—curve inevitably to meet each other at the poles, where, figuratively speaking, all 360 degrees are crammed together on the head of a pin. Measuring the length of a meridian for, say, a provincial or international border—Alberta to the east, in British Columbia's case, and Alaska to the west, in the Yukon's case— was therefore never going to be as simple as drawing a straight line on a plan. Even trickier was the level of international co-operation required to determine the starting point for longitude. If the earth is a circle, where is the point of zero degrees? And where does east really meet west? The dilemma was relevant not only to location and mapping, but to time-keeping. Every fifteen degrees of longitude is equivalent to one hour on the globally accepted twenty-four-hour clock. But where does the clock start ticking?

It took a considerable amount of time for world authorities to agree on the point. On older French maps, for example, the line bisecting Paris is always shown as the prime meridian or starting point. But in 1884, the Washington Meridian Conference finally settled on the meridian passing through the Royal Observatory at Greenwich, England, as the point of zero degrees and the base point of Earth time. The British Columbia–Alberta border running through Peace River country on the 120th meridian lies eight hours behind Greenwich Mean Time. The city of Whitehorse, in the Yukon Territory, nearer the 123rd meridian, is nine hours behind.

One hundred and fifty years prior to the decision of the Meridian Conference, a major expedition to the Peruvian Andes was financed by the French Royal Academy of Science. Eratosthenes' theory on the length of the earth's circumference was not then universally accepted, and the objective of the expedition was finally to settle the matter by measuring one degree of meridian and multiplying it by a factor of 360. It is a measurement that could as easily have been done in comfort in France, but Peru was chosen as a preferred location because of its proximity to the equator. The scientific world was in a state of disagreement over what were then controversial theories expounded by Isaac Newton, to the effect that the earth is indeed elliptical: it is shorter than it is wide. The accepted view prior to that time was that the earth was perfectly round. Measuring the degree of meridian at the equator should, the mathematicians thought, settle the debate once and for all.

The expedition was, however, a trip plagued by illness, desertions, ill-fated love affairs, and murder. The terrain was unspeakably difficult to wade through and climb, infested with dangerous wild animals and biting insects, and frequently saturated in dense cloud that rendered sight measurement next to impossible. Led by two stalwarts named Pierre Bouguer and Charles Marie de la Condamine, the French team nevertheless laboured faithfully for nine and a half years, despite all the obstacles thrown in their path. Unfortunately, as fate would have it, their expedition would also be to no purpose. They were nearly finished when they learned that another team working in Scandinavia had beaten them to it, successfully taking measurements that indicated once and for all that Newton was in fact correct. In an astounding tribute to their dedication to duty, however, Bouguer and Condamine completed their survey so as to verify the other team's findings. The Frenchmen finally made their way home in 1745, a decade after they began their epic task.

Surveying isn't just a matter of mathematics, of course. Economics and politics have historically driven the need for surveys, with the science necessarily following in order to do the job with increasing efficiency and accuracy. Surveyors have always therefore needed to know as much about land law and tax rules as they have about trigonometry. This has lent some confusion to their roles from time to time. William the Conqueror's eleventh-century *Domesday Book*, for example, is really just an inventory of tenancies over lands inspected by surveyors for the purpose of tax collection, although it is frequently described as a survey document.

The word *survey* itself is even of debatable origin, with one school of thought contending that it means "overview" or "superintend," probably from the French verb *surveiller* or possibly from *sur*, "over," and *voir*, "to see." But the French word for surveyor is *arpenteur* or *geometre*, both of which are terms of measurement. Regardless of its derivation, however, the term "surveyor" was certainly in use by the sixteenth century. Indeed, it was already an occupation subject to some criticism, fair or otherwise. In an essay on the origins of the profession published in 2002, American land surveyor Wilhelm Schmidt reported that John Dee, the author of the introduction to a 1570 translation of Euclid's *The Elements of Geometry*, wrote of "the great wrong and injurie…committed by untrue measuring." Andro Linklater writes in his 2002 history of American land surveying, *Measuring America*, that whether by reason of laziness or unscrupulous behaviour, inaccuracies were legion. A contemporary report from the late sixteenth century, writes Linklater, was entitled "A discoverie of sundrie errours and faults daily committed by landemeters [surveyors] ignorant of arithmeticke and geometrie to the damage and prejudice of many of her Majestie's subjects." Some twenty years after that, notes Schmidt, John Nordon wrote sonorously in *The Surveyor's Dialogue* that "I have heard much evil of the profession."

It was perhaps unsurprising that surveyors were prone to accusations of error several hundred years ago, given the relative simplicity of the available tools for measurement. This was compounded by the all too common tendency to cut corners to save time and effort—and money.

In the seventeenth century, and until the late nineteenth century, the basic technology used to determine direction was a compass with a telescope attached, and the fundamental measurement technique in use was triangulation. The latter concept permits the calculation of the length of two sides of a theoretical triangle over the ground, when both the length of the third side and the two angles of the unmeasured sides as they converge toward each other are known. For example: if the distance between two trees has already been measured, and the angles between each of them and a third tree has been read with a compass, then the distance from each of the two first trees to the third can be calculated without having to physically measure it.

Once one such triangle of measurement has been notionally drawn over the ground, further triangles can be added to it with great ease: the introduction of triangulation as a technique effectively made mapping a particular area a simple process of deduction. When mathematicians brought the technique to the attention of surveyors in the first half of the sixteenth century, it was seized on with enthusiasm. Prior to that, a surveyor would have to invest significant effort and time in simply walking along the lines between locations in order to measure them.

Edmund Gunter, a British mathematician of the early seventeenth century, helped considerably by providing a scale to assist in calculating the angles of the notional triangles. Logarithm tables setting out all the possible angle computations were developed later in the same century. Then the inestimable Mr. Gunter also invented his famous Gunter's Chain, a measurement system that would continue in use for centuries and that remains in evidence throughout the former British Empire as the length of a cricket pitch, and in British Columbia as the width of most road allowances. One hundred metal links, marked off in groups of ten links by small brass rings, made up one chain that was sixty-six feet in length. Ten square chains equalled an acre.

Mapmaking techniques were equally primitive, although remarkably accurate under the circumstances. Maps of course had been in existence since the beginning of recorded time, but by the sixteenth century they were becoming increasingly sophisticated. In 1538, Flemish cartographer Gerardus Mercator released his first map of the world. By 1540, he had also surveyed and mapped his native Flanders. Inspired by Mercator, Abraham Ortelius published a modern atlas of the world in 1570.

The medium used was handmade paper, but relief printing processes and intaglio printing were available by the fifteenth century. It would, however, take another two centuries for lithography to be invented by the German Aloys Senefelder around 1796, and then, for the first time, printing useful maps in large editions became practical. The invention of a papermaking machine a few years later propelled mapmaking even further into the realm of commercial usefulness.

There was an immediate and logical consequence to the rapid acceleration of geographical knowledge in Europe: emigration. A combination of archaic feudal land administration systems, combined with the knowledge that so much "empty" land existed west of the Atlantic Ocean—apparently for the taking—propelled thousands upon thousands of hopeful dreamers across the ocean in search of a piece of property that they too could finally call their own. Trading companies with large financial ambitions were just ahead of them, paving the way. By the mid-1770s, Spanish explorers had entered the waters of the Pacific Northwest coast of North America. By 1776, British explorer Captain James Cook was sailing up the Oregon coast and north to the Bering Strait, charting the coast as he went. American ships were starting to join the fray when in 1791 the British Admiralty instructed Captain George Vancouver to survey the Pacific coast of North America "from 30°N to 60°N," or from approximately halfway up what is now known as the Baja Peninsula to what would later become the future Yukon Territory's southern border.

Until just a few years previously, despite the pressing need for charts and maps, there had been no accurate means of measuring longitude at sea—no one had worked out how to compensate for the effect of the motion of water on a clock when attempting to fix a point. For more than a century, would-be colonizers like England and Spain had offered large rewards to the inventor who could solve the problem, to no avail. Finally, in 1759, an English carpenter and clockmaker named John Harrison invented a marine chronometer that fit the bill. Harrison's success was taken further by a man named John Arnold, who refined the marine chronometer into a sophisticated piece of equipment capable of measurement under the most difficult of marine conditions. It was equipped with "Arnold No. 176" that Vancouver began his exploratory work in the North

Pacific in the spring of 1792, aboard the HMS *Discovery*, determining the longitude of Vancouver Island as he went. Despite the glaring omission of the Fraser River on his charts—somewhat ironic given the city at its mouth that would later bear his name—Vancouver's maps were nonetheless extraordinarily accurate and detailed.

The following year, North West Company (NWC) employee and ad hoc land surveyor Alexander Mackenzie also reached North America's west coast, but by foot, and equipped with only a compass, a sextant, a primitive chronometer, and a telescope. On a rock on the east side of the entrance to Elcho Harbour, on Dean Channel near present-day Bella Coola, Mackenzie inscribed his famous message: "From Canada, by land." The date was July 22, 1793. But Mackenzie was not the first man to traverse the land that would eventually become the province of British Columbia, nor the first to qualify for the appellation of land surveyor. The original occupants of the land had employed surveying techniques for thousands of years in the establishment of trails, the location of village sites, the building of longhouses, and the construction of bridges. Paper maps were unnecessary in aboriginal societies that did not rely upon them for trade or for survival and that did not administer a system of individual land ownership requiring recorded evidence of title. The systems of title and ownership employed by First Nations in Canada were indeed so vastly different from those of the newcomers in their territory that the conflict and tragedy that arose from attempts to delineate boundaries between the two cultures and their lands would continue to reverberate into the twenty-first century.

By 1802, Mackenzie's epic journey was incorporated into a new edition of a map of North America by the English cartographer Aaron Arrowsmith. Very little was really known or understood yet about the country west of the Rocky Mountains, but the fingers of European exploration were slowly beginning to prise open its secrets. By 1805, the NWC had established Fort St. John on the Peace River, just east of the Rockies. Hudson's Hope was set up at Rocky Mountain Portage, some fifty kilometres farther west. In the same year another NWC employee, Simon Fraser, celebrated crossing the mountains from east to west by naming the region he found New Caledonia and establishing a company post at

McLeod Lake. Far to the north, Fort Nelson sprang up on the Liard River.

The primary purpose of these settlements in the early part of the nineteenth century was to support trading. While the British government encouraged and supported the companies, it did not yet appreciate how swiftly Americans were moving to the northwest coast and seemed in no hurry to send official representatives into the country. Neither the NWC nor its main competitor, the Hudson's Bay Company (HBC), had sovereign aspirations, let alone any desire to take on the responsibility and cost of land ownership when commerce was their chief preoccupation. All the same, the companies needed to know the best trading routes to use and had a vested interest in occupying those routes for their own, preferably exclusive, use. Naturally, then, it was logical to employ men like Mackenzie and Fraser to effectively conduct observational surveys of the land and rivers they were exploring. By 1808, Fraser had reached the mouth of the great river that bears his name. David Thompson, who had started out with the HBC and who had moved over to the NWC in 1796, arrived at the mouth of the Columbia River in 1811.

Thompson laboured over detailed measurements of the lengths of rivers and the heights of mountains he observed, contributing astoundingly accurate information to the burgeoning material available to British cartographers. Unable to use the heavy and bulky marine chronometers available to Vancouver and his ocean-going counterparts, Thompson resorted to the use of a basic watch combined with astronomical observations to determine longitude. His methods were reliable: he painstakingly and repeatedly observed lunar eclipses of Jupiter's moons, then compared the time difference between observations at his location and at Greenwich. If Jupiter for some reason wasn't visible, Thompson measured the angle of the moon against two fixed astronomical bodies instead.

Thompson's greatest asset was his diligence in recording thousands of observations over the years in his journals, then following them up by physically surveying the ground between his fixed points to fill in the details. The explorer left the Pacific Northwest in 1812, never to return. But his work was not complete: over the next year, drawing on his records and observations, Thompson drew a massive chart of the country west of Hudson Bay and all the way to the Pacific Ocean. It was drawn, says author Stephen R. Brown in the March/April 2001 issue of *Mercator's World*, "with dark ink on twenty-five separate sheets of rag linen, measuring about ten feet wide and six and a half feet tall." When he had completed the map, Thompson gave it to the NWC.

He also provided all his notes and records to the NWC. If the company was grateful for the contributions of its former employee, however, it failed to show it. In 1816 it published a copy of Thompson's map without providing credit to its architect. In 1821, when the NWC and HBC merged, all of Thompson's records were promptly sent to Aaron Arrowsmith, who was still drawing maps back in England. Arrowsmith promptly incorporated the information in his updated *Map Exhibiting All the New Discoveries in the Interior Parts of North America*, originally published in 1795. But again, while Arrowsmith is lauded in cartographic literature today as "the finest mapmaker of his time" and his maps as "among the best at the time of their publication," Thompson received no mention.

Thompson went on to serve for ten years as chief astronomer and surveyor for the British side of the International Boundary Commission work taking place in eastern Canada. But the only recognition of his contribution to the nation's surveying and mapping during his lifetime was given to him by fellow surveyor and explorer Simon Fraser, who named the Thompson River in British Columbia after his colleague. Thompson died in 1857, unrecognized by the authorities for his work.

In the meantime, however, other parties were finding Thompson's work most useful in laying claim to territory in the Pacific Northwest. The only trouble was, they weren't British.

Typical surveyors' camp scene in nineteenth century British Columbia.
OFFICE OF THE SURVEYOR GENERAL

To Measure an Empty Land

Line-cutting on a border survey: date unknown. OFFICE OF THE SURVEYOR GENERAL

By 1905, exactly one hundred years after Simon Fraser peered westward through a gap in the Rocky Mountains and saw the country he named New Caledonia, land surveyors in British Columbia had reached sufficient numbers and enough political clout to incorporate as a professional body under an Act of the provincial legislature.

British Columbia was still a remarkably young province in 1905; the colony had been barely a teenager when it joined Confederation in 1871. But both cadastral and topographic surveying had formed the backbone of provincial settlement from its very beginning. In the sixty-odd years since European settlement began in earnest on what was then the colony of Vancouver Island, to the formal creation of the "Corporation of Land Surveyors of the Province of British Columbia" in 1905, more than 230 land surveyors—some with debatable qualifications but employed as surveyors nonetheless—had already completed a massive amount of work in the province. Land surveying, in one sense, is the oldest European profession in British Columbia. It was among the first official work undertaken to establish a permanent settlement at Fort Victoria, and it has not ceased since. One hundred years after incorporation, little if anything of British Columbia's topography remained to be identified. This is astounding given the size of the land mass involved and the fact that, when Europeans first set foot on land west of the Rockies, they really knew nothing about what faced them in the Pacific Northwest.

A lack of knowledge has never stood in the way of colonial aspirations, however. In the first half of the nineteenth century, both Britain and the United States of America started to send increasing numbers of explorers, emissaries, and even settlers into what was perceived as an "empty" land, the incontrovertible evidence of a substantial existing population notwithstanding. Colonial powers were less blind, however, to the potential wealth of resources that the country west of the Rocky Mountains offered in the region stretching from the southern Columbia Basin to the mouth of the Columbia River and at least as far north as its source in the mountains of British Columbia. As a result, jockeying for position began early in the region then generally known as the Oregon Territory, although often it was executed in what appeared to be a disinterested and seemingly disastrous fashion, especially on the part of the

British. In consequence, the ultimate resolution of international territorial boundaries between Britain and the United States in the west would prove a vexing and long-drawn-out process, rife with mistakes, disagreements, and the very real threat of war between the two countries.

Explorer-surveyors like Alexander Mackenzie and David Thompson were not simply searching for the best east-west trading routes for their employers; in their footsteps they were also establishing invisible lines on which would ride or fall the potential political and economic future of the Oregon Territory and of Britain's role within it. But despite each step forward, no apparent good use was made of the momentum created. While the trading companies seemed acutely aware of the resource potential of the Oregon Territory and of the importance of navigable waterways such as the Columbia River, the British government initially behaved as if it did not.

James Cook ventured no farther east than Nootka Sound on Vancouver Island, and Vancouver kept strictly to his instructions and stuck to the coast. Mackenzie's route, successful as it was, had been far to the north of the rich southern interior. If Britain did understand the future importance to Canada of the Columbia River and of the southern Oregon Territory, it showed an outstanding lack of initiative in instigating a strong push into the region until it was far too late. As a result, Thompson was easily beaten in his efforts on behalf of the North West Company (NWC) to reach the mouth of the Columbia, at what is now the border between Washington State and Oregon. Americans Meriwether Lewis and William Clark had set their flag up six years earlier, in 1805. On July 15, 1811, when Thompson finally showed up, an expedition founded by New York businessman John Jacob Astor already had Fort Astoria up and running.

The Americans were not free of their share of misfortune, either. Despite beating the NWC to the rush, Astor's trading company managed to bungle its operations sufficiently that the British company was able to trade in the region in a virtual monopoly situation for several years. But the fact that the Americans had arrived at the lower Columbia River first would prove crucial to the resolution of which jurisdiction would ultimately gain control of it. After the conclusion of the War of 1812 between

Britain and the United States, the provisions of the 1814 Treaty of Ghent returned control of Fort Astoria to the Americans on the basis, simply, that they had been there first.

Perhaps that was a sufficient wake-up call for the British government. It realized that it now stood to lose control of the entire Columbia River basin, and as a result the determination of a western international border with the United States became an increasingly polarized dispute between the two countries. The British initially had designs on the entire region west of the Rockies as far south as the mouth of the Columbia. The Americans wanted the same thing, at least as far north as the source of the Columbia. The only solution reached was temporary: an agreement was signed in 1818, and renewed in 1827, to share the space for the time being.

Much farther west and a great deal farther to the north, the seeds of another major boundary dispute were being sown. In 1825, an Anglo-Russian treaty settled on the 141st meridian of longitude as a suitable border between the Russian territory of Alaska and British territory north of 54°40' N, roughly the latitude of the source of the Columbia River. But while on paper the 141st meridian seemed a straightforward definition of the boundary to those who signed the treaty, the signatories took little or no account of the terrain it might cross. Next to nothing was known of the region at the time, other than the periphery of its coastal waters. Moreover, the language of the treaty was ambiguous, adding to future uncertainty. The line was to follow "in its prolongation as far as the Frozen Ocean." But whenever the line of the 141st meridian should prove to be more than ten "marine leagues" or about fifty-five kilometres from the ocean, the boundary was simply to be formed by "a line parallel to the windings of the coast, and which shall never exceed the distance of ten marine leagues therefrom."

Easier said than done, given the tortured and mountainous coastline in question. But officials did not have to give any great thought to the definition of that coastline for the purposes of measuring "ten marine leagues," nor to the physical challenge involved in doing so. The task of surveying the agreed line was not pressing at the time, nor would it become so for decades. The pressure for the treaty had arisen from clashing shipping and trading interests in northern waters, rather than from any land-based industry; no other commercial activity of any great consequence was taking place in 1825 in the far north of the region. Even when the United States purchased Alaska in 1867 from the Russians, it was generally considered a strategic folly and of little interest to Canada. The Americans quietly handed over the purchase price of US$7.2 million and took away with them the maps that the Russians had prepared of the agreed border. Nothing more was thought of it at the time.

In the meantime, however, pressure continued to build around the issue of the southern boundary with the United States. American settlers were flooding into the west. Presidential candidate James Polk began fighting an aggressive campaign to push the United States border north as far as 54°40. The British, nervous of sparking another conflict so soon after the last one, stalled for time. By 1843, the Hudson's Bay Company (HBC), anticipating the need to withdraw from its headquarters on the lower reaches of the Columbia River, had decided to move to the southern tip of Vancouver Island instead and to establish Fort Victoria there. It was a more logical location for a company that in 1838 had received from the British government an exclusive hunting and trading licence in the northwest for a period of twenty-one years. It was also a prescient decision. On June 15, 1846, Britain and the United States signed the Oregon Treaty, agreeing that the international boundary west of the Rockies would be drawn along the 49th parallel through the Oregon Territory, and southward from the coast to include within British territory Vancouver Island and most of its satellite islands in the Gulf of Georgia. Had the HBC not moved, it would have found itself located in the United States of America.

Just five years previously and nearly five thousand kilometres to the east, the legislature of what was then the Province of Canada—basically, present-day southern Ontario and Quebec—resolved in September 1841 that "a sum not exceeding 1,500 [pounds] sterling be granted to Her Majesty to defray the probable expense in causing a geological Survey of the Province to be made." The following year, the federal Geological Survey of Canada (the GSC) was established under the expert guidance of director and geologist William Edmond Logan. The fundamental mission of the GSC was to assess Canada's resource potential for industrial mining. Logan, as yet unaware that Canada would soon become much, much bigger, had his work cut out for him.

It would be another three decades, however, before that august organization would begin work in British Columbia. Even by 1843 the European colonizers' knowledge of the interior of the region amounted to very little. James Douglas of the HBC was in charge of Fort Victoria, but for the first few years of its existence little changed; and while by 1846 a few more trading forts had been established in various parts of the region north of the new border, no civilian European settlement had occurred.

The impetus for change was the realization on the part of London that, without support for British immigration to the newly won region, even the Oregon Treaty would not protect it from an effective occupation by either American settlers or American entrepreneurs with an eye on the rich timber and potential mineral sources apparently sitting for the taking. The quickest solution also seemed simple: grant the whole of Vancouver Island to the HBC for a token rental; turn it into a Crown colony; and require the HBC to do the hard work of marketing and disposing of land to settlers at a set price of one pound per acre. Whatever the HBC hadn't disposed of by the expiry of its licence in 1859 would be repurchased by the Crown.

It was an extraordinary transaction, in hindsight, although it would not be the last of its kind. At the time, it was considered a system both appropriate and efficient, and the HBC readily accepted the deal. Despite his hopes, James Douglas was initially passed over as governor of the new colony. To prevent any accusations of favouritism, the British Colonial Office appointed as governor a complete outsider, a young Englishman named Richard Blanshard, who had no previous connections to the colony. Putting his disappointment aside, Douglas immediately and enthusiastically set about the business of encouraging the growth of Fort Victoria into a real town—one that would require real surveyors to lay it out.

Douglas had in fact already had a portion of the area around Fort Victoria surveyed, after a fashion, as early as 1842. A young man named

Adolphus Lee Lewes, employed by the HBC in 1839, had been assigned to work on the west coast in 1840. His father was Chief Factor John Lee Lewes, which may have accounted for his appointment as a "Surveyor" as well as a "Clerk for General Service," notwithstanding little evidence of a surveying education or background. Nonetheless Lewes accompanied Douglas to Vancouver Island in 1842, when Douglas was selecting a suitable site for the fort, and subsequently produced a map entitled *Ground Plan of portion of Vancouver Island selected for New Establishment taken by James Douglas, Esq.* It is certainly the first known plan executed in British Columbia, if not the most technical. But by 1849 it was clear to the HBC that something more was required. Settlers needed more than a vague promise of land to be enticed into immigration; they needed to see hard evidence of their ability to obtain ownership rights. Without surveys, it was impossible to provide that assurance. Unfortunately, the second surveyor hired by the company did little to inspire any confidence in that regard.

Strictly speaking, Walter Colquhoun Grant wasn't really a land surveyor at all. He was an army officer with aspirations to settle on Vancouver Island, and in pursuit of that had secured not only one hundred acres of land near Sooke but the means, through his appointment as "Colonial Surveyor" and at a salary of one hundred pounds per annum, to pay for his land. Grant arrived in Fort Victoria in the summer of 1849, bringing eight other settlers with him. His qualifications were as debatable as those of Lewes, but the HBC seems to have been remarkably accommodating of him. The company was desperate simply to have its first settlers in place in order to meet its obligations to London; if appointing Grant colonial surveyor was the means to do that, then so be it.

Perhaps hoping to hide his failings as a technical surveyor, Grant first suggested that he simply conduct a "general survey" of the whole island. His instructions, however, were much more specific. The company's most urgent need was to obtain a clear delineation of the lands already in use by it around Fort Victoria, and of additional lands that might be necessary for cultivation purposes in order to supply HBC needs. Grant was also instructed to survey his own property while he was at it and to produce a plan. He was, furthermore, to send plans and inventories of all disposed lands to the company on a regular and expeditious basis.

But by the fall of 1849 no plans or inventories were yet forthcoming. Douglas, under pressure from his employer to send survey plans to London immediately, in some desperation suggested Lewes to the HBC as a replacement; Lewes at least had produced a legible plan as and when instructed. Douglas's suggestion was rejected, for reasons that remain unclear. By late spring of 1850 Douglas was driven to write again to London, complaining in strong terms that Grant was simply unable to accomplish any surveys whatsoever. Either miffed or thoroughly embarrassed, Grant tendered his resignation, claiming he needed time to pay attention to his own property. To his credit, he declined any salary. It was little consolation to Douglas, who was so frantic to obtain any form of survey document at all that he even offered Grant a per diem to at least complete the survey of Victoria District.

Grant agreed, but by September of the same year he wrote to Douglas to report that, while he had concluded the survey, the "thick fog and smoke which at present so overclouds the district that I cannot see above 300 yards in any direction, utterly prevents my surveying any more at present with any accuracy." Grant again pleaded a need to return to his own property, which conveniently excused him from finishing "a complete sketch" of his work. In his own defence he wrote, perhaps with some justification: "In justice to myself I may remark that the assistance with which I was furnished was wholly insufficient for carrying on operations rapidly, otherwise I have no doubt the whole would already have been finished." With no sense of irony whatsoever, he remarked that "I have also laid out allotments for all the colonists that have come to the island, Mr. Tod unfortunately being the only one."

Grant is probably best remembered for his unfortunate legacy on Vancouver Island: the ubiquitous scotch broom that he is credited with having casually introduced, thinking it would remind him of home. He is certainly not remembered for his surveying skills. But things were about to improve dramatically. In December 1850 a young Irishman named Joseph Despard Pemberton wrote to the HBC to inquire about the possibility of employment as a surveyor and engineer in the new colony of

Vancouver Island. Perhaps he had heard of Grant's shortcomings—he took pains to describe himself as a man "of thorough business habits and energy." He also had the distinct advantage of actually having studied science and mathematics at Trinity College in Dublin, and at the time of his inquiry was a professor of engineering and surveying at the Royal Agricultural College at Cirencester in England. The HBC snapped him up immediately, offering him a three-year contract as colonial surveyor at an annual salary of four hundred pounds plus a considerable expense account.

Pemberton arrived in Fort Victoria in June 1851 and, to Douglas's delight, set to work straight away. Reports from Douglas to head office in London began to flow thick and fast almost immediately. "Mr. Pemberton...expects to get through a good deal of work before the winter sets in," Douglas wrote happily in November that year. Three weeks later Pemberton was able to send to London sketches of the 3,084 acres he had reserved for the company's use within Victoria District, and by mid-January of 1852 he had shipped a completed plan of a surveyed townsite for Victoria. Supported by a young assistant surveyor named Benjamin William Pearse, Pemberton also quickly put together maps of the Saanich Peninsula, much of Sooke, and extensive portions of the Cowichan Valley and Nanaimo District.

By 1855, Aaron Arrowsmith's nephew and successor John Arrowsmith had published, in London, Pemberton's map entitled *The Southeastern Districts of Vancouver Island.* The measuring of the new colony was well and truly under way.

During an expedition which might last as long as four months, it was usually necessary for survey parties of the past to supplement their stores by hunting and fishing. OFFICE OF THE SURVEYOR GENERAL

The Moon's Bright Limb

Equipment used in the nineteenth century, such as this transit, was primitive compared to contemporary technology, but remarkably accurate in the right hands, all the same. B. JERRITT

One of the challenges facing Joseph Pemberton when he arrived in the new colony of Vancouver Island was that, as a surveyor, he effectively had a blank slate to draw on. Before he could ever set crow's-quill pen to linen to draw a townsite, let alone any specific property boundaries, his first task was simply to decide where to start. That was anything but a simple decision.

Like one piece of a large jigsaw puzzle, any map is only as useful as its reference points. To successfully place that piece of the puzzle, it is critical to know how the piece's contents and edges relate to the rest of the picture. Likewise, a map is useful only if one can, in addition to pinpointing one's location on the map, also identify the area that the map covers within a larger region. Plunk the average person down in the middle of the wilderness with a map that includes their location, without telling that person where they actually *are*, and they may as well use the map to light a signal fire in hope of eventual rescue. The same is true of a survey plan. It is necessary to know where the plan starts or ends in relation to everything else around it. We know, for example, that a property boundary starts at the end of Trillium Way; we know where Trillium Way is because it runs off Wild Cherry Avenue; Wild Cherry runs off Buttercup Lane; and so on. We have reference points for all of them.

For Pemberton to draw up a townsite for Fort Victoria and Victoria District, with accurate measurements of their boundaries and the lots within them, was all very well; but how would anyone know where Fort Victoria was in relation to anything else? What would be the known point that could be used to state with absolute certainty where any particular lot within Victoria District lay? Pemberton's first job was to figure out the best reference points for this far-flung new corner of the British Empire: perhaps a meridian, or yet more simply, a readily identifiable landmark in the area, such as the summit of a mountain. Integrally tied to that decision was the one concerning what kind of survey system to use, for there was certainly more than one option available to him. Pemberton studied several variations of colonial surveying, none of which seemed perfectly suited to his situation. He looked at the rigid rectangular method that had been adopted in New Zealand, referenced to true north, and the 640-acre section and township arrangement used widely in the United

States for pre-emption purposes. Under the pre-emption system, settlers could occupy unsurveyed quarter sections of government-owned land and eventually obtain ownership by carrying out sustained improvements to the land, rather than having to purchase it.

Pemberton also considered closely a then current treatise on the subject of surveying systems written by the former surveyor general of South Australia, Captain Frome of the Royal Engineers. One of Frome's strong recommendations was to ensure that sites located on valuable areas such as waterfront were surveyed with reduced frontages, "so as to distribute this advantage among as many as can participate in it." His other recommendation, one that would be seized on by Pemberton to the gratitude of many future surveyors, was to first conduct a trigonometric or triangulation survey to assist in the laying out of access roads, land classifications, and townsites, before beginning any cadastral or boundary surveys of individual lots within a district. The corners of each lot could then be referenced, or "tied," to the triangulation survey, which, if an identifiable landmark in the area was used, could commence at that spot.

Such pre-planning for roads, municipal infrastructure, cemeteries, and other similar requirements of any future city was of course expensive and time-consuming. Neither consideration was particularly attractive to a commercial enterprise such as the Hudson's Bay Company (HBC), which simply wanted to see settlers coming in and purchasing land as quickly as possible. But as Frome pointed out sensibly, preparing a larger framework in this fashion also avoids awkward and perhaps even more expensive mistakes later on, such as the creation of lots to which no access could be made. In other words, it would create the edges of the jigsaw puzzle, allowing the detailed surveys to be fitted inside it in a logical manner rather than simply tossing random pieces of the puzzle onto the table and hoping they would fit together at the end.

In 1987, in an article entitled "Early Cadastral Surveys", former surveyor general W.A. (Bill) Taylor wrote: "There were two basic philosophies on how best to develop a settlement or country in those early days. Either a trigonometrical survey should be the first requirement, to map what was available and to plan how to divide it up with regard to topography to exploit an economical road access pattern. Or conduct a rigid rect-angular survey with no premapping. Barge right ahead and run the final lines in the beginning and discover what is there after the pattern had been laid down." In 1975 Taylor also wrote in his short publication *Crown Lands: A History of Survey Systems*:

> The adoption of any survey system should take into consideration access, present and future, potential isolation of settlers and cost of survey. A rectangular grid system such as the Dominion Township Grid system of 160 acre quarter sections with road allowances, is the cheapest method of producing the most surveyed acres in the shortest time. However, it has been proven to have had a marked effect on the cultural and psychological development of the settlers. Settlers generally arrive too quickly for adequate surveys to precede them and the Township system was a desperate move to fill the blank of surveyed land available for purchase.

Joseph Pemberton, Taylor writes with admiration, must have been a remarkable salesman, for he was able to persuade the HBC—at least in the beginning—to go to the expense of the eminently more suitable trigonometric survey before laying out a townsite. Assisted by Benjamin Pearse, Pemberton wasted no time. Within a matter of months not only had the HBC lands been surveyed, but land had also been set aside for Richard Blanshard, the governor of the new colony, and for churches, a school, and a park. Pemberton had settled on a more or less rectangular system, but in accordance with Frome's recommendation, the boundaries of lots were tied to the triangulation map that had already been prepared rather than to the compass points of east, north, south, and west. The lots themselves were not uniform in any respect, and ranged consider-ably in size—from as little as twelve acres to as much as 840 acres.

What both Frome and Pemberton had clearly understood was the nature of the land they were respectively dealing with in Australia and on southern Vancouver Island: rocky, irregular coastline and steeply inclined slopes interspersed at uneven intervals with swamp. A township system of inflexible rectangles tied to a rigid north-south or east-west bearing might be suitable for the prairies, or seem logical to bureaucrats in London offices who had never been farther afield than the gentle English fields of Surrey; but it wouldn't work in the difficult terrain of most of the colonies. Pemberton seems therefore to have applied to the system he adopted the practical logic of the terrain in front of him, rather than any uniform "cookie-cutter" formula.

As a result, different plans of the Victoria vicinity look entirely dissimilar, depending upon where in the district they were drawn. Although roughly rectangular in outline, the shape of each lot is different; and the size of almost every lot in the original town plan of Victoria, for example, varies considerably. In the Metchosin District, on the other hand, to which Pemberton and Pearse promptly moved their efforts next, there was a clear attempt to keep the rear boundary lines of the lots more or less parallel to the seashore and to maintain the width of the frontage at about half to one-third of the length of the lots. Along the valley bottom between Fulford Harbour and Burgoyne Bay on Salt Spring Island, surveyed around the same time, each lot is uniform in size and shape—all twenty chains by fifty chains. Both were logical approaches to the topography and likely settlement patterns that the surveyors were dealing with at the time.

If there was one area in which the surveys done by Pemberton under the auspices of the HBC fell short, however, it was that for some inexplicable reason, despite all the efficiency and planning, no allowances were made in the allocation of lots to take land back for roads when it might become necessary in the future. If it was a startling omission, it wasn't one that had any detrimental effect on the way in which Pemberton's employers viewed his efforts. James Douglas—who had by 1851 become governor of the colony after all, following a short and mutually unsatisfactory tenure by Blanshard, and who was perhaps still smarting from his experiences with Grant—was effervescent in his praises for Pemberton at the end of the surveyor's first three-year contract in 1854: "I think it will be difficult to find a person as well adapted for the situation he now so creditably fills, or who will discharge its duties with equal zeal and untiring energy." Perhaps Douglas was anxious that he would lose his efficient right-hand man to more tempting offers elsewhere, but if so, his anxiety proved unfounded. Pemberton graciously accepted the compliments, as well as an offer of renewal of his contract for a further term. He was thirty-three years old. Pearse, his assistant, was just twenty-two.

The two surveyors were each making their mark in Victoria figuratively as well as literally. Pearse was a conservative who quickly became involved in politics: already in 1854 he was agitating for the removal from his post of the colonial chaplain and schoolmaster Robert Staines, with whose radical views both Pearse and Pemberton strongly disagreed. In 1856, Pemberton was elected to the first House of Assembly to sit on the west coast. Both men were also inclined to the arts: Pearse, according to historian Richard Mackie in the *Dictionary of Canadian Biography*, performed in the first musical ensemble west of the Rockies in 1855, and Pemberton appeared as Sir Lucius O'Trigger in a theatrical production of Sheridan's *The Rivals* in 1857.

But it was Pemberton's strategies in property investment, rather than his theatrical talents, that were to leave a greater mark on the Victoria landscape. Governor James Douglas was said to have actively encouraged HBC employees to take up land wherever they could. If so, then Pemberton took his advice assiduously. Almost immediately, the colonial surveyor started purchasing land, and it was all good land; he would eventually own half the property in Oak Bay District.

His method of land acquisition was not without controversy, however. In *More English Than the English: A Very Social History of Victoria*, author Terry Reksten describes an incident in which HBC employee William Macdonald came off the worse for wear in a discussion with Pemberton over land in Oak Bay that Governor Douglas had apparently recommended to Macdonald. Macdonald was seeking advice from Pemberton:

> What did the surveyor think? Pemberton was non-committal and so Macdonald hied himself out to Oak Bay, walked over the land and decided that the magnificent views more than compensated for the rocky outcrops that divided the arable acres. 'I went to the land office and informed Mr. Pemberton of my decision,' Macdonald recalled. 'Mr. Pemberton, rubbing his nose in his usual manner, replied, 'I have taken it for myself.'

In those early years when Pemberton, Pearse, and the other company surveyors based at Fort Victoria were drawing the very beginnings of British Columbia's cadastral and topographical framework, the techniques and equipment they were using were primitive and cumbersome, but despite all of their limitations, surprisingly accurate in the hands of capable surveyors. Surveyor John Trutch, for example, was said by Bill Taylor to have "set a good post...in 1858" on the highest point of Mount Newton, used as the beginning reference point for the surveys of North and South Saanich Districts on the peninsula immediately north of Fort Victoria. The original post is now missing—the victim of a souvenir collector who innocently but illegally removed it in the mid-1950s, thinking it would be better off safely kept in a museum. But because Trutch's original survey was faultless, a government surveyor was easily able to relocate the proper site for the post, more than one hundred years after it was originally set.

To say that Trutch set a good post was high praise indeed, especially coming from another surveyor. Posts are used to mark boundary corners, and to act as reference markers. Once an original post has been set—even if in error—that is where the corner stays forever, whether or not the original post goes missing. That is because property owners must be able to rely on the boundaries they have been told are theirs, without running the risk that those boundaries might change if they prove to have been incorrectly surveyed in the first instance. This is so important a principle of legal boundary establishment that removing survey posts remains a criminal offence today. The trick for contemporary surveyors, of course, is finding the location of the post if the original survey was not well executed.

In the 1850s, there were few established rules or regulations governing how surveys were to be conducted—a matter that would change rapidly as the speed of settlement picked up later on. But even then, surveyors were keenly aware of the importance of the post as establishing the definitive limits of property ownership. The problem was that corner posts in the 1850s and for some considerable time thereafter were made of the most ready and convenient material at hand: wood. It was much simpler to cut a post at the survey site than it was to haul a heavy metal post by hand, as often as not up the side of a steep mountain. Wood, of course, rots quickly in the damp climate of the west coast of British Columbia, and the longevity of the posts was naturally limited.

As a matter of practice, therefore, surveyors rarely used only one means of marking a location. In the 1850s it was customary to place some form of permanent marker under posts: a piece of charcoal, silver coins, a piece of a broken china plate, some broken glass—quite frequently from a whisky or wine bottle, perhaps emptied in anticipation of the heavy work ahead—even, in one case that Taylor relates, a "complete sauce bottle, one of Lee & Perrins from England." Trutch was no exception. As well as placing the post at the top of Mount Newton, he had built a rock cairn, which was still visible. Trutch also blazed at least one oak "bearing tree."

Bearing trees are used to help find the proper location of a post that has rotted or otherwise gone missing. At the time the post is set in place, the surveyor marks a nearby tree with a blaze and the carved letters "B.T.," facing the post. The distance to the post is also carved on the bearing tree, and noted, along with the species and diameter of the tree, in the surveyor's field notes. One tree is useful; two or three are even better, for then more than one bearing and distance can be read and the intersections of the lines drawn from those trees should indicate the site of the original post. Even one hundred years later, it is possible for a surveyor to find the blazes. Robert Allen, BCLS 487, noted in 2005:

> We still use [old] bearing trees where required. Over time, the blazes on the bearing trees will grow over and all that you can find is a small black line down the tree where the blaze was. By carefully cutting into the old blaze, you can often see the original carvings. Also as the blaze grows over, the carved "B.T." and distance fill in with wood and if you are really careful, you can get a reverse image of the carvings. The oldest bearing trees that I [have] found went back to 1881 and 1886.

The relocation of such previous survey posts continues to form a substantial part of modern surveying work. Having set a good post in the first place, John Trutch should rest easy knowing that the inevitable re-survey of the site was very straightforward. The more accurate the

CAMP
No 2
JULY 5/91
C H DAWSON. SUVYR
R H GIBSON. CHMAN
EA HARVEY. do H5
H PLOTT AX
G D BOLE do
W BLIZARD. cook

original work, of course, the easier it is. The accuracy depended on two factors, in varying degrees: the skills of the man and the quality of the equipment. Contemporary land surveyors are extremely loyal to the work of their predecessors: most of them have experienced the pleasure of finding an old post in the exact spot it was meant to be. They know too that their successors will also, one day, be relocating their work. But as with most occupations, a skilled and conscientious surveyor was capable of a high level of accuracy, notwithstanding poor equipment; a less conscientious one would not produce reliable results even with the best of tools.

In the early days of land measurement in the province and well into the twentieth century, the toolkit was still basic. A plumb-bob or plumb-line—a piece of pointed brass or iron suspended from a string—could be used to establish a vertical line, but it was at the mercy of the wind. The Gunter's chain was the basic unit of measurement, but even metal chains were subject to stretching, and the use of a chain that had not been tested for length could result in outstanding errors. Provincial land surveyor William Draper wrote an article in 1941 about pioneer surveyors of the Fraser Valley, saying: "While a chain is theoretically sixty-six feet long, in practise the old link-chain that was used in those days had a thousand wearing surfaces, and the links would stretch; and unless it was checked every day and corrected the sections would not measure the same." The chains were also heavy. Stretching a sixty-six foot, eight-pound length of metal in a straight line, and holding it in place long enough to let down a plumb-line at either end, was no mean feat. Eventually lighter steel tape was invented as an alternative to chains, but it too was subject to stretching. In use by as early as the 1870s, the steel tape was also not widely available until manufacturers began mass marketing it at the turn of the twentieth century.

In the field, however, even the most basic of equipment could fulfill a surveyor's need. Requisite to the range of skills required of surveyors was the ability to repair any equipment at any time, given the impracticality of returning hundreds of miles to home base for a replacement. In *Tales of a Pioneer*

Bearing tree in North Vancouver area carved by G.H. Dawson, PLS 7. At latest the tree was blazed in 1894, but it could have been as early as 1889. CHAPMAN LAND SURVEYING

Surveyor, written by one of British Columbia's early surveyors, Charles Aeneas Shaw, editor Raymond Hull notes that Shaw repaired his cook's watch: "[It was] an old English watch with a 'barrel' drive—the mechanism was driven by a tiny chain, scarcely larger than a coarse thread, wound around the mainspring barrel. The chain broke, and since time-keeping was important for the barometric observations, Shaw took the watch apart, removed the broken link, and rejoined that chain with rivets made by grinding down a sewing needle on a whetstone."

Hull also provides what may be apocryphal directions for replacing the cross-hairs in a transit:

i) Make a wire loop a little larger than the diameter of the instrument tube.
ii) Catch a spider and drop it to make it extrude a filament.
iii) Catch a section of the filament on the wire loop.
iv) Using the loop as a handle, place the spider filament exactly in position on the reticle of the transit. Treated with care, it should last for years.

Surveyors made use of levels and levelling rods to measure elevations; chronometers to measure time and longitude; and logarithm tables to determine the trigonometric functions of bearings. Linen and ink, vulnerable to any moisture—even an inadvertent sneeze—were used to draw their plans. But it was the compass, for better or worse, that was used to establish magnetic directions. Opinions vary on the usefulness of the compass as a surveying tool—certainly, for rough or remote surveys requiring a lesser level of accuracy, a compass might be sufficient. But as early as 1917, B.C. land surveyor Connell Higgins was already calling on his colleagues to abolish even the limited continued use of the compass in timber surveys. The compass, wrote Higgins in a paper presented to the 1917 annual general meeting of land surveyors, "is the faithful friend of the mariner...but when we impose on it the task of laying out a straight line, then I contend that we are asking it too much and elevating it above its legitimate field."

Higgins, perhaps unfairly, was critical of early surveyors. While he praised the work of some, he also believed that high enough standards had not generally been met. "I think we all know that some poor survey work has been done in this Province," he wrote. He blamed, to a large degree, the compass work that had been undertaken in an attempt to locate boundary lines. This was not necessarily the fault of the surveyor— the challenges presented to the effective operation of a compass in British Columbia were legion. Iron and magnetite deposits, of which there were many, would affect the magnetic integrity of the compass. Likewise electrical storms, or an axe or other metal tool inadvertently left in a vest. On a steep slope, where lines of sight could not be completed to the top, interruptions to the measurement increased the risk of error. There was even, Higgins wrote, "sometimes an inaccuracy in the free motion of the needle through frictional electricity developed on the glass surface of the compass-box by rubbing on one's dry clothes while being carried from place to place."

Fortunately, other types of instruments weren't far behind. The great benefit provided by the transit, the American version of which was first assembled in 1831 by Philadelphia manufacturer William J. Young, was the ability to swivel a mounted telescope on a horizontal as well as a vertical axis. It included a compass, and circles to measure horizontal and vertical angles, and thus greater precision could be achieved by a surveyor. Transits were in use everywhere within a relatively short time, despite the unwieldy wooden boxes that the instruments were carried in, and the even heavier tripods required in the field. In 1845 Jonas Phelps and William Gurley founded the Gurley Manufacturing Company in New York State. William's brother Lewis bought Phelps out within a few years, and the Gurley transit, wrote American surveyor Wilhelm Schmidt in *Bearings* magazine, became "a staple of the profession—a 'gun' both reliable and hardy, a precision instrument you could sling over your shoulder between set-ups." The word "gun" quickly joined the vernacular for an instrument used to "shoot" angles and bearings.

It would have been difficult enough in the nineteenth century, with the tools then available, to survey flat, open ground on a clear day. But British Columbia isn't flat or open, for the most part, nor are clear days guaranteed at any time. It was far more likely that surveyors would have to deal with the sight-inhibiting difficulties posed by fog, pouring

Among the reminiscences of all surveyors in British Columbia from the mid-nineteenth century to the present day are the tortured memories of mosquitoes in the summer months. Smudge fires helped both man and horse get some respite from their misery. Pictured here is the Cariboo camp of W.S. Drewry, 1912 or 1913. MRS. JOANNE DREWRY

rain, gusting wind, smoke from the ubiquitous summer forest fires, and clouds of mosquitoes. The mosquitoes posed a double threat: men could literally become incapacitated from the number of bites they received, and they were frequently sent home from field parties because of their inability to keep working. Bears were an ever-present threat. Packrats stole supplies; wild horses would lick the tops of pickets for the salt and push them over.

Great physical strength was required. Surveyors would have to cut down trees to follow a line of sight, and good axemanship for cutting line was critical. The sheer logistics of travel were mind-blowing. With no means of long-distance communication or any form of speedy travel, the entire season would be spent in the field, requiring a level of planning akin to that needed for a military campaign: hiring of local guides, and of crew for packing, cutting line, and cooking; purchasing food, equipment, horses for packing gear, feed for the horses, and so on, for up to five months at a time. To add to their woes, the surveyors would frequently be called upon to carry out additional duties, such as the careful gathering of botanical specimens for the benefit of the chief botanist in London.

Given the challenges they had to overcome, surveyors were able to

The legend on this image, presumably of members of W.S. Drewry's support crew in the Cariboo around 1912, reads: "Jack and Tom shoeing." Pack horses were essential to survey party transportation until as late as the mid-twentieth century. Occasionally the combination of rugged terrain and lack of available feed precluded the use of horses, however. MRS. JOANNE DREWRY

achieve an extraordinary level of precision in measurement in the nineteenth century and the early decades of the twentieth century. It is not surprising, however, that even by the end of the 1850s, an eagerness for an even greater level of regulation and more detailed instructions was becoming evident. A number of significant events underlined that necessity emphatically over the following decade. By the end of 1858, the still-sleepy colony of Vancouver Island and the brand-new Crown colony of British Columbia, created in November of that year, were also about to witness a veritable explosion of new immigrants. Hard in their wake came the demand, from both immigrants and government, for certainty around their property rights. That meant a resounding and urgent need for land surveyors, and in far larger numbers than the handful that had been serving Fort Victoria and its environs and making limited forays into the interior. When news of the discoveries of precious metals spread beyond the colony, the need to conduct a proper survey of the border along the 49th parallel could no longer be delayed. Governor Douglas needed help.

It arrived on Christmas Day, 1858.

More Than the Average Ground Control

A survey party portaging canoes at Murchison's Rapids, North Thompson River, November 1871. BENJAMIN BALTZLY/LIBRARY AND ARCHIVES CANADA PA-022618

On December 25, 1858, Colonel Richard Clement Moody arrived in Victoria to take up his appointment as chief commissioner of lands and works and lieutenant-governor of the newly created colony of British Columbia. Moody was also the commanding officer of an elite group of men who had been sent to the colonies to undertake two specific tasks: laying out and building townsites, roads, and bridges, and surveying the international boundary along the 49th parallel.

The Columbia Detachment of the Royal Engineers was not an arbitrary choice on the part of the authorities. Judge Fredrick Howay told an audience in Vancouver in 1909: "It was a picked body—selected out of a large number of volunteers for this service, and chosen with the view of having included in their ranks every trade, profession, and calling which might be useful in the circumstances of a colony springing so suddenly into existence as British Columbia had done." The Royal Engineers, known as REs, were also military men—a vital qualification in Governor James Douglas's urgent request for law enforcement in the region.

As usual, the need for such law enforcement was driven by economic considerations. The topography of the province of British Columbia is challenging—wave after wave of steep and icy mountain ranges, muskeg country to the north, and massive rivers raging through canyons and mosquito-infested forests. But the same geological forces that created the rugged terrain are also responsible for immense reserves of minerals beneath its surface. Gold had been discovered on the Thompson River as early as 1856, and by the summer of 1858, with further discoveries in the Cariboo region of the interior, as many as 25,000 people, gold fever burning in their veins, had rushed into the country. The trickle of settlers turned into a flash flood. When London realized the significance of the potential revenues to be generated, the new Crown colony was hastily created. Governor Douglas of Vancouver Island also took on the governorship of the colony of British Columbia.

Even before then, Douglas had realized he would need backup. In August 1858 he wrote to Secretary of State Sir Edward Bulwer-Lytton, requesting the assistance of "even a single company of infantry." Fortunately for Douglas, Bulwer-Lytton had already introduced into the British House of Commons the draft legislation required "to secure this promising and noble territory from the hunger of gold." A letter from Bulwer-Lytton to Douglas written in early July crossed with the one the governor sent in August; it told him that Lytton did intend to send to British Columbia at the earliest opportunity an officer of the Royal Engineers with a company of "Sappers and Miners."

The term "sapper" originated in the military role of tunnelling under enemy positions to place explosives. While that was not a role envisaged for the work to be undertaken in the new colony, the name stuck. In fact, while Douglas was hoping for help in law enforcement, Bulwer-Lytton had other priorities: "This force is sent for scientific and practical purposes, and not solely for military objects. As little display as possible should therefore be made of it." In another letter sent a few weeks later, he elaborated on his choice of the Royal Engineers:

> The superior discipline and intelligence of this force, which affords grounds for expecting that they will be far less likely than ordinary soldiers of the line to yield to the temptation to desertion offered by the goldfields, and their capacity at once to provide for themselves in a country without habitation, appear to me to render them especially suited for this duty; whilst by their services…in carrying out the numerous engineering works which in the earlier stages of colonization are so essential to the welfare and progress of the community, they will probably not only be preserved from the idleness which might corrupt the discipline of ordinary soldiers, but establish themselves in the popular goodwill of the emigrants by the civil benefits it will be in the regular nature of their occupation to confer.

Bulwer-Lytton was a passionate supporter of the men of whom he spoke so highly, and their welfare was important to him. The terms of their employment were generous: thirty acres of land in British Columbia were to be given to each man at the end of his service (later increased to 150 acres), and all married men were to be allowed to bring their wives and children, an unusual concession at the time. Bulwer-Lytton also ensured that the engineers were provided with an extensive library of books which he had personally chosen. He had already predicted that the

Royal Engineers would have a future in British Columbia that went well beyond a military role; he wanted to ensure that they were as prepared as possible.

Each member of the detachment was required to know a trade, such as carpentry, tailoring, or stonemasonry. Also required were a solid education in mathematics, land surveying, mapping, and engineering at the Royal Military Academy in England. The engineers had been taught methods of accurate draughting and even, to some extent, traditional landscape painting—in the absence of cameras, the engineers were expected to produce documentary sketches in the field to accompany any surveys. By the early 1860s, cameras were available for this purpose, but they were still generally regarded as too large and cumbersome to be usefully employed in the field. A competent artist was held in much higher regard than such an unwieldy, heavy, and unreliable instrument.

By the time Colonel Moody arrived in Victoria at the end of 1858, two shiploads of engineers had already arrived in British Columbia and commenced work under the leadership of Captains John Grant and Robert Parsons. Their first task was to build their own quarters, at Derby, on the south bank of the Fraser River, the site of present-day Langley. The project was already under way when Moody arrived to inspect the construction site early in 1859. The colonel was considering where to locate a capital for the new colony, but the fort at Derby appeared to him to be a poor choice given its proximity to the United States border. International tensions were still recent enough to make Derby feel too vulnerable, and Moody promptly instructed his men to move everything west to the site of the future city of New Westminster, also on the Fraser River but with a far more comfortable margin of colonial territory between it and its southern neighbour.

Moody's decision was, however, also an immediate cause of tension in what had quickly become a difficult personal relationship between him and Governor Douglas. Douglas, of course, could envisage the likelihood of the two neighbouring colonies merging in the foreseeable future, with Vancouver Island becoming a small and potentially irrelevant satellite of the larger mainland colony. He would therefore have preferred the capital to be at Victoria, where his power was centred. But locating the capital at Victoria was a technical impossibility, given that the town was, for the time being at any rate, located in a different colony. Douglas was a relatively long way away from New Westminster, however, and Moody had already started work on construction. For the time being, Moody had the advantage and paid little attention to Douglas, despite the fact that the governor was his superior. New Westminster was incorporated in July 1860 and would remain the capital until 1868, two years after the foreseen merger took place in 1866. Notwithstanding his early fears, Douglas would finally get his way.

In the meantime, however, Moody was occupied with his new role as chief commissioner of lands and works on the mainland. He was in completely unfamiliar terrain and may initially have felt a little out of his depth. The system of survey he seems to have selected for the new colony was the one already in use in Oregon and Washington State land districts—a rigid 640-acre section and square-lot township system, tied or referenced to the nearest meridian. Despite his apparent sensitivity to the still relatively recent tensions between their two jurisdictions, he wrote to the surveyor general in Washington State, James Tilton, asking for copies of survey instruction manuals. "Any suggestions of a practical character which your experience may lead you to consider as likely to be of service to me, with respect to officework the modes of calculating the distances *sic* and to the checking and examination of the work generally will be most acceptable and valued by me as highly as I feel convinced they will be cordially offered by you," wrote Moody. His obsequiousness must have worked, for he received at least one manual, parts of which were promptly copied for further use and found their way into at least one set of survey instructions.

In July 1859, Moody instructed a surveyor named Joseph Trutch to use the American rigid square-lot system to survey Sea and Lulu islands at the mouth of the Fraser River. He was precise in his requirements:

> You are hereby instructed to take as the initial point of Survey the fixed point near Semiahmoo where the 49th parallel intersects the ocean...from [there] you are to run a meridian line to be named the 'Coast Meridian' which meridian [at 122°45' N] you are to extend

Northward to the Northernmost limits of the District...

At each Block and section corner post to be set and established with four bearing trees...and marked in all respects as in the United States land survey.

In his instructions Moody made a number of amendments to the system: sections were reduced in size to 160 acres, and townships were renamed "blocks." Governor Douglas was no more happy about this decision than about the choice of capital; less than one month earlier, he had written tetchily to Moody: "It has been represented to me that the method of surveying intended to be pursued by Mr. Trutch is one which is very imperfect and highly objectionable, and which...has led to much inconvenience and endless litigation. This is a matter of detail connected with your Department into which of course it is not necessary for me to enter, but I deem it right to mention the matter notwithstanding."

Once again, Moody ignored Douglas. Trutch proceeded with the survey, although it would be the first and last of its kind used in British Columbia. Before the year was out, Moody had switched to a more flexible variable-sized district-lot system, better suited to the terrain with which he was faced. While it did not look greatly different on the ground, it married lot sizes to their specific location rather than drawing arbitrary square lines over land that was patently neither flat nor square in shape. As Douglas had reasonably pointed out, it was a system much less prone to arbitrary outcomes that would lead inevitably to disputes.

If he could sometimes behave in a mercurial fashion and appear obstreperous, Moody was, however, also a highly effective leader. Under his guidance, the Royal Engineers would complete the surveys and construction of an astounding number of roads, bridges, and townsites in the space of a mere four years between their arrival in the colony and their recall to England in 1863. They laid out not only New Westminster, but much of the future city of Vancouver and its immediate neighbours; the towns of Yale, Hope, Douglas, Lillooet and Lytton in the interior of the mainland colony; roads from Douglas to Lillooet, Hope to Similkameen and to the Cariboo; and, after an observatory was established at New Westminster, they recorded a phenomenal number of astronomical observations as a basis for future mapping. But the most enduring legacy of the Royal Engineers—or at least, the one for which they may be best remembered—remains their survey work on the international boundary between the colony of British Columbia and the United States of America.

"If you look along the International Boundary between Canada and the United States in any forested area," declares the official literature of the current International Boundary Commission, "it will appear simply as a six metre or twenty foot cleared swath, a long open vista stretching from horizon to horizon, dotted in a regular pattern with white markers. Over mountains, down cliffs, along waterways and through prairie grasses, the line snakes 8,891 kilometres or 5,525 miles across North America." The boundary between Canada and its southern neighbour contains 5,528 boundary monuments and 5,700 triangulation stations along its length. British Columbia's share of that length measures 2,168 kilometres, or 1,347 miles—and it was the Royal Engineers who would, along with their American counterparts, measure it first.

It had been a straightforward matter in 1846 for officials in Washington, D.C., and London to determine on paper that the boundary should simply be a line drawn along the 49th parallel. For the purposes of politics and empire, that sufficed. But as mineral strikes became increasingly regular occurrences on both sides of the border, specific property rights and revenues became a matter of intense importance to both the individuals concerned and the governments that stood to benefit economically.

The need to draw a physical line on the ground was apparent, but the logistics of drawing the line were another matter altogether. The 49th parallel crosses almost every kind of terrain, from river deltas to mountain peaks and glaciers. The magnetic fields of those giant mountains played havoc with compasses. The rivers had to be crossed in canoes or on rafts, without any shift in the line occurring. Trees had to be cut across the six-metre swath with hand-wielded axes. It was a massively ambitious task, further complicated by both international politics and yet another serious personality clash among the three men most responsible for the success of that task.

Both Britain and the United States appointed their own boundary commissioners to oversee the survey, but in the absence of any spirit of international co-operation at the time, the commissioners were instructed to conduct their work separately. Archibald Campbell was the American appointee for the entire project. At first, the British appointed a commissioner whose powers were limited to determining the marine portion of the boundary, between the mainland and Vancouver Island only. Campbell and Captain James Prevost, the British commissioner, met in June 1857 to discuss the best method to undertake this component of the boundary survey. They disagreed immediately, and their disagreement would escalate almost to the point of open warfare over whether the San Juan Islands should be in British Columbia or the United States. A British pig straying into American territory on the San Juans was, happily, the only casualty; but sensitivities were so high that the porcine British trespasser and its untimely end at the hand of an outraged American farmer nearly sparked a declaration of hostilities between the two countries. In the end, what is now known as the "Pig War" never happened. The parties chose arbitration over conflict and a decision was eventually made in 1872 by the chosen arbiter, Kaiser Wilhelm of Germany, in favour of the Americans.

In the meantime, in February 1858 the British finally appointed Captain John Hawkins of the Royal Engineers as the commissioner responsible for surveying the land portion of the boundary from the coast eastward to the Rocky Mountains. While Hawkins made his way to Vancouver Island, arriving in July after numerous delays at sea, Campbell lost his patience and simply went ahead and got started. Their first meeting in August was already tense as a consequence; it also immediately resulted in a fundamental disagreement over the level of demarcation required along the boundary. Rather than being staked out by vulnerable wooden posts, the boundary was to be marked with sturdy monuments made of rock and cement, in which brass plates would be placed to identify each monument individually. Campbell, wanting to keep costs down, thought it sufficient to place the monuments only at the "striking natural features of the country," including streams and permanent trails, that intersected the boundary. Hawkins, on the other hand, wanted to place boundary markers every mile "on open ground."

Both teams proceeded in their own way, working from separate base camps. The Americans stayed ahead of the British, something Campbell rubbed in repeatedly to Hawkins in the limited correspondence that took place between them. "Not finding any of your parties in a position to render aid," he wrote in one letter, "we undertook the work alone. You will thus perceive that while you are prepared to consider the best means of opening [a trail]…we are undertaking it…For some wise purpose, it has been our privilege to become the pioneers in this Herculean task, [which we] are likely to enjoy…until we reach the Rocky Mountains." Hawkins could be equally insulting, blasting Campbell's men for incompetence in what appear to have been quite unjustified attacks. In one account, Campbell is described as "a fussy, cross little body who can't bear to be thwarted."

Under the circumstances of such divisive leadership, it seems a miracle that the surveying teams were able to complete their task over the next four years. But the men were professionals, and the teams on each side went to work with gusto, despite the difficulties and the challenges of the terrain facing them. The surveyors started work at a small beach dividing British territory at Tsawwassen from a small and anomalous tip of American land called Point Roberts, a location that would eventually prove to be about 800 feet or 240 metres north of the actual 49th parallel. This was not the consequence of careless surveying, writes historian Alec McEwan, but of "the limitations of nineteenth century technology, and…inevitable discrepancies" caused by the adoption of astronomic rather than geodetic coordinates and by gravity. Astronomic observations, notes McEwan, were difficult to make and weather-dependent. Such discrepancies would eventually show themselves at numerous locations along the border upon the emergence of more sophisticated technology. Under the circumstances of the time, however, the locations were remarkably accurate.

Campbell had been more prescient about those circumstances, and about the sheer difficulty of marking every mile of the boundary, than Hawkins had. Campbell, of course, had the advantage of having started work earlier. As the survey teams worked their way east, they found that many points were simply inaccessible; portions of the mountain ranges between the Fraser Valley and the Okanagan, for example, included sections as long as twenty-three miles that went unmarked despite Hawkins's wishes. Nearer the coast and in the more open valley lands between mountain ranges, however, it was possible to mark whole swaths of the line continually with iron posts or rock cairns.

Lieutenant Charles Wilson performed multiple roles as record keeper, commissariat, transport officer, and secretary to the British survey team. He kept detailed records that included many personal observations on the scenery, conditions, and work at hand. Life on the "line," or indeed on any of the survey projects being undertaken by the Royal Engineers, was far from easy for the men or the officers. Wilson travelled extensively along the work line, bringing provisions and mail to the camps and reporting on progress to his superiors. Rain, snow, wild animals, summer heat, and forest fires were common distractions. Among the most disconcerting challenges were the ubiquitous mosquitoes, to the point where work had to be stopped for several weeks in the low-lying Sumas prairie portion of the Fraser Valley. Trying to keep "the 'squitters" off, wrote Wilson, required men to wear protective clothing from head to toe and to puff desperately and constantly on a pipe. And the strain clearly showed: "Washing is a perfect torture, [the mosquitoes] settle en masse upon you perfectly covering every portion of the body exposed, we sit wrapped up in leather with gloves on and bags around our heads and even that cannot keep them off. None of us have had any sleep for the last two nights and we can scarcely eat, exposing the face is such a painful operation."

The pack animals suffered equally, if not more. "Each mule as it is packed is obliged to be led into a circle of fires continually...two...mules have been blinded, and six of our horses were so reduced that we had to turn them out onto the prairie and let them take their chance of living, I never saw anything like the state of their skins one mass of sores...we are all of us," concluded Wilson soberly, "a good deal pulled down by want of sleep and continuous irritation." If mosquitoes were not enough to put up with, the ordinary hazards of working in the wilderness also took their toll. Men drowned in the rivers; sapper James Duffy froze to death west of Lillooet, in the vicinity of the road and lake now named after him (although, for some reason, spelled "Duffey"). Avalanches and falling trees caused serious injury and further loss of life. Occasionally, human folly got the better of someone: one packer took a bullet through the thigh when moving a bag in which an engineer had stowed a loaded revolver.

Not all was hardship and constant difficulty, although sometimes the notional perks of the job proved to be the further undoing of some of the men. Food rations were generous, and alcohol even more so. "We are allowed a pint bottle of wine and a bottle of beer per diem," wrote surveyor James Anderson. "A keg of brandy is generally kept as it is very acceptable sometimes on a cold night when we have to sit up until sunrise observing the stars." The effects could, however, be deleterious: "just when we were starting some soldier was found missing," wrote Anderson, "and he was known to have been pretty drunk about an hour before...we were delayed about three hours, which disgusted us not a little." Of another engineer that Anderson described as "most intelligent and gentlemanly," and who yet was still only a private soldier, Anderson also suspected that "drinking has been the cause of it all, for there are more cases of drunkenness recorded against him than any other man we have out here."

The engineers entertained themselves in the wilderness as best they could. While some succumbed to alcohol, others invested their time in more productive activities. Lieutenant Wilson was very fond of dances and similar festivities, and records in detail the preparations for such entertainments. Of a ball held at Esquimalt headquarters, near Victoria, Wilson wrote enthusiastically: "The rooms were decorated and arranged by me...I had the floor well waxed to make it slippery." The engineers also enjoyed great hospitality in the communities and forts they encountered along the route. Historian Patricia Johnson wrote in 1955 in the historical journal *The Beaver* that the surveyors were well cared for at Hudson's Bay Company posts, which provided useful bases for their operations. At Fort Colville on the American side, fine entertainments and feasting were always in order on special occasions such as Christmas.

At Colville the American and British commissioners met for the third time in November 1860, finally with greater success and cordiality, and with next to no disagreement. By the end of 1861, the field work of surveying the line was complete on both sides and the parties retired to their headquarters to finish their paperwork. But matters were not over. It was not sufficient, of course, for each side to simply rely on their own work—it was necessary to compare notes to ensure that the surveys had in fact been accurately conducted along the 49th parallel—and, most importantly, that they matched. By the time official maps had been produced, however, several years had slipped by. When those maps were compared, there were a number of differences between them. Once again that was the result of imperfect technology and geological reality—the gravitational pull of the mountains had severely affected the compass readings, for example—but equally it demonstrated the different approaches taken by the two teams, and their separate agendas.

Agreement was tentatively reached simply to "split the difference"—to draw a line halfway between two differing points and call that the border. This simply added to the confusion, however, and appeared to defeat the purpose entirely of establishing certainty on the ground for settlers, prospectors, and businesspeople who wanted to be able to rely on the monuments that had been erected, supposedly along the actual border. To complicate matters further, the original survey documents prepared by both teams, which might have helped resolve some of the differences, appeared to have gone astray. In fact the American reports had never been finalized because of the chaos generated by the U.S. Civil War, which had begun in 1861. The British reports were equally jinxed; more than thirty years later, they were discovered at the Royal Observatory at Greenwich, England.

A meticulous re-survey of the boundary was eventually undertaken in the early years of the twentieth century. Then the two countries agreed that the boundary would be physically marked by both sides together on the ground, even where it did not correspond exactly with the 49th parallel. With improved instruments and greater co-operation, new lines were cut to replace the old, and new monuments were erected. In the end, the later surveyors found that surprisingly few corrections had to be made. Despite their many challenges, the Columbia Detachment of the Royal Engineers and their American counterparts had completed an ambitious task with diligence, and had done it astoundingly well.

In 1863, the detachment was disbanded. Wilson went to Jerusalem, to conduct a survey of the city in order to improve the water supply system. Moody and many others returned to England, or moved to other foreign service, never to return to British Columbia. In the five years of their assignment to the colony, they had left a legacy of settlement that is unparalleled. But not all of them left. Some, taking up their free land, decided to stay with their wives and families and to embrace a future in a land they had come to love. Sergeant William McColl and Lance Corporal George Turner set up a partnership as land surveyors, as did John McClure—whose son Samuel would become a well-known architect in due course—and James Turnbull.

Trails to the interior had started to become real roads. Towns had sprung up along the Fraser and Thompson rivers. In 1863, the first *British Columbia Gazette* was published, another legacy of the engineers. A suspension bridge had been built over the Fraser River north of Yale. On the land immediately north of the mouth of the Fraser and south of a bay named Burrard Inlet, several town lots had been laid out. In the meantime, two surveyors named Edgar Dewdney and Walter Moberly had commenced building a trail from the settlement of Hope eastward through the Similkameen Valley towards Princeton.

In Victoria, Governor Douglas had not been sitting idle. Pre-emption legislation was in place, establishing proper procedures for settlers taking up unsurveyed agricultural land. When surveying pre-emptions, property boundaries were to be run as nearly as possible to the cardinal points of the compass, and the dimensions of lots were constrained so as to prevent unfairly long, narrow waterfront properties from being created. Surveyors were required to avoid awkwardly shaped lots and to withstand the strong objections raised by pre-emptors who did not like the outcome of the survey. Pre-emption was an inexpensive way to place settlers on the land quickly, but the lack of a prior survey could cause serious problems. When the legal property boundaries of a section were finally surveyed, sometimes years after the initial pre-emption, it was occasionally found that those boundaries differed significantly from what the settler had thought he or she owned—to the extent that homes were sometimes built across boundaries, or even right outside property

Royal Engineer Captain Parsons's house, facing the Fraser River in New Westminster. From the Capt. Robert Parsons collection, 1860. A. NEILD/LIBRARY AND ARCHIVES CANADA PA-099727

lines. Engineer Captain R.M. Parsons wrote astutely to Moody in 1861:

> For the survey of pre-empted lands before all things I imagine it is necessary that persons of strict integrity be employed, as it will be difficult to check their work for a long time to come. They should be men of judgment also and hold a position that will give weight to their opinions for they will have to regulate the rude approximations to boundaries made by the pre-emptors themselves, so as to accord with the existing laws and to endeavour to prevent portions of land between pre-empted properties being rendered valueless by inconvenient and irregular outlines.

In 1861, the first Land Registry Act was passed on Vancouver Island, introducing a system of guaranteed land title based on what had become known as the "Torrens principle," after Robert Torrens, the British official who had created the system for land registration in South Australia in 1858. The basic principle was simple: the owner registered on the paper title to land held "indefeasible" or guaranteed title "against the world." While there were exceptions to the principle, the essential object was to eliminate the reigning confusion over land ownership in the colonies. Squatters, for example, were taking over land that had already been pre-empted, and multiple errors were also arising from the uncoordinated creation of unregistered land deeds. The Torrens principle has been retained in land registration systems in British Columbia ever since its introduction, with some technical variations over the decades. "The individual person...must have his faith in the system," wrote A.A. Milledge, land registrar of the New Westminster Land Registration District in a paper delivered in 1962 to the Corporation of British Columbia Land Surveyors. "When I speak of conveyancing, I include the work of surveyors in making surveys for the plans that represent the work done in the field. That confidence of the public in our system must be preserved."

While the systematic regulation of land surveyors and their work in the colonies remained a thing of the future in 1864, more and more surveyors were trickling into the region all the same, in search of adventure and new prosperity. Prosperity was a dubious goal, but they would certainly find adventure.

In addition to surveying knowledge, surveyors have always had to have many extracurricular skills – in this instance, butchering the camp meat. OFFICE OF THE SURVEYOR GENERAL

No Push-Button Era

Alberta Boundary Commissioner R.W. Cautley, circa 1915. OFFICE OF THE SURVEYOR
GENERAL

In 2005, Hans Troelsen, BCLS 551, wrote the following in an obituary of Robert (Bob) Peck, BCLS 379 (September 24, 1926–January 1, 2005):

> He was a surveyor, not just in the professional sense, but in the way he keenly observed and considered human events as life unfolded around him. He loved the sweet mystery of an unadjusted traverse that closed to within a few seconds. He loved heavy hand-knitted wool socks, well-worn boots and old sweaters with leather elbow patches. He loved a warm dry fireplace after a long hard day in the bush. He loved the meandering curvilinear pathways of life and was intrigued by what today's adventure would bring him tomorrow... He believed in traditional values such as trust, honesty, integrity, friendship, reliability, tolerance, and above all, loyalty. He believed there is a special adventurous spirit that lives in the hearts of prairie boys because he was one...[a spirit] that comes from always trying to look over that horizon, so far in the distance.

The character of the men and women who have been involved in surveying British Columbia has not particularly changed since the earliest years of the province. Surveyors were and remain a distinct breed. Many others like them have engaged in other activities and professions, of course: pioneers in every walk of life, from farming to mining to engineering. But the land surveyors of British Columbia and their families share characteristics and backgrounds, flaws and merits, histories, experiences, and attitudes that are almost inseparable. They are also similar to each other to an uncanny degree.

Their numbers have always been few, which offers a partial explanation. Clinging together in their minority, they have formed enduring friendships and married into each other's families. Many of them have passed on the mantle from father to son—and, in 2005, for the first time, from father to daughter—creating even stronger links in the chain of land surveying history in the province. They have always had a strong sense of being at the heart of history in the making, as is evident in their field notes and reports over the decades. They have demonstrated a professional pride in their work and a sense of solidarity with their forebears and each other that are almost unparalleled in any other profession. At

the same time, they have without exception been independent characters able to speak their mind and even, at times, strongly disagree with
each other.

What formed such strongly defined characters? Who were these
people who could come to work in an environment so completely outside
of the comfort zone of ordinary mortals and, for the most part, thrive?
Many of them were well equipped to do so—the Royal Engineers, for
example. Most were eager; but many had no previous experience in the
skills or physical fortitude required to cope in British Columbia's rugged
terrain. They came from England, Scotland, Ireland; from eastern Canada
and the United States of America. Some had studied extensively; others
learned as they went. Almost without exception they were middle- or
upper-class men, youngest sons, with the opportunity to make their
fortune and create a life of adventure far from the gentle dullness of British civilization and the limits it placed upon them. They took everything
that faced them in their stride, coping in different ways: with humour,
camaraderie, pride in their work, a sense of purpose in drawing lines
upon the land, serving their government well, and giving settlers defined
boundaries to their properties. But between the lines of many of the
early reports and field notes is writ much hardship, for both surveyors
and their families. For all the tales of laughter and success, there are also
many stories of loneliness, alcoholism, breakdown, and suffering.

"Work and survival in the wilderness engendered stature in our
pioneer surveyors," wrote former surveyor general Gerry Andrews in
1990 in the BCLS journal, *The Link.* "Wisdom and skill meant success.
Ignorance and ineptitude invited disaster." Modern technology, mourned
Andrews, "denies such wholesome experience" to the young surveyors of
modern times. Whether that is a good or bad thing may be a moot point
to those "young surveyors" who have not had to cope with the hardships
that their forebears endured. The "old" surveyors had no choice.

The governors of the young colonies could also ill afford to pick and
choose their employees from the limited ranks of those who were available. Charles Westly Busk was an English land surveyor who had studied
engineering and had come west with the Canadian Pacific Railway in the
1880s. Busk remarked in his reminiscences some fifty years later that,

upon coming to Victoria, he had little trouble finding work:

> I established myself in a couple of rooms on Yates Street until I could look around and learn something of the country and opportunities in my profession. As a preliminary I called on Sir Jos. Trutch and the Surveyor-General, and from both learned that as I owned a theodolite and level and allied instruments it was to be presumed I knew how to use them, and accordingly no examination nor licence was necessary—all I had to do was to get the offer of some work and then go and do it. I secured an office on Bastion Square, opposite the entrance of the then jail, an old H.B. Co. fort surrounded by a wooden palisading. I soon secured sufficient employment in making surveys, tracing old corner posts, etc., to keep me busy and meet living expenses.

In fact, despite Busk's recollection, since 1861 the chief commissioner of lands and works (at that time, Colonel Richard Moody) had been empowered to appoint "Sworn Surveyors" who were required to supply to the government a bond of one hundred pounds. It was a significant sum, required as surety that they would "well and efficiently survey such piece of land as they may be required to survey." The chief commissioner would appoint any such "Sworn Surveyor" at the request of a purchaser of land, and at the purchaser's expense, the appointee would perform a survey of the property. By Busk's time, the 1884 *Land Act* required all Crown land surveys to be made by a "Surveyor approved of and acting under the instructions of the Chief Commissioner of Lands and Works or the Surveyor-General." George Fountain, BCLS 245, wrote in 1937:

> Rumour has it that any person wishing to practise as a Land Surveyor merely journeyed to Victoria, was introduced to the proper Government official and, if favourably received, thereafter could hold himself to be a Provincial Land Surveyor. However, this cannot be entirely the whole story, as a fairly competent method of selection and control over the early Surveyors must have been kept, either by setting a comparatively high standard for admission or by selecting only the better qualified men to do the Government

surveys, for, with some exceptions, these early surveys were of good quality and the surveyors themselves seem to have been men of considerable prestige in the community.

The list of sworn surveyors, which grew rapidly in the remaining decades of the nineteenth century, comprised a typically adventurous array of characters. Joseph Westrop Carey was an Irishman born in 1830 and raised in County Cork where, according to retired history buff H.B. "Barry" Cotton, BCLS 290, he studied land surveying before leaving his native shores at the age of fifteen for Boston, Massachusetts. By the time Carey reached Victoria in 1859, he had undertaken surveying work in California, Arizona, and Mexico. Tales of the Fraser River gold rush brought him north on the steamer *Brother Jonathon,* in the company of an eccentric shipmate by the name of Amor de Cosmos.

De Cosmos would immediately found the *British Colonist* newspaper in Victoria and go on in 1872 to become premier of the province, for a brief and inglorious period of fourteen months. But Carey also marked his own small place in provincial history. Bent on finding gold, he initially headed up the Fraser in search of his fortune. Prospecting and Carey were ill-matched, however, and he may have been quite relieved to be employed by the U.S. boundary commission as a survey assistant on the 49th parallel surveys. Even this may have proved too much eventually, for Carey found himself back in Victoria before long. Although he continued to work as a land surveyor, conducting the original surveys of many of the Gulf Islands in Georgia Strait, he is better remembered for his foray into Victoria's local politics. In 1884 he successfully won the mayor's seat and, according to Cotton, plunged straight into controversy. Carey refused to pay a legal bill that had been incurred by the previous administration. Such was the extent of his stubbornness that even when the sheriff put the assets of the city up for sale by court-ordered public auction in order to pay the debt, Carey would not budge. Before the critical moment of actual sale was reached, a group of horrified citizens paid the bill themselves. Unsurprisingly, Carey was not re-elected.

If Carey's sense of adventure demonstrated itself in his eccentric behaviour, in others it showed more plainly in an unquenchable search for new experiences. Such were the restless spirits of men like William Bauer that even the wilds of British Columbia could not slake his thirst for new explorations. Bauer would eventually settle in Vancouver, but not before ranging as far afield as the Malay Peninsula to build railroads for the King of Siam, and the Yukon Territory in the wake of the Klondike gold rush in 1897. Land surveyor Colonel William Holmes went to China to conduct road surveys in the midst of the intense and dangerous politics of the 1930s in that country. For others, wars would prove irresistible: almost without exception, and on each occasion on which they were called, British Columbia land surveyors dropped their tools and flocked to sign up to fight for their country in foreign fields.

These men were drawn to the occupation of surveying by its discipline and its magic, and by that sense of adventure. "In 1864 a company of Royal Engineers began the survey for fortifications on the Point Levis side of the river opposite Quebec," wrote Arthur Cotton (no relation to Barry) in 1929. "It was then that I, as a boy [of twelve], saw a survey party for the first time, and I think I can say it was that that led me into the profession. I was with them every chance I could get." Cotton worked his way west, witnessing the Riel Rebellion and the battle of Batoche in Saskatchewan in 1885, and playing a cautious background role: "It is better to be a live surveyor than a dead hero," he remarked discreetly in his reminiscences. By comparison, "the survey of the North-West Territories was more like a picnic than anything else. There were no hardships or privations to endure." Cotton went on to become a surveyor in British Columbia, despite the hard work that he had already witnessed:

> When I look back and think of the labour that chaining entailed then, I am greatly impressed. Gunter's chain was the only one in use. The chainmen were armed with that and a set of ten iron pins and a brass one to mark the end of the ten chains or tallies. I wonder how the chainmen of today would enjoy it, eighty times to the mile, and if the country is hilly, many times oftener! I have very often chained fifteen miles a day with an eight pound link chain. Try it and see how laborious it is!

> They were strong and physically fit, or they would not have been able

to survive. Some didn't, like the unfortunate sapper Duffy. Duffy was a friend of sapper James Turnbull, of whom Moody said: "I always selected him for isolated and difficult enterprises, demanding hardy endurance, skill and judgement." A contemporary of both Turnbull and Duffy was Lieutenant Henry Spencer Palmer, also a member of the Royal Engineers. In the summer of 1862, Palmer undertook a four-month reconnaissance trip up North Bentinck Arm and the Bella Coola River, 440 miles north of Victoria, looking for a route to the Fraser River. His lengthy report to Colonel Moody on the subject reveals a man of both extraordinary powers of endurance and a wonderfully poetic nature.

Of the arduous nature of the journey and the glorious but atrociously difficult country he was seeing, Palmer wrote: "The steamer course winds through an archipelago of surpassing beauty...By the few who, for trading and other purposes, have penetrated these arms of the sea strange stories are told of the grand and gloomy character of the neighbouring scenery...near Knight's Canal, we hear of a river which flows for 15 miles through a magnificent glacier tunnel 100 feet in height." The mountains of North Bentinck Arm spurred him to his own lyrical heights: "Piles of mountains...in singularly tumbled though rounded masses....snowy peaks, pine-clad slopes, rugged cliffs and precipices, naked, shapeless masses of trappean and granitic rocks projecting upwards to vast heights...these, in constant succession, form an aggregate of sublime and wild, though strangely desolate...scenery."

That same scenery would prove heartbreakingly difficult for Palmer's party to traverse, although Palmer remained laconic in his report: "It would be tedious to describe at length the various obstacles that opposed our progress and the sundry shifts to which we were put in prosecuting our difficult journey." He found he could recommend neither the North Bentinck Arm as a route to the Fraser nor the Bella Coola Valley as a suitable area for settlement: "The country traversed after leaving the Bella Coola Valley is excessively sterile and unproductive...I cannot say that I passed on the entire journey a single tract of land likely to afford encouragement to settlers, though perhaps, as a desperate resource, it might be possible to reclaim at considerable outlay...portions of the swamp lands." Palmer did make a shrewd observation on the frustrating nature of exploratory surveys: "The experience of this country has shewn that the first road through an uninhabited forest district is rarely on the best line, and that it is only when settlement affords opportunity for detailed exploration that the most favourable route in detail can be discovered."

The women who followed their men to British Columbia were no less hardy. They faced many of the same privations, if different emotional hardships. They endured the same long and difficult sea voyage to reach the colonies as did their husbands. Some endured childbirth while on board in open seas, and not all survived the trip. Those who did reach Vancouver Island were quartered in clusters of dwellings that could be described as equally "rude" as those Palmer had observed up Bentinck Arm—two-room buildings with few amenities. They were women of fortitude, or it is doubtful they would have come, or stayed. Women who had typically been used to the help of servants and governesses took for granted that they would simply have to manage on their own, and they did. Left alone for months at a time in Victoria or New Westminster, they appeared to have many entertainments to fill their days—teas, sporting amusements, the occasional ball or banquet when the men were in town. Few, if any, travelled with their surveying husbands, who were based in the two main settlements rather than in the interior.

It must have been unbearably lonely at times. Whether married or single, childless or in charge of a brood, all but the most privileged immigrant women faced exceedingly difficult conditions in the colony. Occasionally, they suffered great misfortune, and even tragedy. In 1861, for example, the schoolmistress in New Westminster was summarily removed by Colonel Moody. Hinting at wanton behaviour on the unfortunate young woman's part, Moody wrote, bringing the matter to the attention of Governor Douglas, that her "misconduct [was] of a nature proving her entire unfitness for the charge of children...An unfortunate misplaced sympathy on the part of many of the detachment...makes it impractical for me to obtain the services of another teacher..."

On November 4, 1859, Amor de Cosmos reported sadly in the *British Colonist*:

On Friday last, while the town was still in a great state of excitement about the murder of the three Italians by [Indians] at the mouth of the Fraser...news arrived that Mrs. Crote, the wife of one of the Sappers, had murdered her family and cut her own throat; and I am sorry to say it turned out to be true...it appeared she had been in a desperate way for some time about being out here. And when the news of the murders...arrived, it turned her brain completely, and she was heard to say that sooner than the Indians should kill her children, she would kill them herself.

Loneliness was not the sole purview of the women. Together with hardship it brought out poetry, humour, drunkenness, and creativity in surveyors, in a variety of arresting forms. Many of them excelled at amateur theatre and frequently performed in shows. Benjamin Pearse, who succeeded Joseph Pemberton as surveyor general in 1864, not only performed himself but also helped found the Victoria Amateur Orchestra in 1879. Ashdown Henry Green, a famous Indian Department surveyor of the late nineteenth century, was a renowned ichthyologist, identifying nine new species of fish in British Columbia during the course of his career. Sapper Peter Leech surveyed part of the Alaska boundary with British Columbia in the mid-1860s. His sense of humour was wry, to say the least: terminating his line directly over a grave, he reported with a straight face to his superiors that "one half of the corpse was in English, the other half in Russian American territory." Breaking all the rules on the inviolability of the post placement, the line was later discreetly moved.

Stanzas from an anonymous poem entitled "The Song of the Transitman" capture the heartache of the way of life well:

Twenty years on location, wandering through the land,
Crossing the raging torrents, a courageous little band,
Mapping the hills and valleys, for the Company making gold,
Twenty years on location...twenty years and I'm old.
This is the song of the transitman as he lay in his room alone
In a cheap hotel, as drunk as hell, as he stiffened out like stone
The only reward for his lifelong work a man without a home.

Drunk the transitman may have been, but from the earliest days of

the regulation of surveyors it has been incumbent on them to act with "due sobriety." They are a contradictory lot, all the same. On the one hand, Ernest Bolton Hermon, the president of the Association of Provincial Land Surveyors in 1894, bemoaned that "the public have fallen into the error of considering as a surveyor every person who can set up an instrument, read an angle, look wise, and drink whisky." On the other, a predilection to drink was accepted from the beginning.

Royal Engineer Captain Parsons wrote diplomatically to his superiors in 1858 that "I think it will be more conducive to discipline [to] keep the soldiers out of the temptations of a town for a short period..." Indeed, the ability to knock back a fair share of the hard stuff was and remains a matter of pride among surveyors. It was incumbent on a man to ensure a packed bottle of whisky accompanied the field provisions if his wife was expecting a child to be born in his absence; on the estimated date of birth, he could celebrate with his comrades. But no excuse was really required, and several bottles would be standard components of any field stores. Woe betide the hapless assistant who spilled or mislaid his party chief's personal stash—a sin almost more unforgivable than dropping the transit.

In her 1976 book *Because of Gold,* author Bronwen Patenaude recounts an anecdote from 1899, when a survey crew arrived in Quesnel en route into the wilderness. "As most of them were out on their first job, foot loose and fancy free, they drank too many intoxicating beverages which made them quarrelsome and unmanageable." According to Patenaude, bartender John McLean had the unconscious surveyors carted by wheelbarrow to what he thought was a safe distance out of town, only to find them revived by the fresh air and eager to return. McLean gave up and joined in, wrote Patenaude, and ten days later the surveyors finally left McLean and his staff "completely ragged and worn out"—and terrified in case they returned.

Despite all their eccentricities and human weaknesses, the early surveyors left their mark on British Columbia in an honourable and indelible fashion. In their observations and reports they contributed vastly to the knowledge of the province as it was in their time. In their wake a roll call of place names now pays tribute to the men who blazed new trails and opened up the country for new settlement by European immigrants. The geographical naming policy of the province captures this concept aptly: "Geographical names are not just labels on maps and road signs; they convey aspects of the history and promise of an area that might otherwise be overlooked or forgotten by visitors and later generations. Whether preserved on maps, in texts, or through an oral tradition, they reveal patterns of settlement, exploration and migration, and mirror outside influences to our history."

The names of early surveyors therefore constitute a veritable who's who of place names in British Columbia. Along almost every road we drive in the province, or in parks we visit where once surveying parties huddled in the rain and tangled salal, desperately fighting off mosquitoes, are written the names of surveyors. Here are but a few: Mounts Warre and Vavasour in the Rocky Mountains; Bell-Irving River in the Nass Valley and Mount Bell-Irving, east of the Stewart–Cassiar highway; Graham River in the Peace country; Henderson Creek in the Similkameen; and Mount McGregor and Mount Revell in the Kootenays. Towns, roads, and suburbs by the dozen also capture surveyors' names—Port Moody, Duffey Lake Road, Hamilton Road. Part of New Westminster is still known as Sapperton.

At the dawn of the 1860s, however, many of these names were yet to be placed on the blank map of British Columbia. For the men and women who had come to the colonies just one or two years previously, the work had only just begun.

The Touch of Civilization

The Royal Engineers cutting on the 49th parallel in British Columbia, circa 1861.
LIBRARY AND ARCHIVES CANADA C-019426

By the 1860s, the potential wealth of British Columbia was widely known. The colonial government was faced with an inward rush of people from all over the world, particularly from the United States of America, eager to extract the colony's resources and, more to the point, to export the revenue thus derived.

Establishing the physical borders of the province on its southern boundary along the 49th parallel had been vitally important in helping ensure that British Columbia's wealth would be harvested for the benefit of Britain. But if Americans were to simply immigrate in overwhelming numbers and settle the country regardless, that thin line of rock and concrete monuments alone might not be enough protection. It was an economic and political strategy that had already worked well for the Americans in Oregon, Idaho, and Washington, after all. Accordingly, the British government also hastened to sponsor numerous forays by surveyors into the interior of both the mainland and Vancouver Island. They were instructed to explore and report back promptly on the opportunities for settlement and for critical transportation and commercial trading links. Hand in hand with those government efforts, various privately sponsored entrepreneurial expeditions took place as well.

Things moved with astonishing speed, given both a distinct lack of available financial government resources and the daunting territory that faced the colonists. Land surveyors were involved literally every step of the way. That is an accurate description, in fact, of expeditions that for the most part took place on foot, if not by canoe, or in rare instances on horseback. Horses were more often used as pack animals, but even that wasn't possible on steep or snowbound terrain where feed was unavailable. Despite the limitations on fast and efficient access, however, by 1861 surveyors Edgar Dewdney and Walter Moberly had already completed their work on a road eastward from Hope to Princeton, in the Similkameen Valley. By 1863, the Royal Engineers had made roads into all the areas of the mainland colony where mineral strikes had been occurring, including the Fraser River canyon, Lillooet, and the Cariboo. A government lands and works department had been created, and a government printing office in which the first *British Columbia Gazette* was produced.

In 1864, administrative roles tumbled over dramatically. Both Governor

James Douglas and Surveyor General Joseph Pemberton retired. Pemberton continued his political career briefly, then went into real estate investment as a full-time occupation. Joseph Trutch took the reins as chief commissioner of lands and works on the mainland, and Benjamin Pearse took over as surveyor general of Vancouver Island. In the same year, further gold strikes in the east Kootenays brought another rush of prospectors and miners flooding into the region immediately west of the Rocky Mountains. Dewdney was instructed to continue surveying and building his road from Princeton all the way east to Wild Horse Creek on the Kootenay River.

As the numbers of settlers and entrepreneurs coming into the colony shot up, the need became urgent again to create detailed regulations to govern such matters as the proper staking of mineral claims and the pre-emption of lots. More and more individuals were pre-empting or "staking" 160-acre lots throughout the southern interior, at a pace far exceeding the ability of government surveyors to keep up. While obtaining a survey immediately was highly desirable, it wasn't possible in most instances. In the absence of a prior survey, pre-emptors were advised by the government simply to place stakes at the corners of their desired properties.

But most individuals had little idea of what 160 acres really looked like, as well as a poor eye—or perhaps an overly ambitious one—for judging where boundaries might really lie between the stakes. As a result, gaps frequently existed between a property owner's understanding of the boundaries of his lot and the subsequent survey plan—and between the survey plan and the actual property, if the survey itself was not well executed. By the point at which pre-empted lots could be surveyed, enough time may have passed for the settler to undertake significant improvements on the property—or at least, on what he or she thought was the property. The risk of litigation was high if the results of a survey differed from the owner's expectations. Both property owner and surveyor could discover to their dismay that the owner had cleared and worked on land he did not own—land that may well have been pre-empted by someone else in the meantime, or which the government was unwilling to grant to him.

Despite the first efforts that had been made in 1860 at placing regulatory controls over the process for pre-emption, huge technical and physical challenges remained in marrying later surveys to previously pre-empted land. This was true even in areas, such as New Westminster, that already had been extensively cleared and surveyed. By letter dated April 20, 1860, Colonel Moody made this clear in no uncertain terms to an auctioneer by the name of Holbrook. Holbrook was attempting to sell town lots in New Westminster that had been surveyed, but the plans did not include any specific dimensions for the lots, which was a major flaw from Holbrook's perspective. Moody defended the lack of precision, however, by pointing to the posts that had been placed to indicate the corners of the surveyed lots: "I purposely abstained from defining the exact dimensions of the lots…knowing that the obstructions arising from the forest and the nature of the ground would physically preclude absolute accuracy. The lots…[are] defined by the original pickets then existing on the ground…" Evidence of Moody's frustration at the limitations he faced, and the lack of understanding from members of the public such as Holbrook, shows in his sarcasm: "I regret any inconvenience to you or to others from assuming it was practicable to lay out lots on the ground with absolute precision."

The difficulty in establishing precise boundaries on plans may have been instrumental in the early development of the virtually unbreakable rule that the location of the posts prevails over any other understanding, written or otherwise, of where the boundary or corners of a property may lie. But until those posts were in place, there was no guarantee of security, even if a property had been staked. A plaintive petition from one Henry Hunter to the government in 1888 described the problem that had arisen for him with respect to the eighty-odd acres he had staked on the Fraser River, seven miles below Hope, in 1867:

> At that time I…did not think there was more than about 80 acres of this land at all fit for agriculture…I was told I would get all the land within my stakes not exceeding 160 acres. I therefore recorded 80 acres, more or less, and carefully staked off and mapped it…
>
> Mr. Woods came to survey my land and land adjoining [in

August 1886]...I desired to stick by my lines and stakes as to boundary. He contended he could not take my lines; he must run by the cardinal points.

Bound by the regulations, Woods was unable to abide by poor Mr. Hunter's stakes. Moreover, Hunter had expected to get a full 160 acres despite the fact that he had only recorded eighty when he registered his pre-emption. He was to be disappointed: as he had been told, the fine print in the legislation used the words "more or less," and "not exceeding," and did not guarantee a pre-emptor that exact amount of land. Since he had not staked and recorded 160 acres, he was advised that he was not entitled to any more than his eighty acres. "Any argument I could advance," wrote Hunter sadly, "was of no avail."

Hunter's situation was easily, if not happily, resolved. But in numerous other incidents of a similar nature, the lack of fine print had precluded such a clear-cut resolution. That spurred a further raft of legislation in the early 1860s to govern matters such as pre-emption, miners' boards, gold claims management—errors in staking or surveying mineral claims were even more volatile, given the revenues at risk—and the authority of the chief commissioner of lands and works to accept surveys made by any "metes and bounds" as he saw fit. In 1865, an "ordinance for regulating the acquisition of land" in British Columbia was passed by the colonial legislature. The ordinance stipulated, among other things, that all Crown lands were to be sold subject to resumption of public rights of way, thus avoiding in the future the access problems typical of Pemberton's early surveys around Victoria. Problems would still ensue, but for a different reason. One hundred and twenty years later, former surveyor general William "Bill" Taylor, BCLS 282, would fume in *The Link* about the timidity of the Department of Highways in enforcing the rights of way resumptions: "In this matter, politics is really emasculating the survey system...Ignorance, timidity and fear of political embarrassment prevents the system from working as well as it should."

Ignorance may well have been a characteristic of government in the 1860s, but timidity and fear of political embarrassment seemed to be distinctly lacking. Instead, a conspicuous spirit of entrepreneurship seemed to prevail throughout the colonies; a consequence, perhaps, of the fact that British Columbia effectively began its life as the corporate child of the Hudson's Bay Company. Surveyors were no exception, as Pemberton had already proved in Victoria. James Orr, a land surveyor who had successfully run for a seat on the legislative council for the mainland colony in 1863, was also typical. Orr certainly conducted a number of exploratory surveys for the government, but he also staked 160 acres in the Similkameen Valley, dabbled in mining quite successfully, applied unsuccessfully for the licence to run a ferry over the Kootenay River, and in 1864 obtained a prospecting permit for petroleum and coal oil around Quesnel. Surveyors, of course, generally stood to benefit financially from the drive to find new trading routes and easy access to the interior, since they were employed as members of any exploratory team tasked with assessing the prospects of a new region.

But financial benefits did not always outweigh the problems when entrepreneurial vision far exceeded practical reality. Alfred Pendrill Waddington may well have been the most visionary—and the most disastrously unrealistic—of them all. Waddington has been described in much the same breath as both "a champion and steadfast promoter" of his ambitions and an "irresponsible developer." In 1861–62 the English businessman sponsored a prospective commercial route to the Cariboo goldfields via Bute Inlet, just south of Knight Inlet, and up the Homathko River. The reasoning behind the expedition was that, if it was feasible to support a rail track along the river, access to and from the goldfields by a combination of steamer and train would be a great deal faster and cheaper than using the horse trail via Hope, Yale, and the Fraser canyon.

British Columbia's highest mountain is named after Waddington, despite the fact that the entire project was misconceived, was riddled with deceit and disaster, and left Waddington financially ruined. The expeditions up the Homathko also eventually resulted in a tragic altercation between his crew and local aboriginal people. But while Waddington may have suffered the economic downfall—and perhaps some smidgeon of embarrassment, although if he did feel it he hid it well—it was two land surveyors who were faced with undertaking the actual expeditions up the Homathko, very nearly at the cost of their lives.

Robert Homfray had been largely engaged in surveys of Victoria and of Derby, on the mainland, prior to accepting the contract with Waddington to assess the viability of the Homathko route. He was not the first to take a crew up the river, so he had some sense of the daunting journey in front of him. It was "without doubt the hardest looking part of British Columbia that I have yet been into," wrote Major W. Downie, who in June 1861 had been the first European to travel up the Homathko. Downie had ventured only twenty-seven miles upriver. Even so, "this," he stated firmly and quite unequivocally, was "no place for a road." But businesspeople in Victoria did not want to hear such depressing news, and if Homfray had any anxiety about Downie's assessment, Waddington was undeterred. Waddington even took it upon himself to venture several miles up the river in September 1861, although he turned back in fairly short order on the pretext of returning to Victoria to report on what lay ahead. He instructed his lieutenant, Thomas Pryce, to continue up the river to explore further, but to Waddington's disappointment, Pryce returned quickly. One month later, muttering that this time someone competent was in charge, Waddington sent Homfray off to complete the expedition.

Homfray was well aware of Pryce's failure to reach the Cariboo. He also received a warning en route, from the aboriginal people living in Desolation Sound, about the difficulties that lay ahead. They tried to dissuade him from what they knew could only end in disaster: the river, they told him, tumbled down sheer canyons in unstoppable, giant rapids; glaciers poked their snouts almost into the water, and avalanches were a constant threat; and in some tight corners, log jams almost buried the entire river. It seemed an impossible task to manhandle a canoe up such a torrent, even in the low water of late autumn. How a rail route could even have seemed a possibility under the circumstances is difficult now to conceive. But even after his guide had turned back, after it became impossible to use a canoe, after most of their supplies had been lost in the river and the weather had turned to snow and freezing rain, Homfray persevered until he too was finally turned back—this time by an unwelcoming group of aboriginal people.

Homfray discreetly kept his horrendous experiences and disappointing report between himself and his employer, who while not amused was still not put off. In fact, Waddington somehow persuaded *The Colonist* newspaper to report on December 21, 1861, that the river was "found to be navigable for light-draft steamboats for 40 miles...then an easy portage to avoid a canyon 350 yards in length." Waddington also wrote to Governor Douglas that the Homathko was a "fine, level valley" and navigable by steamboat for at least forty miles from the river mouth. Thomas Pryce had told Waddington that he had travelled far enough to see the "bunch grass" lands of the Cariboo that lay beyond the mountains. It was a description, Barry Cotton wryly noted in 2004, which was "fanciful in the extreme," although it may well have been information garnered from the locals and simply extrapolated into a best-case and extremely optimistic scenario. Regardless, Waddington's dream was not yet vanquished. With encouragement from the government, the following summer he sent the most experienced surveyor he had yet engaged, Hermann Tiedemann, to undertake a practical assessment of the route.

Tiedemann was not only a surveyor, but an engineer and architect who had trained in Germany. He had arrived in Victoria in 1858 and gone straight to work for Pemberton as chief draughtsman in his office. Tiedemann's architectural talents were not wasted: he is credited with having designed the lighthouses at Race Rocks and Fisgard Island near Victoria as well as Vancouver Island's first legislative buildings, known as the "Bird Cages" because of their unusual appearance. Completed in 1864, they were eventually replaced in 1898 by the current imposing structure designed by Francis Rattenbury. Such urban enterprises clearly did not satisfy Tiedemann, however, and he seems to have required little encouragement to resign from his desk job and undertake the feasibility study for the Homathko River route. Far more experienced than his predecessors, it took Tiedemann a mere seven days from the head of Bute Inlet to pass the same point Pryce claimed to have reached. Unlike Pryce, however, Tiedemann observed not bunchgrass plains but "peak after peak, thousands of feet in height and clad in perpetual snow...below us a dark chasm, in perpendicular walls of granite, the Homathko River... Probably," Tiedemann noted dryly, "[Pryce] took the snow-clad peaks for bunch grass in his dream."

The Grand Canyon of the Homathko River, 1875. CHARLES HORETZKY/LIBRARY AND
ARCHIVES CANADA PA-009138

From there, things went downhill. Tiedemann nearly drowned
beneath the glacier that now bears his name, and his party lost most
of their provisions and much of their equipment. Nearly a month later,
"reduced almost to a skeleton and hardly able to walk," he stumbled into
Fort Alexandria in the Cariboo, about seventy-five kilometres north
of present-day Williams Lake. Astoundingly—and to Waddington's
immense gratification—Tiedemann did conclude that a trail was possible, by carrying a plank road around the cliff faces of the canyon. But the
surveyor had been travelling in summer, with the water already lower
than in the spring. More than a decade later he had the opportunity to
test his theory, constructing a tentative plank road on the river while
conducting a survey for the Canadian Pacific Railway. The plank road
was washed away almost immediately in spring freshets.

Where Tiedemann and Waddington differed was on the prospective

The Homathko River, twelve miles upstream from its mouth, July 1875. CHARLES
HORETZKY/LIBRARY AND ARCHIVES CANADA PA-009134

cost of the route. It was a standard part of an exploratory surveyor's job to
estimate the costs of a route and the cheapest and most effective method
of construction. Waddington happily advised a public meeting in August
1862 that the total cost of building a road would be around $220,000.
That was a not insignificant sum in those days, but it was at least realistic
in terms of receiving both government and public support. Tiedemann,
however, estimated the cost at $316,810—for just five miles of rockwork
in the canyon alone. Clearly that had not been what Waddington wanted
to hear; Tiedemann advised Surveyor General Joseph Trutch some years
later in his own defence that he had communicated all of his estimates
to Waddington, "but [they] were so received by him as to prevent my
having further connection with him."

In the meantime, however, tragedy waited in the wings—a tragedy
that would also sound the final death knell for Waddington's dream.

The indomitable entrepreneur continued to forge ahead, sending dozens of road builders into Bute Inlet in 1863 and 1864. Tensions were almost immediate with the Tsilhqot'in, or Chilcotin, people at the upstream end of the river. While some were hired as packers—and it was the Tsilhqot'in who had assisted Tiedemann when on the brink of starvation and failure the previous year—nonetheless, they were also deeply concerned by the intrusion and events occurring around them. There may well also have been individuals who felt personally mistreated by the white men.

Those concerns eventually spilled over into a deadly attack in April 1864. More than a dozen members of the survey party and settlers in the area were killed over the ensuing days, and out of unreasoned revenge rather than an objective desire for justice, several Tsilhqot'in men were subsequently hanged. It was the point of no return for Waddington's venture. While the *British Colonist* sympathized effusively with him in its May 12, 1864, issue—"This gentleman has toiled hard, and fought nobly and manfully against the insuperable obstacles which have presented themselves"—no appetite remained to support such a dangerous venture, and his dream was finally over.

The saga of the Homathko was not complete. Despite all the impracticalities of the route, Tiedemann returned in 1872, the year Waddington died, to survey the route for the Canadian Pacific Railway (CPR). Marcus Smith, chief of the CPR survey team in British Columbia, seemed to have been as determined as Waddington to make the route work but would prove equally unsuccessful. Smith, who was described as "cantankerous" and "not popular with the crews," did however have a way with words. He wrote of the scenery as being "awfully sublime," and the turbulent water muttering and "groaning like troubled spirits." Despite its beauty—Smith also wrote that "wherever a handful of soil could rest it was sprinkled with wild flowers amongst which bloomed the sweet lily of the valley"— the Homathko's wildness would prove untameable.

Dreams were still alive and well in other parts of the colony, however. Some were plausible, some as doomed as the Waddington road. Far to the east, Captain John Palliser of the Waterford Artillery Militia had been charged in 1857 by a British imperial commission to search for viable rail routes through the Rocky Mountains. Palliser and his team identified and conducted preliminary surveys of several passes that might accommodate a rail line, including the Kicking Horse Pass, so named after a recalcitrant pack horse kicked Dr. James Hector, a geologist and member of Palliser's party. It was the pass through which the CPR line would eventually run, although Palliser himself recommended against it. Facing a veritable sea of mountains, and with the little knowledge yet available to him of the interior of British Columbia, it was Palliser's view that the only feasible transcontinental rail routes ran far to the south of the new border. Although Palliser did at least produce a map of the area covered by his surveys, it lacked sufficient detail to be of much use. "The time has now forever gone," lamented Palliser gloomily, to be able to achieve such a route through Canada.

In 1865, another audacious venture was begun. Land surveyors Peter Leech, John Maclure, and James Mahood quit their jobs to help survey a proposed telegraph link between Europe and Russia. The Collins Overland and Western Union Telegraph was to run through what would later be named the Bulkley Valley after the expedition leader, Colonel Charles Bulkley, and was one of the most exciting forays into global communication that had yet been undertaken anywhere in the world. Provincial Ordinance No. 54 of 1865 authorized one Perry Macdonough Collins, an American citizen, to survey and construct the portion of the telegraph line crossing British Columbia. It was desirable, said Her Majesty's government, to co-operate cordially with the United States and Russia in this international project. Co-operation with aboriginal people did not seem to be as pressing an objective; the ordinance also empowered Collins to build defence posts that might be "necessary for the proper use or defence of the said International Telegraph line against Native tribes within the said Colony" despite there being little or no evidence that aboriginal people were about to engage in open hostilities with the colonizers on any kind of systematic or orchestrated basis.

Mahood went to Siberia in October 1865 to begin work on the eastern end of the proposed line. In less than six months, he and his companions traversed nearly three thousand miles of unmapped wilderness between them, evaluating the best route to take. Maclure started from New

Westminster and headed northeast. The government took advantage of the situation to share with the telegraph company the cost of building the first road eastward along the Fraser River. At least two other land surveyors participated in this part of the "Telegraph Trail" as well: Joseph McKay and Walter Moberly.

The surveying teams and construction crew strung wire up as fast as they could go. Their motivation was a competing Atlantic cable link being worked on by another American entrepreneur, Cyrus Field. By the spring of 1866, more than one hundred men had laid hundreds of miles of telegraph line, connecting New Westminster all the way to Quesnel. It was an outstanding feat. It was also, unfortunately, to no avail: Field successfully connected his Atlantic link in early 1866, which the Quesnel crew learned painfully over their very own wire. At least they heard immediately. After a brief spurt of further work, in the hope that the competing line might still not function properly for some reason, they abandoned the project. In Siberia, Mahood and his team, out of reach of any fast means of communication, would not hear of their downfall until more than one year later, in June 1867.

In 1866, the two Crown colonies of Vancouver Island and British Columbia had merged into one colony of British Columbia. Joseph Trutch was appointed as surveyor general of the united colony, and in 1871 British Columbia joined Canada as its newest province. Trutch became British Columbia's first lieutenant-governor. His final act as surveyor general was to publish the first official general map of the province. In the meantime, little changed in terms of the systems of property and township surveys between 1860 and 1873, when a new Land Act was passed.

Prior to Confederation, the colonial government had repurchased Vancouver Island from the HBC and in 1870 had fixed the price of surveyed rural Crown land at a dollar per acre. A lands and works office had existed since 1858, with responsibility for surveys and mapping, but upon British Columbia becoming a province in 1871 a new and official department of lands and works was established, under the charge of the surveyor general and commissioner of lands and works. Benjamin Pearse took on the additional role of commissioner, so that he was responsible

Members of the first parliament of British Columbia. Third from right is land surveyor Walter Moberly. CHARLES GENTILE/LIBRARY AND ARCHIVES CANADA C-088878

for not only surveys, mapping, Crown land management and public works but also, interestingly, the oversight of any government immigration schemes.

It was a great deal of responsibility, so it is not surprising that less than a year later the role of surveyor general was carved off into a separate bureaucratic position, which Pearse would continue to hold until 1872. In the Land Act that was passed the following year, specific measurements were ascribed to lot sizes: the longest side was to be around 1,078 yards—just under fifty chains—and the shortest side about 768 yards, or 35 chains. A number of alternative lot sizes were permitted. A formal township system was introduced in 1874, setting township sizes at six miles square with thirty-six sections, all to be tied into the international boundary on the 49th parallel and to the coast meridian.

Despite the increasingly specific rules applying to land grants and to surveying, the 1870s, according to surveyor William Draper in a paper about pioneer surveys that he wrote in 1941, saw some spectacularly creative surveying. In 1873, James Mahood—he of the infamous Siberian experience—retraced the twelve miles of the coast meridian that Joseph Trutch had first run from the international boundary at Tsawwassen in 1859. According to Draper, Mahood deliberately destroyed all of Trutch's posts and replaced them with his own. By the time he arrived at the next parallel, he was four chains short of Trutch's original measurements. The problem, explains Draper, was not that Mahood was a bad surveyor. On the contrary, he is praised for having kept a "uniform" chain. But Mahood generously kept a uniform chain that was longer than sixty-six feet, so as to ensure that each 160-acre section would remain that size even if the one-twentieth road allowance was eventually taken off.

His motivation was noble, if technically and legally incorrect. At least it was also consistent, enabling later surveyors to work out what had occurred without much difficulty. Consistency in the use of a wrong measurement, in some respects, had greater merit than did erratic measurements that could not be easily followed. Draper describes an unnamed surveyor who regularly omitted posts—whether to save time, effort, or money is unclear—and another who, upon seeing how crooked the line he had run with his compass had turned out to be, simply wrote in his notes: "Strong local attraction here" and continued on his way.

The terms of Confederation would in time have a substantial impact on almost every surveyor in British Columbia. The new province began to benefit almost immediately from Confederation, as the Geological Survey of Canada (GSC) started preparations to begin detailed and ambitious exploratory work in the west, at the federal government's expense and in furtherance of the transcontinental rail link that was one of the fundamental provisions of the deal. The promise by the federal government to build a railway not only would provide work for land surveyors for the next fifteen years and beyond, it would significantly affect the survey systems used in British Columbia and place a permanent stamp on the province by its impact on the future city of Vancouver.

The thirteenth term of Confederation seemed less directly related to surveying activities, but it would prove otherwise. It would also be of the utmost significance in terms of the future relationship between the aboriginal occupants of British Columbia and European settlers:

> The charge of the Indians, and the trusteeship and management of the lands reserved for their use and benefit, shall be assumed by the Dominion Government and a policy as liberal as that hitherto pursued by the British Columbia Government shall be continued...tracts of land of such extent as has hitherto been the practice of the British Columbia Government to appropriate for that purpose, shall from time to time be conveyed by the Local Government to the Dominion Government in trust for the use and benefit of the Indians...

The trouble with the language used was that prior to Confederation, British Columbia had been neither particularly liberal in its policies nor generous in its reservation of lands for the use and benefit of aboriginal people. While the stamp of settlement had become indelible on the face of the province, a relationship of any kind between the provincial government and the First Nations of British Columbia, amicable or otherwise, seemed distinctly lacking.

What links did exist between the original aboriginal settlers of the country and the new pioneer immigrants tended to be with surveyors working for the government. For the surveyors, first in the field to conduct exploratory surveys and subsequently tasked with the laying out of Indian reserves, this was a mixed blessing. For aboriginal people, colonization altogether—as far as they could see from the work of the land surveyors they were encountering—was an unmitigated disaster.

Some Strange Instrument

Barry Cotton working on the Columbia Cellulose surveys in 1950. The transit has been set up on a large tree stump to gain better sighting. This was a common strategy, from the time of the earliest surveys in British Columbia, especially when a large tree was directly in the path of the desired line. H.B. "BARRY" COTTON

By the early 1850s, when the bare bones of Fort Victoria were slowly being clothed with the fabric of settlement, the aboriginal peoples of British Columbia had already experienced a distinct impact from the handful of European explorers, surveyors, and settlers they had encountered. Within the space of a few years, the impact would become resounding.

Compared with the tens of thousands of native people estimated to have been living in the territory during the mid-nineteenth century, colonists numbered far less than a thousand all told. But only twenty-five years later, a noticeable change had already occurred. By 1881, when a census of the province's population was taken, aboriginal people numbered just under 26,000, or about half of the total registered population. Smallpox and measles epidemics had already wreaked havoc, killing as many as nine out of ten people in places like Haida Gwaii (then more commonly referred to as the Queen Charlotte Islands). As early as 1862, Lieutenant Henry Spencer Palmer had commented sombrely in his report on the Bentinck Arm explorations upon "the gradually progressing extinction of the race, clear evidence of which is afforded by the sight...of the ruins of deserted lodges, once the habitations of large families of Indians that have gradually dwindled away by death until the few survivors have incorporated themselves with the larger bands." Palmer blamed this in part on war with the Haida Nation, but also on the "immoral habits of life" of native people. More realistically, aboriginal populations had simply been wiped out by disease. "Smallpox," acknowledged Palmer in the same report, "has this year contributed a sad quota of death."

Aboriginal people were also already being subjected to distorted and incorrect colonial assumptions about their culture, their predilections, and their humanity. Use of the term "Indian" to describe them was unhelpful: apart from being geographically incorrect in its application to the aboriginal people of North America, it served only to cement in place an almost insurmountable barrier between those people who were labelled as "Indian" and those who were not. The same attitudes would also effectively dictate the way in which land rights would be managed by the government. Aboriginal people and their rights were considered, in general, to be inferior to settlers and their rights. But conflicts between settlers wanting to pre-empt large tracts of land and aboriginal people used to occupying that same land were inevitable. In anticipation of such conflict, a policy was developed during the early 1850s to set specific parcels of land or "reserves" aside for Indians to live on and grow food. It was hoped that by providing them with their own land, native people would be satisfied and refrain from interfering with settlement.

Under the circumstances of incredibly rapid colonial occupation pressing up against large numbers of bewildered and increasingly resentful aboriginal people, a reserve system may have seemed to the government to be a good compromise that would protect native interests sufficiently while pacifying less moderate settler attitudes. But there were two significant problems with the policy. The concept of private land ownership as Europeans understood it, let alone permanent occupation of only one small fixed piece of property, was completely alien to aboriginal people more accustomed to travelling seasonally, living in winter villages, hunting and fishing in a large and otherwise unoccupied territory, and trading their goods with neighbouring communities. Families or even groups of families or communities might consider a particularly good fishing spot, for example, to be theirs to use exclusively. The notion of stewardship rights and responsibilities belonging to a particular aboriginal group in relation to land and resources within their territory was customary. But no system of registered title existed, nor did a limit on freedom of movement generally. The drawing of lines around their homes to notionally enclose them permanently must have been almost inconceivable.

Furthermore, criteria for determining boundaries of the "Indian reserves" were also coloured by colonial thinking. The government did not consider that native communities needed nearly as much land as settlers did. It also quickly determined that valuable agricultural property, and land ripe for mineral extraction, must be of little or no value to aboriginal people. After all, they did not seem to be using the land for those purposes to any great extent. Naturally, reasoned the government, it would be much better utilized by tax-paying settlers who would develop it for productive, revenue-generating use. Indian reserves could not, and would not, be created at the expense of agriculture, industry, and urban expansion. Accordingly, land set aside by government for reserves was often of the poorest quality, and had little or no access to water.

This did not mean that the authorities were not sympathetic to the impact of colonization on native people. The root causes behind the murder of members of Waddington's survey and road-building party in the Chilcotin region two years previously had quickly been recognized by the authorities: "The Indians have, I believe, been most injudiciously treated," wrote police commissioner Chartres Brew to the colonial secretary of British Columbia on May 23, 1864, after inspecting the scene of the murders. "It was known that the Indians were little removed from a state of starvation, yet not the slightest effort was made to obtain the goodwill of the Indians, or to guard against their enmity...The women, particularly the younger ones, were better fed than the men, as the price of prostitution to the hungry wretches was enough to eat...if a sound discretion had been exercised towards them, I believe this outrage would not have been perpetrated."

Some government authorities were very well intentioned towards aboriginal people, if misguided in their ideas for solutions. In developing land use, pre-emption, and reservation policies both for settlers and for aboriginal people, Governor James Douglas endeavoured, on the surface at least, to avoid discriminating against the latter. In doing so he was supported by British government policy, which was directed at protecting native interests. In July 1858 Edward Bulwer-Lytton wrote to Douglas instructing him: "I have to enjoin upon you to consider the best and most humane means of dealing with the Native Indians. The feelings of this country would be strongly opposed to the adoption of any arbitrary or oppressive measures towards them. I commit [the question] to you, in the full persuasion that you will pay every regard to the interests of the Natives which an enlightened humanity can suggest."

It was Bulwer-Lytton who had first written to Douglas to ask his opinion about the idea of Indian reserves. But while the goal was to reduce the potential for conflict between settler and native occupation of Crown lands, the government's bias was clearly in favour of settlers from the beginning. Aboriginal people would be provided with the exclusive use only of their own villages and of specific portions of land in their region which they were accustomed to using for agricultural or similar purposes. Douglas, who envisaged reserves being selected by aboriginal people themselves and therefore likely generous in size, advocated the policy wholeheartedly from the beginning: "I conceive the proposed plan to be at once feasible, and also the only plan which promises to result in the moral elevation of the native Indian races, in rescuing them from degradation, and protecting them from oppression and rapid decay." His enthusiasm may have been overstated, for it quickly attracted a warning from his masters in London. "Bear in mind," he was sternly cautioned, "The importance of exercising due care in laying out and defining the... reserves, so as to avoid checking at a future day the progress of the white colonist."

Unlike settler land, which was owned by the individual who had pre-empted it, the new Indian reserves were also to remain in Crown ownership. The objective of that was twofold. Many of the new reserves were being located in areas into which settlers were also rapidly moving. It was originally hoped that the reserves would therefore be temporary, that their occupants would be encouraged to move off land they didn't own and to pre-empt land in their own names instead on the same basis as anyone else. The reserves would become redundant, and the land would be available for general settlement. And, as they moved off reserves and into the system of private land ownership, native people would eventually become integrated into the new society of British Columbia.

Despite the hope that the creation of reserves would serve to avoid conflicts between settlers and aboriginal people, significant problems quickly appeared. Indian reserves on Crown lands were protected from pre-emption by settlers by the land ordinance of 1860. But how was a settler to know whether or not a particular piece of Crown land had yet been made into a reserve? And how would an aboriginal person comprehend why a settler was insisting on cultivating fields or erecting buildings on land that he or she used to freely gather medicinal plants, or hunt—and, moreover, was telling them that they were now "trespassing"? A dispute resolution mechanism was created in 1869 to deal with boundary disagreements between native people and settlers, but according to Anne Seymour, a historian with the Legal Surveys Division of Natural Resources Canada, no record exists to indicate that the mechanism was ever used, successfully or otherwise. Until and unless Indian reserves could be readily identified, any dispute resolution procedure was of little use, and the problems were bound to continue.

The process of reserve creation required first a determination of where the reserve should be located, and then a survey of some kind to establish the boundaries of the reserve. This was by no means to be an easy task for the land surveyors instructed to do the work. They faced a number of challenges, not the least of which were a lack of money on the part of government to pay for surveys, and insufficient numbers in their ranks. There were simply not enough authorized surveyors available to expeditiously conduct full legal surveys of each Indian reserve, let alone all of the pre-emptions rapidly starting to dot the map of southern and coastal British Columbia. The logistics of travel to any remote communities were of course physically onerous. But perhaps most challenging of all for the surveyors concerned was an utter lack of consistency in the directions they received from Victoria or New Westminster from time to time; and on occasion, outright conflict in what they were told to do.

Under the terms of treaties that Governor Douglas had signed with some Vancouver Island nations during the early 1850s, "village sites" and "enclosed fields" were to be reserved and the members of the nation would be free to hunt over unoccupied lands. But what that meant in terms of surveying specific areas of land was far from clear. No provision was included in the "Douglas treaties" to determine what constituted a "village," let alone where its boundaries might lie. Nor were aboriginal people accustomed to "enclosing" or fencing in their fields. Wild camas grew where they grew; potato patches needed no fences. It was extremely difficult for surveyors to comply with instructions to survey and mark off Indian reserves so vaguely described.

Another dilemma arose with respect to the existence of European settlements, no matter how small, in areas covered by the Douglas treaties. When Joseph Pemberton started surveying reserve land in the Victoria area during the 1850s, it was after he had completed his triangulation surveys for the region. A number of private properties and a townsite had already been surveyed as well, all more or less neat polygons tied in to the orderly, straight lines of the triangulation survey. The local Indian villages and fields to be reserved under the treaties, however, were much more haphazard in shape because they were based on loose descriptions of the villages and other areas concerned. From Pemberton's perspective as a surveyor, of course, it was highly undesirable to consider drawing irregular or oddly shaped boundaries around the Indian reserves if that would conflict with the tidy and regular lines of his existing surveys. Accordingly, notwithstanding the obligation under the treaties to locate villages and fields where they actually lay, Pemberton opted for convenience over obligation and laid out the reserve boundaries to conform to the triangulation surveys instead.

By comparison, the approach that Douglas took to providing instructions for the surveys of reserves seemed to be governed largely by two factors: his desire to be fair, and cost. By the early 1860s, his instructions to the chief commissioner of lands and works (at that time, still Colonel Moody) were to lay out the boundaries of reserves according to the wishes of the aboriginal community itself. It was a simple administrative way to settle both location and size in one move, and from his perspective, it was indisputably fair to the native people concerned. At the same time, despite the evidence of uncertainty arising from the lack of defined boundaries around the new land reserves, he thought it sufficient to mark them out simply with "conspicuous" wooden posts, a relatively cheap option but debatable in its accuracy. In his desire for quick results, Douglas believed that proper surveys could wait until there was sufficient money in the government's coffers.

Colonel Moody complicated matters further, qualifying Douglas's instructions as he thought fit. According to Cole Harris in his history of reserve creation in British Columbia, *Making Native Space*, when Moody passed on to his surveyors in the field Douglas's instructions that reserves were to be laid out as "pointed out by the Indians themselves," he added the words "within reason." Moody would also caution his surveyors to ensure that reserve sizes were not artificially inflated.

Once in the field, the reality was that surveyors simply had to use their own judgment based on the circumstances facing them. As a result, final reserve sizes depended to some degree on who the surveyor was and how he interpreted his instructions. Captain Parsons of the Royal Engineers simply passed the buck, referring the final decision to the local district magistrate. Sapper Turnbull, surveying in the Fraser Canyon region near Yale under Parsons's authority, took a conservative approach: those reserves are some of the smallest in the province. William Cox, on the other hand, who marked out reserves in the Okanagan region in 1861, followed the original directive from Douglas to the letter. Surveyor William McColl did the same in the Fraser Valley in 1864. Those reserves were, by contrast, the largest in the region—at least until Joseph Trutch arrived on the scene.

Trutch took over from Moody as chief commissioner of lands and works in 1864. No great friend to Douglas, and of an entirely different frame of mind when it came to aboriginal people, Trutch's leanings were evident from the start. He immediately outlawed native rights of pre-emption of Crown lands, effectively confining aboriginal people to living on the reserves. To Trutch, European settlement was the first and foremost priority, and no interference was to be brooked from the Indians. He also began taking steps to reduce the size of the Okanagan and Fraser Valley reserves, which he considered "entirely disproportionate" to the number of aboriginal people in residence on them. He attacked the validity of instructions that had been issued to surveyors prior to his tenure, asserting that any reserves already laid out under that authority had been laid out illegally. "The subject of reserving lands for the use of the Indian tribes does not appear to have been dealt with on any established system during Sir James Douglas' administration," Trutch wrote to the acting colonial secretary on August 28, 1867. "The rights of Indians to hold lands were totally undefined...no reserves of lands specially for Indian purposes were made by official notice in the *Gazette*, and those Indian Reserves which were informally made seem to have been so reserved in furtherance of verbal instructions only from the Governor." By 1867, according to Cole Harris, Trutch was instructing surveyors to "interfere as little as possible with lands already taken up by whites." He had also limited the size of reserves to ten acres per adult male plus necessary grazing land. By the following year that had been reduced further, to ten acres per family. The cost issue remained unchanged: surveys were to be conducted "as cheaply as possible."

Correspondence regarding William McColl's surveys during this period illustrates the difficulties facing surveyors under Trutch's authority. McColl was instructed in April 1864 by the Surveyor General's Office to survey reserves on the Fraser River, between New Westminster and the Harrison River. In his written instructions the hapless surveyor was given one month to set out corner and intermediate posts in order to lay out "whatsoever land the Indians claim as theirs." It took McColl one month and eleven days, but as he reported to Trutch on May 16, he had an excuse in hand: "I beg to inform you that, in addition to the written instructions, I had further verbal instructions given to me by Sir James Douglas, to the effect that all lands claimed by the Indians were to be included in the reserve; the Indians were to have as much land as they wished...I also...have laid off more reserves than what was originally intended...a considerable larger amount of work than what was expected."

Trutch, naturally, was horrified. He disputed Douglas's authority to have given McColl any additional instructions: "Acting on this latter indefinite authority, rather than on [his] written instructions, McColl marked out reserves of most unreasonable extent," complained Trutch. He accused McColl of not having actually surveyed the reserves but merely estimating distances in his sketches: "He seems to have merely walked over the ground claimed by the Indians, setting up stakes at the corners pointed out by them...and then to have estimated the acreage contained therein." Trutch was of the view that the reserves should be reduced substantially, as being "of no real value to the Indians and utterly unprofitable to the public interests." Seeking approval from London, he wrote to the acting colonial secretary recommending that the government "disavow absolutely McColl's authority to make these reserves of the extravagant extent laid out by him, and instead to survey off the reserves afresh."

Trutch's attitude was best illustrated in his own words: "The Indians have really no right to the lands that they claim, nor are they of any actual value or utility to them; and I cannot see why they should either retain these lands to the prejudice of the general interests of the Colony, or be allowed to make a market of them." He was nervous of the reaction the reserve reductions would stimulate on the part of the native people affected, all the same. "Very careful management of the dispositions of the Indian claimants would be requisite to prevent serious dissatisfaction; firmness and discretion are equally essential...to convince the Indians that the Government intend only to deal fairly with them, and the whites, who desire to settle on and cultivate the lands which the Indians have really no right to and no use for."

The Colonial Office readily agreed with Trutch, albeit in slightly more diplomatic terms: "There is good reason to believe that Mr. McColl very greatly misunderstood [his] instructions...and he has in consequence created reserves of and far beyond the wants or expectations of the Indians," replied colonial secretary William Young to Trutch on November 6, 1867. But Young could give Trutch little assistance when it came to advising him on how to pacify the understandably resentful aboriginal people affected by the reserve reductions. Trutch was to direct the work of reserve reduction, Young wrote hopefully from far distant London, "in such manner as shall avoid any misunderstanding or complications with the Indians."

In the end, Trutch had much the same experience as many other surveyors given the task of marking off small and insufficient plots of land as reserves: he met little resistance. At least, his subsequent report suggests that outcome: "The Indians...are ready to abide by any decision the Governor may make as to the extent of land to be reserved for their use...They are only anxious to retain their villages and potato patches and such moderate extents of land around them as may be finally reserved by Government for them." The majority of the reports of reserve surveys from that period sound similar: "Indians satisfied"; "they expressed themselves satisfied"; "Indians to which these three reserves belong to were perfectly satisfied"; "Indians, with one unimportant exception, well satisfied"; even "Indians submissively satisfied."

There appear to be few, if any, equivalent contemporaneous written reports by aboriginal people, voicing their reactions in their own words or from their own viewpoint. The records of interaction over the creation and survey of reserves largely exist in reports such as Trutch's and in the field notes and diaries of the surveyors instructed to lay out reserve boundaries. Naturally, they are coloured by the perceptions and attitudes of those individual surveyors. Those varied widely. Trutch perhaps represented a viewpoint at one end of a cultural spectrum that was generally accepted by a society focused intently on making its fortune in a new land rich in natural resources. But he was by no means made of the cloth from which most surveyors were cut. At the other end of the spectrum, many surveyors working in the field harboured a genuine sympathy and liking for the people they encountered and tried hard to satisfy their needs, despite instructions that limited their ability to do so. Survey crews also often hired aboriginal people to work with them as packers, paddlers, guides, and cooks. Many positive experiences were recorded, indicating mutual respect; in as many instances, however, a gulf of expectations and cultural understanding, despite the best of intentions, resulted in a frustration that reveals itself starkly in the written records.

On December 3, 1868, surveyor Edward Mohun reported on his work at Katzie, on the lower Fraser River. "On the map furnished me...the reserve is shown to have a frontage of about 20 chains," he wrote. "The chief claims 40 chains...At Matsqui about 80 acres was laid out, which has caused great dissatisfaction. The chief says it is nearly all swamp; that it cuts off the burial ground and the potato patches...and he wishes his west boundary about 20 chains lower down the river." Mohun did his best to help: "I promised to lay his complaint before you," he wrote to Joseph Trutch, "as what he states is true, and he trusts that you will give directions to have his western boundary removed lower down." The final reserve size was about sixteen acres larger than Mohun's survey at Matsqui, so it seems that Trutch may actually have been sympathetic to that particular complaint.

James Launders's experience surveying reserves in the Chilliwack region the same year was similar to that of Mohun. With respect to Sumass No. 2 reserve, Launders noted that

> The Indians were not well satisfied; they wanted all their original claim.
>
> The reserve which I was directed to survey on the opposite bank of the Fraser River was not accepted by the Indians, it was to contain 20 acres, but there is no land above high water mark

for 3 miles along the right bank of the river; small patches...are cultivated by separate families and the largest would not exceed ½ an acre. They wished me to put down 4 stakes at the corners of each of these strips and could not comprehend my non-compliance. After going with or meeting them on the ground twice I had to abandon the hopeless task of giving them satisfaction.

I would recommend that some further enquiry be made or something be done to secure to them in some way these patches... the reserve around their village...is liable to floods, and [they] would not have it. I therefore did not survey it.

As settlement progressed in British Columbia, things did not become any easier for either aboriginal people or the surveyors tasked with drawing reserve boundaries. Five years after the province joined Canada in 1871, an Indian Reserve Commission was jointly established by the federal and provincial governments with a view to allocating and surveying the remaining reserves in the province. Four British Columbian land surveyors worked extensively with the commissioners over the next twenty-odd years: Ashdown Henry Green, Edward Mohun, Captain William Sugden Jemmett, and Ernest Meeson Skinner. And, whereas the commissioners changed from time to time—Gilbert Malcolm Sproat was a commissioner for several years before Trutch's brother-in-law Peter O'Reilly took over as the sole commissioner after 1880—the approach by government to the issue did not change at all. The policy on the size and number of reserves remained consistently restrictive. That meant the work of surveyors was not about to get any easier.

Reflecting on the records left by the commissioners and by their staff of discussions between them and aboriginal people, Cole Harris remarks: "Theirs was not talk among equals...one cannot but be struck by the deep inequalities embedded in this colonial encounter." Sproat, unlike Trutch, felt that James Douglas had not been too liberal in his instructions to provide to the Indians what they wanted; indeed, his writings indicate a commitment to satisfying their needs and to understanding that theirs was a different way of life. Sproat thought that seasonal encampments, for example, should be considered to be permanent villages for the purpose of reserve allocations. But even Sproat was limited by an entrenched bias in favour of settlers. His instructions to the surveyors, according to Harris, required them to make any of their decisions on reserve size subject to "the controlling necessity for settling up the country with white settlers." If that meant survey lines would "run through favourite Indian camping places and berrying grounds, and perhaps... cut the tribal race course in two," that was of trivial consequence. Any allocations that Sproat did attempt to make that Victoria considered to favour the Indians unduly were overturned or simply ignored. Finally, he resigned in 1880, and Peter O'Reilly took over.

O'Reilly was not only related to Trutch, he was a man of a like mind. For nearly eighteen years he would dominate the way in which reserves were systematically created, for the most part, on the poorest land and of the smallest size possible—and, because O'Reilly rarely travelled from Victoria to any of the aboriginal communities affected by his decisions, with little or no consultation with the people concerned. It was left to the hapless surveyors to deal with the inevitable reactions.

Resistance was stronger in some areas than others. The Nass Valley was one of the few places O'Reilly did visit, albeit briefly. According to Daniel Raunet in his history of the Nisga'a land claims, *Without Surrender, Without Consent,* after O'Reilly's departure William Jemmett was prevented by the Nisga'a from carrying out any surveys. Chief Tat-ca-kaks of Lakalzap lodged an affidavit in protest against O'Reilly's arbitrary decisions over reserve boundaries, stating that "we are not satisfied with Mr. O'Reilly coming and measuring off our land...we have never been willing that our land should be surveyed." Chief Skadeen of Gitlakda-mix said much the same thing a few years later: "the reserve is not large enough for us to live on...Mr. O'Reilly did not do right...because I did not want our land surveyed he said he would take my power away and give it to someone else. God gave us a good survey when he gave us the land."

In 1983, Chief Frank Calder recounted the events when the first surveyors came to Gitlakdamix:

So...there's five people across, over Gitlakdamix. And they're looking through some strange instrument…By God, yes, it's a tent, there is smoke coming out beside the tent, and they counted five people…

The Queen wants to survey a line down the river, you know. So far down that way it's gonna cross the river and then it's gonna come back up, and it's gonna go a ways behind your village, and it's gonna cross the river again and come down here. That's what we're doing [they said].

Eight o'clock every canoe beached started heading across. Every Nisga'a has a Hudson Bay musket. They marched up. Never argued to ask them what they were doing. They just said, 'Get off my land.' The guys left. Who wouldn't leave with all these guys with their muskets?

The Tsimshian at Metlakatla did not fare so well as the Nisga'a. With the help of a former missionary, William Duncan, the Tsimshian did resist the imposition of a reserve system for a number of years, rejecting any attempts at surveys. But in the spring of 1885, Duncan left Metlakatla to visit England. In his absence, surveyor Samuel Tuck was sent out to attempt once more to establish reserve boundaries. This time, he succeeded—or at least, thought he did. When he returned the following year to complete his work, he once again met complete resistance. His stakes were pulled out and his instruments were taken from him. Finally, he was forced to leave altogether. In retaliation, a gunboat and police were sent in to arrest the key offenders and protect Tuck as he completed his work. Defeated at last, several hundred Tsimshian people left Metlakatla and moved north to Annette Island in Alaskan territory, from which location they would never return.

The field notes of various surveyors of the era make compelling reading, highlighting the gulf between government intentions and First Nations' expectations. Ashdown Henry Green witnessed O'Reilly's meeting with the Homalco at Orford Bay on August 8, 1888. The Homalco wanted fishing sites protected, a concept that O'Reilly simply could not grasp:

William, Chief: …Mr. Sproat did not come here. I told him I wanted the river; he did not go to the head of Bute Inlet…I am sorry my land is not surveyed that's why I am glad to see you.

Commissioner: I intend to give you the good land about your houses, but what is the use of giving you these bare rocks?

Sometimes, surveyors were simply frustrated in their efforts by circumstance or deliberate, but subtle, evasion. James Launders visited Burrard Inlet north of Vancouver on September 21, 1869: "Mr. Brew... accompanied us to the above Indian Ranch to speak with the Indians about their land. The chief was not there at the Ranch therefore there was nothing definite settled. Rain," he added gloomily, "all day." On September 2, 1891, Francis Devereux was working his way up the Nass River with the help of a native guide. "Began traverse of shoreline from camp," wrote Devereux in his field notes, "but could not find the tree which was blazed by the commissioner, and after a thorough search, my Indian informed me that we were not in the proper place for it." Devereux struck camp and forged his way north a further seven miles, only to discover that he had been in the right place at the beginning, despite what his guide had told him. Unsurprisingly, Edward Mohun found that it was next to impossible to hire native people from one community to help him survey another community's reserve. Mohun also complained at having to pay a per diem of $1.50 to "my own Indians" because a colleague had agreed to pay that rate to "his Indians."

In 1905, land surveyor Arthur Wheeler published his detailed report on the surveys of the Selkirk Range in southeast British Columbia. Wheeler wrote:

It [must not] be overlooked that most of the early travelling in these regions was by paths and trails previously mapped out and travelled by the Indian inhabitants, their lines of communication when passing to and fro on hunting expeditions. The Indian applies his natural ability in this respect in a wonderful manner and, as a rule, his selection of routes is seldom at fault. They furnish fair samples of engineering skill, while his knowledge of topographical formation...enables him to see at a glance the proper place to look for a road...it is likely that the passes entered and recorded by Sir George Simpson and Capt. Palliser's parties were travelled

Indian routes. To those journeying through the mountain wilds, the difference of an Indian trail and no Indian trail becomes very apparent.

Wheeler—whose positive attitude towards aboriginal people was one too infrequently expressed in the records—was writing about the transcontinental rail link that had been forged through the mountains during the mid-1880s. By that time, the attention of the dominion government had already largely turned away from native people and the reserve-making process, and was more focused on railway-making in British Columbia under the terms of Confederation with the province. The work of surveying Indian reserves was far from complete, and a handful of surveyors would continue that work into the early years of the twentieth century. Nearly one hundred years would pass before the voices of aboriginal protest against their treatment would be raised again with any strength, let alone heard. For the time being, they were being drowned out by the roar of train engines. The settlement of British Columbia was about to expand at a speed unprecedented elsewhere in the country. Land surveyors were ready and waiting on the platform of change.

8

A Sea of Mountains

A bearing tree carved in 1920 and found on September 17, 1991, by David Bazett, BCLS 576, on British Columbia's central coast. DAVID BAZETT

Never in British Columbia's entire history have its residents been united on a political issue. Confederation with the Dominion of Canada on July 20, 1871, was no exception. Some embraced their province's entry into Canada, others felt betrayed. Many felt that, despite the downside of ceding control to Ottawa, it was worth the trade-off: "It is very awkward as a Dominion officer having to apply to Canada for orders," wrote provincial Supreme Court judge Henry Crease to C.W. Franks on November 13, 1871. "It seems further than Home used to be but the prospect of a Rway. sometime before the Greek Calends makes rough places smooth."

The promise of a transcontinental railway had been a compelling force behind the colony's decision to join Confederation. By the late 1860s, the only means of transportation through the interior of British Columbia were horse trails and wagon roads. The Dewdney Trail had been completed as far as east Kootenay, but it was a slow and inefficient journey. Travellers from the east coast of the continent had to take passage by sea around the southerly route of Cape Horn, then north again to San Francisco or Victoria, or endure an arduous cross-country trip by wagon trail. Both options were expensive journeys that took several months. In the meantime, more and more valuable mineral discoveries were being made in the interior—some too close to the United States border for comfort. The political threat from the south had not disappeared with the completion of the boundary surveys. Significant pressure was building in Victoria as entrepreneurs lobbied government aggressively for effective and economical means to travel and freight cargo to the east.

Rail was the only feasible, long-term option—but the colonial government could not afford the cost. Indeed, in the spirit of its successors over the years, it had already run up a debt exceeding $1.5 million. A marriage with Canada that brought both a dowry of a railroad and a greater sense of national security seemed not only strategically wise, but economically inevitable. British Columbia's negotiators—Joseph Trutch among them—struck what appeared to be a good deal. Under the terms of union, the colony's debt would be assumed by Ottawa, which also committed to the completion of a transcontinental link by no later than 1881, at its expense. It was also agreed that the dominion government would pay British Columbia the sum of $100,000 a year in perpetuity. The trade-off for that stipend would later be regretted, but seemed desirable at the time: the granting to the Canadian Pacific Railway (CPR), the chosen railroad builder, of twenty miles of land on either side of the railway for its entire length. The objective was to encourage development and settlement, at both the expense and to the profit of the CPR. What was not foreseen at the time of creation of this "railway belt" were the vast complications that would later arise in terms of land titles and surveying systems.

The more immediate problem, however, was that the ink was barely dry on the papers of Confederation when it became clear that work on the railway would see significant delays. Flip-flopping governments in Ottawa caused a hiatus in progress lasting several years. Arguments between the provincial government and the dominion government as to where the western terminus of the railway should be located also caused delays. Victoria wanted the terminus to be on Vancouver Island, but Canada considered that running the line as far as the mainland coast would be a sufficient fulfillment of its obligations. But any initial lack of political will from Ottawa to see the project through paled in comparison with the physical requirements of building the railroad across British Columbia. The sheer difficulty of establishing a route through the Rocky Mountains and then through the seemingly even more impenetrable Selkirk Range posed surveying challenges that would take more than a decade to overcome.

Charles Aeneas Shaw was a British Columbia land surveyor who spent a significant portion of his career during the late nineteenth century working on surveys for the CPR. In the foreword to Shaw's book *Tales of a Pioneer Surveyor*, editor Raymond Hull provides a compelling description of the surveying techniques employed by the early railroad surveyors in looking for routes through the mountains. Following the planning of the general route for the line by the CPR engineers, the surveyors were sent into uncharted country to reconnoitre the most suitable options for locating the line. "If the line was to cross a height of land, the leader had to tramp the countryside, climbing trees, scrambling up mountains, looking for the most favourable point to make that crossing," wrote Hull. "Suppose the line were moved to the other side of the valley. Would it increase or reduce construction costs? How would it affect the costs of operation?" Hull points out that a longer route with easier grades might be more cost-effective than a short, steep route, but both had to be thoroughly explored. Climatic conditions also had to be considered, as solid ground in winter might become swamp in summer, and a sluggish stream in the fall a roaring torrent in the spring. Altitude, curvature of the future line, avalanche routes, the proximity of potentially rich mineral deposits, accessibility to good timber and a water supply—all these things and more had to be assessed by the surveyors and reported upon.

Once the feasible routes had been established, they were all then surveyed properly with instruments, and precise measurements of all aspects of the trial lines—altitude, distance, angles, and direction—were recorded. Those lines would be cleared of brush and trees, bearing trees blazed, and posts placed to indicate a change in direction. The data gathered allowed draughtsmen to plot the lines on a plan, and engineers to calculate the specific costs of construction. Based on that information, a decision could be made on the final route to be used. That, however, was not the end of the survey work: a specific "location survey" then had to be conducted, to make all the final improvements possible in the chosen line before construction would even begin. All of this sounds straightforward on paper. In the steep terrain of the mountains—where game was scarce, snow was frequent, and every item needed for the job had to be packed in on foot, into places horses couldn't go—the process was far from simple to implement.

When the dominion government promised British Columbia a railway line in 1871, it wasn't unreasonable to think it would take all of ten years to complete. As it happened, construction took significantly longer than ten years. The famous last spike in the line was driven into the ground at Craigellachie by Donald Alexander Smith, the future Lord Strathcona, on November 7, 1885. But when Sir Sandford Fleming was appointed by the CPR in 1871 as the engineer-in-chief to oversee the survey and construction of the line, the inevitability of significant delays was not yet obvious. Fleming did not waste any time, and survey parties were organized as quickly as possible to begin exploratory work.

Fleming's instructions to the chiefs of his survey teams were succinct:

Each party is placed under the control of an Engineer, whose duty it will be to maintain proper discipline…In conducting the survey, the engineer of a party is expected to be at its head every day, exploring in front and to the right and left, in order to see what obstructions may be in the way and to determine the best manner of avoiding them.

A pair of light steel climbers will be furnished to each party in order to enable the engineers in charge to climb a tree with facility…

The following is the outfit of each man: two pairs of pants, two coats, three flannel shirts, three pairs of drawers, six pairs of socks, one pair of mitts, two pairs of strong boots or shoepacks, one towel, one brush and comb, and a few other small articles; the whole personal outfit must not exceed thirty pounds. The number of firearms in each party is to be limited to one rifle and one double-barrelled gun.

Among the many British Columbian land surveyors engaged to work on the transcontinental link were Ashdown Henry Green, Edgar Dewdney, Charles Perry (formerly of the Royal Engineers), Charles Hanington, George Hargreaves, Edward Mohun, and Herman Tiedemann. These men and their crews were sent out in divisional teams denoted with a letter of the alphabet. Party Q, for example, travelled up to the headwaters of the Fraser River. Parties U and V, led by John Trutch, worked between Kamloops and Burrard Inlet. Parties S and T, led by Walter Moberly, went to the Rocky Mountains.

Despite Palliser's gloomy conclusion that no route through the Canadian Rockies was viable, he had not entirely dismissed the potential of the Kicking Horse Pass as having potential at least for a road: "In that pass Dr. Hector has observed a peculiarity which distinguishes it from the other we had examined, viz: the absence of any abrupt step at the commencement of the descent to the west," wrote Palliser in his report. That feature made it reasonable to consider that a railway line could in fact be constructed through the pass.

Palliser's negative view of the Rocky Mountain routes may have been

A CPR survey on the Kemano River, June 1874. CHARLES HORETZKY/LIBRARY AND ARCHIVES CANADA PA-009290

coloured by the hardships his survey team had suffered during the three years they spent in the field. The challenges that they faced had to be met and overcome by all future survey teams, as well as the railroad construction teams. Part of their job was to assess not only the technical feasibility of the potential routes, but also to suggest the most economical and practical ways to utilize them in constructing the railroad. In doing so, they were required to test every possible aspect of the routes under consideration. That meant, of course, enduring all the consequences of exploration in previously uncharted, high alpine terrain. "Very little vegetation appears along the summit of the watershed," wrote Palliser of the Kananaskis Pass. "[It] is overspread with masses of stones and rocks, and the only animal we have seen is the siffleur (Hoary Marmot)." Food was scarce. It was impossible to pack sufficient supplies into such remote country, and hunting was necessary to supplement their meagre fare. "It is excellent eating when fat," said Palliser of the hapless marmots the team encountered. At Vermilion Pass there was no game at all, and the survey party suffered extreme hunger. Its members were forced to carry on travelling until they reached the western slopes of the mountains, where they were able at last to capture some game.

Apart from Palliser's party, other surveyors had been exploring the various mountain passes for rail route potential well before 1871. As early as 1864, an explorer named J. Jenkins created a detailed map of the Columbia River area north from Wild Horse Creek up to and including what was known as the "Big Bend" of the river (now long vanished under the waters of Kinbasket Lake, after the construction of the Mica Dam in the 1970s). Despite the prevailing belief that the Selkirks were impassable, Jenkins made note of several Indian trails across the mountains, including one that would in fact have successfully taken him through them, had he completed what he apparently intended to do. At a place on the river that he recorded on his map as being called Gil-Ces-Che-Sin, Jenkins noted: "Proposed to cross the great bend of the Columbia here with 1 Indian, intending that the other should go round with the Canoe: but they objected on account of the Rapids, and Portaged…" Without the assistance of his guides, Jenkins did not pursue the trail further. Despite the creation of his detailed map and notes, no apparent note was made in Victoria of the existence of the trail. It does not appear that Jenkins ever returned to try again.

The next surveyor in the area was the province's assistant surveyor general, Walter Moberly. By 1865 Moberly had established a route through the Monashee Mountains (then known as the Gold Range) at Eagle Pass, west of present-day Revelstoke and the Selkirks. As Reverend George Monro Grant described it in 1885 in "The Canada Pacific Railway," an article he wrote for *Century* magazine, Moberly had been sent into the area to explore after gold had been found nearby: "One day, not far from Shuswap Lake, among tangled mountains choked with dense underbrush and fallen timber, valleys radiating to every point of the compass, but leading nowhere, [Moberly] saw an eagle flying to the east up one of the valleys. Accepting the omen, he followed and discovered the pass which he called after the eagle, though it might more fitly be called by his own name."

Moberly's name would not grace any of the mountain passes that the railway would eventually cross. But he may be the best remembered surveyor, after Fleming, to be involved in the construction of the CPR line. Moberly was a colourful character, beset by problems and challenges wherever he went. Later in life, he would become pompous and self-congratulatory, rewriting the events of forty years previously and reinventing himself in his public writings as a man greatly wronged by the authorities in his various endeavours—including his work on the CPR line—and as a benefactor of all British Columbians in his work surveying what he referred to as "his" railway. But if that was somewhat exaggerated, Moberly's memory does without a doubt deserve respect. He flung himself with passion into all his work in British Columbia with an unfailing integrity towards his crew and his objective, whether it was the survey of a Vancouver site, his work on the Cariboo Road, or the construction of the new trail from Hope to Princeton with Edgar Dewdney.

Moberly had spent his early surveying years working in Ontario, where he had first met Sandford Fleming and made a favourable impression. He had arrived in the Crown colony of British Columbia in late 1858, taking on contract surveying work for the government. The hapless but sincere Moberly, who at times invested much of his own money to ensure that his projects were completed, found himself ill-served by a government that did not feel inclined to reimburse him. Moberly complained in his memoirs that it left him a "ruined man" and that it took him eight years to pay off all his debts. He had a brief fling with politics, running successfully for election in the Cariboo East riding at the end of 1864, but resigned after only one session to accept the position of assistant surveyor general. Moberly's first love was to be in the field—and by 1865 his ambition to discover the key to the Selkirks' lock was his single-minded objective.

A variety of routes through the Rockies were already known to be possible options for a railway, but the impenetrable Selkirks remained the bigger challenge. Failure to find a pass would mean that the railway would have to detour a significant distance to the north to go around the Big Bend of the Columbia River, at much greater expense to the CPR. Moberly desperately wanted to find the pass that would mean a more direct route. "If a pass could only be found across the Selkirks," writes George Grant, "he felt that his work would be completed." However, like his predecessor Jenkins, Moberly would not be the one to receive that credit.

After finding the Eagle Pass in 1865, Moberly crossed the Columbia and started working his way up the Illecillewaet River. There are differing accounts of what happened next. According to retired land surveyor Barry Cotton, one pass up the east fork of the river seemed to hold promise, and Moberly sent his assistant up to explore. His journal entry for July 13, 1865, recorded the failure of that attempt: "Perry...did not reach the divide, but reported a low wide valley as far as he went. His exploration has not settled the point whether it would be possible to get through the mountains by this valley, but I fear not. He ought to have got on the divide, and his failure is a great disappointment to me..."

In Grant's version of the story published in 1885, however, there is no mention of an assistant. According to Grant, Moberly was thwarted first by taking a wrong turn up the north fork, subsequently by losing his Indian guides, and finally by the onset of winter snows in the mountains. "Reluctantly," writes Grant, "Moberly had to content himself with putting on record that the easterly fork of the Ille-Cille-Waet should be examined before a route for a transcontinental railway was finally determined on." Arthur Wheeler, one of Canada's most distinguished surveyors and an author of some talent, wrote a detailed account of the surveying of the Selkirk Range in 1905. Wheeler also mentions Perry, the assistant, but makes no mention of any exploration of the east fork of the Illecillewaet River.

A different version of events again appeared some years later. In 1909, Moberly wrote a lengthy paper entitled "Early History of Canadian Pacific Railway" for the Art, Historical and Scientific Association of Vancouver.

The passage of time had perhaps lent him a creative perspective as to what really happened, but by then he had polished his own version of events masterfully, and entirely to his own credit. "It will be seen that six years before British Columbia became a province of the Dominion I had made discoveries that insured to Canada a capital line for the present Canadian Pacific Railway through the mountain region of Canada principally at my own expense," he wrote loftily. "I may say that to find a line for my proposed railway had now become the ambition of my life, for I had now got a tolerably good idea of the immense value and importance, both commercially and politically, my proposed railway would be to the British Empire, to the Dominion of Canada and to British Columbia."

Notwithstanding that he had recorded in his diary on November 16, 1871, that he had "never had the opportunity to examine thoroughly" Rogers Pass—and indeed, had again missed the opportunity to do it that year—Moberly now unequivocally claimed credit for its discovery. But his failure to traverse the east fork properly lost him the glory all the same. More than ten years after Moberly had attempted to break through the Selkirks, one Major A.B. Rogers would be the one to finally locate the pass via the east fork and, to Moberly's great and lasting bitterness, have his name enshrined upon it permanently. That bitterness is reflected in his response more than thirty years later, which was simply to dismiss Rogers Pass as the wrong route after all: "From my own exploration of the valley of the Illecillewaet River made in 1865, and of its southeasterly branch and Rogers Pass made in the year of 1866 by one of my assistants, Mr. Albert Perry, nearly twenty years before Major A.B. Rogers explored the pass, it is my opinion that the location of the Canadian Pacific Railway across the Selkirk Range of mountains is a very serious mistake," he wrote in 1909. Moberly now claimed that the Selkirks were completely unsuitable for a railway traverse; and that he had always thought the route around the top of the Big Bend would have been far better. As to Rogers Pass itself, Moberly thought that if anything, "It should be named Perry's Pass, as he was the first white man to traverse it."

Moberly's sentiments on the correct route through the Selkirks were, however, heavily influenced by events that had transpired after 1871 and by the way in which the final CPR route through Kicking Horse Pass had been settled. If Moberly's preferred route through Howse Pass had been selected, then indeed a route around the Big Bend would have seemed a more seamless continuation of the line. But in his choice of pass through the Rockies the beleaguered surveyor was yet again thwarted—this time, by his boss.

Moberly had left the country for a few years after his disappointment on the Illecillewaet. But in 1871 Sir Sandford Fleming took him on to undertake the surveys of the proposed line through the Rockies. Unfortunately, their relationship was flawed almost immediately by a firm difference of opinion as to which pass was most suitable, and in the end it would be completely poisoned by that difference. Fleming favoured the Yellowhead. Moberly preferred the more northerly Howse. Perhaps in an attempt to pacify Moberly and to rule out the merits of Howse Pass, Fleming gave him the authority to run a trial location of Howse Pass. In his enthusiasm—or perhaps stubbornness, believing his opinion would be borne out in the field—Moberly immediately began planning a full-scale location survey. Having spent several months making advance arrangements, he was about to set out when he received word from Fleming that the line was to be located through the Yellowhead. Devastated, he quit the country not long afterward and handed over his responsibilities to a man named Marcus Smith. Moberly was not present to witness the irony that, in the end, the line would run neither through the Yellowhead nor through Howse Pass, but through Kicking Horse Pass to the south.

Moberly might well have been pleased, however, had he witnessed an exchange between his nemesis, Rogers, and land surveyor Charles Aeneas Shaw in 1883. Shaw was in charge of the final location surveys through Kicking Horse Pass, working just ahead of the railway construction crews heading west over the Rockies. No love was lost between the two, for Shaw had re-surveyed much of Rogers's work through the Kicking Horse and reported it to be not only faulty, but located in such a way that it would cost the CPR in excess of one and a half million dollars more than it should. The powers that be had agreed with Shaw's conclusions, so when Rogers and Shaw finally encountered each other in late 1883, the following exchange, as recounted by Shaw in *Tales of a Pioneer Surveyor*, was not surprising, if perhaps a touch embroidered for effect:

Charles Aeneas Shaw, PLS 34: part of survey party, west fork of Kettle River, date uncertain but possibly late nineteenth century. OFFICE OF THE SURVEYOR GENERAL

We passed down the Kicking Horse Valley and finally reached the supply depot in the Columbia Valley. Major Rogers came out to meet us…he had evidently forgotten me, for his greeting was, "Who the hell are you, and where the hell do you think you're going?"

I answered sharply, "It's none of your damned business, to either question. Who the hell are you, anyway?"

He answered, "I am Major Rogers."

I then said, "My name is Shaw. I've been sent by Van Horne to examine and report on the pass through the Selkirks."

This made him fairly froth at the mouth. He said, "You're the ------ prairie gopher that has come into the mountains and ruined my reputation as an engineer," coupled with considerable more profanity.

I was now getting annoyed, so I jumped off my horse and, seizing him by the throat, shook him until his teeth rattled. I said, "Another word out of you, and I'll throw you in the river and drown you."

This quelled him.

Construction of the CPR line in British Columbia finally began at Yale on May 15, 1880. In the meantime, the intended development and settlement benefits of creating the railway belt had yet to show themselves. If anything, the belt's creation resulted in significant delays to settlement; at a minimum, it created huge complexities and problems that even in the early twenty-first century continued to cause bureaucratic and political headaches for the provincial government.

The various disputes between Ottawa and Victoria over such matters as the proposed western terminus of the line, combined with delays caused by a change of government in Ottawa, had effectively resulted in a development limbo in the railway belt instead of a development boom. The final location of the rail line in British Columbia was not settled until 1883; only then could the forty-mile-wide strip of land, amounting to 17,150 square miles, or 10,976,000 acres, be transferred from provincial jurisdiction to the dominion government. The amount of land transferred was staggering in its sheer size. Another 3.5 million acres of land was transferred in what became known as the "Peace River Block," to compensate Canada for gaps in the railway belt where land had already been granted to settlers prior to Confederation. On Vancouver Island, a further 1.9 million acres—about a quarter of the entire island—was granted in 1884 to the dominion government in exchange for building the island railway, the Esquimalt and Nanaimo line. It had been reluctantly conceded by Victoria that the western terminus of the transcontinental link would end at Burrard Inlet rather than in Victoria. However, the province insisted that Canada honour its obligations under the terms of union by arranging for the building of an island railway.

Unlike the rest of the railway belt, the Vancouver Island land grant (which quickly became known as the Esquimalt and Nanaimo or "E&N" grant) was to be held on trust in the name of the dominion government but to remain under provincial jurisdiction for surveying and

An engineering survey party poses at Moberly House, in the Columbia River valley. They were working on closing the 233-mile gap in the CPR main line between Stephen and Savonas, in the fall of 1884. CANADIAN PACIFIC RAILWAY ARCHIVES NS.1341

land subdivision matters. The remainder of the belt fell under dominion control in its entirety. Jurisdictional problems reared their heads immediately, as did property-rights disputes.

Until 1884, it had been impossible to effectively continue the process of issuing land, mineral, water, and timber grants in the various portions of the railway belt, let alone to start to designate townsites near or at the proposed station stops along the route. The pressure on the provincial government to grant land to settlers in those areas in the meantime was growing—land speculators were chomping at the bit—but nothing could be done. That did not mean that pre-emptions did not continue, particularly on Vancouver Island. Even though the province could not legally grant any land or other rights to settlers, it continued to permit pre-emption in the E&N grant and to issue pre-emption records, and surveys of many of the pre-emptions were also completed. The province then turned the survey plans over to the dominion government to give effect to the grants after 1884.

The settlement legislation of 1884 that had given effect to the transfer of land to the dominion had in fact preserved the rights of such settlers to a certain degree. Land already pre-empted, leased, or purchased was excluded from the railway grant. Even squatters' rights were protected: "each bona fide squatter who has continuously occupied, and improved any of the lands…for a period of one year prior to the first day of January 1883, shall be entitled to a grant of the freehold of surface rights of the said squatted land." All the same, as is often the case with the federal government, there was a gap between words and action, and the post-1884 period was rife with settler lawsuits against the government.

At the same time, the dominion government began issuing grants itself. Disputes over mineral rights also began to broil between Ottawa and Victoria. "Talk about a constitutional crisis," wrote former surveyor general Bill Taylor, in 1987 in *Early Cadastral Surveys.* "The feds…issued grants to settlers and endeavoured to withhold the mineral and timber rights to themselves. This was not satisfactory to B.C. because if B.C. had dealt direct with the settlers, these mineral and surface rights would have been granted at that point in time…B.C. managed to get justice for most of the settlers…but it cost the Province dearly in further grants. The result is a title searcher's nightmare." On the other hand, it might have been seen as a provincial land surveyor's dream: work for surveyors was guaranteed for the foreseeable future. Not only did the various pre-emptions and grants have to be sorted out, usually through detailed boundary surveys in order to determine title, but the E&N grants themselves required survey. Taylor writes proudly of the land surveyors' achievements during that period: "The survey of the E&N Land Grant boundaries was carried out quickly and accurately by the Province. A creditable piece of work by competent, imaginative surveyors."

Surveys of the railway belt and the Peace River Block were dealt with differently than were those of the E&N grants. Having become dominion lands, they were surveyed in accordance with what was known as the fourth system of dominion land survey, or a rectangular township system, with instructions issuing from the surveyor general of dominion lands in Ottawa. This wasn't necessarily a simple matter; in *The Selkirk Range*, Arthur Wheeler states that it was impossible to lay out the base and meridian lines of that system, "owing to the mountainous character of the country." The roadbed of the railway, remarks Wheeler, made a much more sensible reference point because it had already been precisely surveyed, and it was a given that it ran dead centre through the railway belt. In the end, the railway did become the baseline for the more than five hundred miles of survey lines required west of the Rockies, and the reference point for surveys extending from it. Reference points were placed principally on telegraph poles, as indicated by the letters "CPT" (Canadian Pacific Traverse). Even by 1905, writes Wheeler, many of the poles had already been replaced by newer ones, and with them went the CPT markings. Whether any at all remain today is doubtful.

A mix of dominion land surveyors (DLS) and some provincial land surveyors (up until 1891, generally denoted by the letters "LS" after their names) worked on the initial surveys in the railway belt. But jurisdictional disputes between the dominion government and the province continued to haunt the work of surveyors. In volume two of his 1967 history of Canadian land surveying, *Men and Meridians*, Don Thomson writes: "The railway belt…continued to be a bone of contention for almost half a century…It became impossible to ascertain precisely what lands in the Belt belonged to the Dominion and what lands to the province. In some instances where the lands clearly belonged to the Dominion, these had to be surveyed and dealt with by the provincial authorities," because the dominion government had adopted the province's township system already in use when the railway belt lands were transferred. The Fraser Valley was one area where this occurred; the surveys subsequently became referred to as the "fifth system" of dominion land surveys.

One result of this jurisdictional maelstrom, writes Thomson, was that surveying operations in the belt came to a standstill at one point. "When a [dominion] surveyor arrived at a place where lands had been laid out or occupied under provincial authority he had to abstain from making any surveys in that vicinity. If he decided to proceed anyway his surveys could not be confirmed because such were not made as directed by regulations governing him." Numerous stormy meetings ensued between the surveyor general of Canada, Edouard Deville, and the provincial commissioner of Crown lands, I.W. Smith. Proposals and counter-proposals for the appropriate ways to survey and finalize the boundaries of the belt see-sawed back and forth between Ottawa and Victoria. Not until the mid-1890s was a compromise resolved that would permit the surveyors to carry on their work with any sense of certainty.

Taylor provides an entertaining summation of the situation in *Early Cadastral Surveys:*

> The best thing the Federal Government did in connection with their surveys and grants in the block was to provide a very clear statement that every parcel sold was entitled to access to the nearest route...This right to access was guaranteed...but it has fallen down many times through [provincial] political timidity to enforce it for a private benefit. The actual survey of the railway belt was unorthodox but understandable in view of the mountainous terrain...The trick was to locate the traverse station, which was usually referenced by only one bearing and distance to a nearby CP telegraph pole. No wonder one needs not to be too fussy when dealing with this survey. It is no longer possible to identify the traverse stations.

By comparison, the Peace River Block, surveyed two decades later in the early part of the twentieth century, was a breeze; all jurisdictional issues between the two governments had been more or less resolved by that point.

In the meantime, however, the increasing expansion in British Columbia of dominion lands, either in the form of Indian reserves or of railway grants, had sparked the beginning of what would become a long-running tension between dominion and provincial land surveyors. Naturally, both types of surveyor were keen to get the work of surveying dominion lands; initially at least, provincial land surveyors may simply have assumed that they had every right to conduct surveys on dominion lands. Certainly numerous LS-designated surveyors were involved in the Indian reserve surveys, and more than twenty are recorded as having participated in the railway belt surveys.

Members of the Geological Survey of Canada in British Columbia, July 22, 1871.
From left to right: L.N. Rheaumis, R. Mclennan, A.S. Hall, W.W. Ireland, G. Watt,
A.R.C. Selwyn, A. Mclennan, W. Moberly, C.E. Gillette, J. Richardson, Mr. McDonald.

But dominion land or DLS-designated surveyors were starting to flood
into the new province after 1871, riding the wave of the terms of union
that had not only paved the way to the creation of vast tracts of dominion lands but had authorized—indeed, obliged—the Geological Survey
of Canada (GSC) to begin work in British Columbia. George M. Dawson,
the diminutive geologist who would leave his name on numerous land-
marks in both British Columbia and the Yukon Territory, carried out

many topographical surveys in the province for the GSC between 1875 and 1890, helped by crew members from the east. But Dawson was also occasionally assisted by provincial land surveyors such as James McEvoy, LS, in the Kamloops region in 1888.

Some dominion land surveyors simply signed up to provincial qualifications and earned the LS suffix after their names, but they remained in the minority. The vast majority preferred to simply retain their dominion status, and by 1874 they were becoming increasingly concerned by the inroads that they were witnessing on their "turf" by the provincial land surveyors. On April 24 of that year, a group of dominion land surveyors from Manitoba and the North-West Territories met in Winnipeg and formed an association "for the better organization of the profession." That group would eventually become the Association of Manitoba Land Surveyors. In 1882, the Association of Dominion Land Surveyors (ADLS) was formed, in part to protect the interests of its members under any perceived threat from provincial surveyors muscling in on their jurisdiction.

At the 1885 annual general meeting of the ADLS, two resolutions were passed on the subject. First, a delegation was to be sent to the minister of the interior to persuade him of the "necessity and justice" of ensuring that only DLS-designated surveyors be authorized to survey dominion lands in British Columbia. They also decided to apply for statutory incorporation, perceiving perhaps that would lend them greater authority. The dominion government was not persuaded in either case at the time. In 1886, therefore, the association went a step further, resolving to cancel the commissions of any DLS surveyor who was signing plans of dominion lands prepared by anyone without a DLS qualification. A case was also again to be made to the government that DLS surveyors were being treated unjustly if provincial land surveyors in British Columbia continued to be employed on dominion lands.

Again, the ADLS was rebuffed. In 1888, the Department of the Interior provided it with a legal opinion to the effect that the government was under no obligation to employ DLS surveyors on the railway surveys in the west or to prepare the necessary plans. In some respects that is unsurprising, given that the new minister was Edgar Dewdney, a man loyal to British Columbia's interests. Despite that, the ADLS would not give up. In 1889 a letter was again sent to Dewdney, remonstrating with him regarding the employment of William Jemmett and Ernest Skinner on the surveys of Indian reserves:

> These two gentlemen…not only have never received any commission to practice from [the Board of Examiners for Dominion Land Surveyors]…their names are not included in the list…of those authorized Surveyors of [British Columbia] land…The association [wishes] to respectfully point out the injustice done to those who have become legally qualified to survey Dominion Lands…
>
> It is not necessary to point out the great trouble which may, and is quite likely to arise owing to faulty surveying of Indian reserves by those who…are not legally or professionally qualified…

The employment of Jemmett and Skinner was the thin end of the wedge, as far as the ADLS was concerned. "None but duly qualified Dominion Land surveyors should be employed by the Government in the survey of Dominion Lands, no matter for what purpose the surveys are made," the ADLS stated emphatically. This time, the association was successful. The deputy minister of justice agreed, and after 1890 only qualified DLS surveyors were permitted to survey dominion lands. To solve the thorny issue of legalizing the surveys of reserves and the railway belt that had already been completed by provincial land surveyors, the deputy minister of the interior decided that the easiest method was simply to include the lines of existing surveys on dominion township plans. By doing so, the surveys were duly incorporated into official survey documents prepared by qualified dominion surveyors, thus "on the approval of that survey in the manner prescribed by law they would become legalized."

It was a neat and pragmatic solution, not unlike the one adopted in the 1890s to deal with surveys that had been completed in the railway belt. Canada had proposed in 1890 that "in all cases where the land sought to be acquired has already been surveyed under the authority of either Government, such survey shall be accepted as conclusive and the grant issued thereon." British Columbia agreed. Both approaches to

Dr. George M. Dawson (third from left) and party at Fort McLeod, B.C., July 14, 1879.
GEOLOGICAL SURVEY OF CANADA/LIBRARY AND ARCHIVES CANADA PA-051137

Food was enormously important to men working long days in the field. Large survey parties usually employed a camp cook." OFFICE OF THE SURVEYOR GENERAL

dealing with regularizing completed surveys without requiring them to be repeated were worthy of the times. There were still nowhere near enough surveyors, federal or provincial, to keep up with the amount of available work. For with the rolling of the first transcontinental train into Vancouver in 1887—the terminus had been extended from Port Moody, which had received the very first CPR train to arrive on the west coast in 1886—British Columbia was witnessing development around the mouth of the Fraser River and Burrard Inlet at an unprecedented pace. The provincial government was scrambling to keep up with the regulatory and administrative framework required to cradle rapid urban expansion and rampant property speculation. Technological advances were also occurring at a dizzying pace.

Land surveyors in the province had to do something to keep up, and they had to do it quickly.

9

An Exacting Level

A boat-building camp at Dease Lake, 1887. GEOLOGICAL SURVEY OF CANADA/LIBRARY AND ARCHIVES CANADA PA-052787

The 1890s stand out on their own, both in terms of British Columbia's general history and in terms of its surveying story. A convergence of events that had occurred in the province during the first four decades of European settlement was lending itself to what could, at the very least, be described as interesting times for surveyors. There certainly seemed little excuse to be idle.

Not only had the first CPR train that steamed into the west coast port of Vancouver in 1887 brought with it carloads of dreams and ambition, it had also freighted in an era of land development expansion and speculation that was unprecedented in the region. Between 1890 and 1900, writes Robert Cail in his detailed history of Crown lands disposal in British Columbia, *Land, Man and the Law*, eighty-seven railway companies were incorporated in the province. Survey work on the Vancouver Island line during the 1880s prompted speculation of its own in island newspapers: "Is the railway to be extended to Gabriola Island?" the *Nanaimo Free Press* asked hopefully—if somewhat unrealistically—on October 15, 1884.

In 1891, a new Mineral Act entitled miners to Crown grants of land upon payment of the sum of twenty-five dollars per acre, in lieu of having to develop their claim as if it were a settlement property. The new statutory provision created a massive demand for detailed surveys as miners sought to protect the boundaries of their valuable claims with the utmost precision. Determined prospectors, who had worked their methodical way into the southern interior of the province in the 1880s and early 1890s looking for gold, found instead masses of silver and lead in the west Kootenays. The mining industry took off. Surveyors were called upon to establish "Mineral Monuments" through a series of triangulation networks in the Kootenays. Ernest Cleveland's work in this regard was used to produce the first coloured contour map in British Columbia, in 1898. An economic recession in 1893, brought on by the repeal in the United States of the 1890 Silver Purchase Act, which had formerly guaranteed high prices for British Columbian silver, caused the mining industry to stumble temporarily. Although it regained some of its momentum during the later part of the 1890s, silver mining in the province would never again enjoy the extraordinary levels of activity that took place immediately after the first discoveries in 1892, and it was near to having run its course by the end of the decade.

The Klondike gold rush of 1897, however, brought thousands more dreamers through Vancouver and Victoria on their way to the Yukon. With them came the pressure to locate routes through British Columbia to reach the northern goldfields. These and other developments associated with provincial mining activity created a demand for hydroelectricity and more railroad building. If the valuable minerals being found in the Kootenays were to be transported west to Vancouver or east to Ontario rather than south into the coffers of the Americans, the creation of rail links from the centre of mining activity in the west Kootenays to the main CPR line at Revelstoke was becoming critical. The 1890s therefore saw a frenzy of railway location and building, and collateral development along the chosen routes. In 1891, the Vernon & Nelson Telephone Company was incorporated to create a province-wide telephone system. It would subsequently become the British Columbia Telephone Co. Ltd. (now the contemporary company called Telus). At the time of its incorporation, there were already more than three dozen local telephone companies in operation. A hydroelectric plant started operating in Rossland in 1898, followed almost immediately by another plant on the Goldstream River, near Victoria.

During the late 1870s and the 1880s, George Mercer Dawson and his team had mapped much of the interior of the province for the Geological Survey of Canada (GSC), including the Fraser and Peace rivers, large sections of the Rocky Mountains, Kamloops, the Cariboo, and the Stikine, Dease, and upper Liard rivers. Dawson suffered a physical handicap that had stunted his growth significantly—in photographs from his travels his head barely reaches the shoulder height of some of his colleagues, and his back was permanently disfigured. Despite that challenge Dawson managed to cover an astonishing amount of terrain while completing his mapping work for the GSC, and in 1895 he became its director. By 1896 his fame and prestige were such that he was invited to become president of the Geological Society of America. Dawson City in the Yukon and Dawson Creek in British Columbia were named for the small but august geologist.

Dawson's work in British Columbia was not completely without controversy, although that controversy seems to have been kept quietly behind bureaucratic doors. In 1889 an experienced dominion land surveyor named William Stewart Drewry was engaged by the Department of the Interior in Ottawa to conduct triangulation surveys in the railway belt, with a view to establishing reference points for more detailed sectional surveys later on. Drewry was a dedicated individual, and while working close to the Rocky Mountains found much evidence of mineral wealth. In 1890, he wrote to his manager in the technical branch of the department in Ottawa, a Mr. Dennis, to ask whether or not he should also collect information regarding the mineral resources in the region being surveyed, considering the extent of his discoveries.

Dennis then wrote to the deputy minister of the interior, A.M. Burgess, on October 31, 1890, to ask for advice. He had informed Drewry, he said, that it was the duty of any surveyor working for the dominion to obtain all reliable information regarding the resources of the districts visited by them; he also considered Drewry "one of our best men and any information given by him can be thoroughly relied upon." The trouble, continued Dennis, regarded "the publication of facts in reference to mineral wealth on this side of the summit of the Rocky Mountains...such facts will probably contradict the published reports of the Geological Survey. The question arises, is it desirable that a discussion as to the value or reliability of the reports issued by the Geological Survey should arise between the two departments?"

It seems likely there was no love lost between the Department of the Interior—at least, in the person of Dennis and the GSC. This might be especially so if they were competing for surveying budget funds, because Dennis went on somewhat cryptically to say: "You are fully in possession of my views regarding the practical value of these reports." The implication was that his views were not positive; all the same, Dennis clearly didn't want to go into print on the public record contradicting the GSC reports without the backing of his boss. His dilemma was resolved by a prompt and thinly veiled reprimand from Burgess on November 5, 1890, encouraging a full public report from Drewry on all information in his possession. Such information, wrote Burgess diplomatically, need not necessarily be considered as contradictory to the reports of the GSC so much as "supplementary to them. It would of course be very desirable," Burgess also stated firmly, "that Mr. Drewry's report should be couched in language which would not give any room to the Geological Survey people to suppose that he desired in any way to reflect upon them, because that would be doing himself and the Department with which he is connected an injustice." Nothing much has changed within the bureaucracy in over a century: the last thing senior officials need is dirty linen between their department and another aired in public, and more importantly, in front of their political masters. Practicality must have prevailed in Ottawa, for there the matter seems to have ended.

Back in British Columbia, increasing development was resulting in an indirect but important effect on the work of surveyors. Well before the 1890s, litigation was already alive and well in the province and starting to have an impact. In his 2004 paper "Cadastral Survey Practice, 1851–2004," former surveyor general Don Duffy wrote about the 1884 case of *Johnston v. Clarke,* which established firmly in British Columbia law "the principle that original posts in their original positions govern the corners, even if not set as intended, due to surveying errors." In 1876, surveyor William Jemmett had corrected an earlier survey by another surveyor named Saunders. The court undid Jemmett's work; notwithstanding his good intentions to correct the first survey, it was more important that an innocent public could rely on the original setting of the posts and carry on the development of property without risk that the boundaries might later change.

Up in the Nass Valley, the Nisga'a people hadn't yet thought about resorting to legal action. By the time they would get around to it in the 1920s, the dominion government would promptly bar native people from the pursuit of land claims without the permission of the minister of Indian affairs. In the meantime, however, the Nisga'a started to organize themselves in the 1880s to discuss their land difficulties with Victoria. Their chief objection was to the way in which surveyors kept arriving in their territory to draw lines around small plots of land, on which the Nisga'a were being told they had to live from then on. Together with the Tsimshian, the Nisga'a paid a fruitless visit to Victoria in 1887. Undaunted, in 1890 they decided to form a land committee to deal with the problem. Fortunately—for they might have given up immediately in sheer disbelief had they known it would take 109 years to have their claims dealt with to their satisfaction—the Nisga'a had no idea of the scope of the struggle ahead of them.

Land surveyors in the province were more fortunate in the protection of their interests. Despite the small number of surveyors in British Columbia and the disproportionately large amount of available work, surveyors seem to have been perpetually haunted by the spectre of insufficient financially rewarding employment. The pressure from the Association of Dominion Land Surveyors to exclude provincial land surveyors from what it considered its turf had not gone unnoticed, and resentment levels were high. The fact that the requisite qualifications to practise as a surveyor were not being consistently met was also an irritant to qualified men in the field. Certainly some were required to sit and pass examinations to prove their knowledge and skills. But the chief commissioner of lands and works had the authority to license surveyors without requiring any such examination or standard to be applied to their experience or academic backgrounds. By 1890, the muttering in the ranks was becoming loud. If provincial surveyors were to retain a hold on the work they had been getting—and moreover, make sure that not just any fly-by-night newcomer could arrive in British Columbia and muscle in on their action—then they had better do something about it, and quickly.

On October 16, stalwarts William Jemmett, John Kirk, Arthur Cotton, John McKenzie, Albert Hill, Charles Woods, and a colourful Québécois named Narcisse Gauvreau met in New Westminster to discuss what might be done to resolve the situation. The purpose of the meeting, wrote Patrick Brennan, BCLS 396, in *The Link* in 1979, "was to seek the cooperation of the surveyors of the Province to raise the standard of the profession, to promote an interchange of ideas, and to increase their scientific knowledge for the benefit of themselves and the public." All noble purposes, to be sure, but such co-operation could also serve to provide surveyors with far greater leverage with government and the public than they had as individuals.

The merits of joining forces were obvious, and on December 1 of the same year twenty-two surveyors visited Victoria to meet with Surveyor General William Sinclair Gore. The meeting lasted two full days, at the end of which a new Association of Provincial Land Surveyors of British Columbia emerged with Edward Mohun as its first president. Mohun had moved on from Indian reserve surveys and in 1890 had won the contract to design and build a sewer system for the city of Victoria (Mohun's work was robust, for the system was still in use by the region in 2005, notwithstanding vigorous protests from environmentalists objecting to the emission of raw sewage into the ocean). Under Mohun's leadership, the association started placing immediate pressure on the government to recognize its authority.

The *British Columbia Gazette* of January 3, 1891, names eighty-two authorized land surveyors on the official list issued by Gore (eighty-three, if it is assumed Gore counted himself among their numbers). The first regular meeting of the new association took place on January 29, and a resolution was passed immediately to petition the government to enact a law to "protect the authorized surveyors of this Province in the performance of their duties, to prevent unqualified persons acting as surveyors, and to provide for duly qualified persons from time to time being admitted to practice." The petition also suggested that a board of examiners be constituted to test candidates for entry to the profession and to govern the professional conduct of authorized surveyors. The statute, the surveyors thought, could also be administered by them, since they were the ones who knew best what it was all about.

The Provincial Land Surveyors Act was passed with astonishing speed on April 20, 1891, and must have seemed satisfactory to its proponents in most respects. Henceforth British Columbian land surveyors receiving their commission to practise were entitled to add the letters "PLS" after their names, to denote their official status. James Herrick McGregor became PLS 1. While they had not yet gained control over the rules governing the profession, at least strict rules now existed to prevent any miscreant pretender to the profession from conducting his business without authorization. These rules were to be administered by officials appointed from the ranks of the provincial land surveyors. Candidates had to jump through two levels of examination hoops. Unless he could first show that he had suitably equivalent experience in another jurisdiction, the candidate had first to have articled for three years to a provincial land surveyor in British Columbia, generally referred to as a "master." To qualify to article, the student must have passed an examination demonstrating proficiency in various subjects, including "penmanship and orthography," and knowledge of "quadratic equations...the first four books of Euclid, plane trigonometry, and the use of logarithms."

At least twelve months of the three-year articling period had to be spent in conducting field work. At the end of the three years, the would-be surveyor not only had to pass further examinations on such subjects as practical astronomy and measurement of areas, "including their calculation by latitude and departure," but had to be "capable of intelligently reporting" on surveying operations. He also had to produce "satisfactory testimony as to his character for sobriety and probity." Given the proliferation of drinking stories attached to every era of surveying in British Columbia, usually related with great relish by the participants, it is difficult to imagine many masters who could have produced such testimony with respect to their own habits. But perhaps the testimony as to sobriety may simply have been produced on the "honour among thieves" principle: with a wink and tacit acceptance that after enduring the rigours of the field, it was beyond reasonable expectation of human nature that surveyors would not soften their hardships with a whisky or several around the campfire.

For students, life in the field would have been even more stressful. Not only did they have to endure long days of hard physical labour; they then had to settle down in their tents at night with a lantern and their books to study theory, ignoring mosquitoes, rain, and bears among their many distractions. Frank Green was studying for his PLS examination in January 1898, writes Edward Affleck in the November 2001 *Link*, while working with a survey party on the location of the Columbia & Western Railway over the Monashee Mountains between Castlegar and Christina Lake. According to Green's diary, he spent two months shovelling snow along the location line, frantically snatching study breaks whenever he could. In order to reach Victoria by April 4, when the six days of examinations would commence, Green had to leave Christina Lake on March 23. According to Affleck, he walked through the snow to Cascade City, caught the stage for Bossburg, Washington, and thence the train to Nelson, back in British Columbia. From Nelson, Green caught the train to Revelstoke via the Arrow Lakes connection to the main CPR line, which would take him to Vancouver, from where he could catch a boat to Victoria. He arrived on March 31. With five days in hand to cram, Green wasted not a moment. He was the only one of the six candidates who passed, becoming PLS 45.

In 1892, Edgar Dewdney returned from Ottawa to take up the position of lieutenant-governor, the second surveyor in the province to be so honoured in the space of only twenty-one years. The same year, B.C. Surveyor General Tom Kains wrote one of the most comprehensive analyses of survey systems for the province to date in his annual report to the chief commissioner of lands and works on Crown land surveys. Kains thought it high time to expedite further development through allocating government funds to an extensive topographical surveying and mapping program:

> The Province of British Columbia...has now arrived at such a stage
> of her existence that circumstances demand the commencement
> of a systematic survey, to be gradually carried on and completed
> and which would prove of direct economic value...there is room
> for additional hundreds of thousands of population and a vast
> scope for the safe investment of capital. Security in title to land
> and minerals demands a mode of...defining their geographical
> location; while the question of the enormous value of good maps
> in attracting people and capital has been...settled.

"In the earlier history of this Province," Kains said, "the expenditure necessary for such a class of work would not have been warranted." Now, however, he considered it time for the government to start spending, and topographic maps that would indicate elevations, drainages, access routes, and water sources were a priority in easing the expansion of settlement. A.O. Wheeler described a topographical map in this way in a paper he delivered to the Corporation in 1914:

A topographical map usually consists of contour lines, which represent the projection on a plan of imaginary lines following the inequalities of the surface at given intervals of altitude:—Say that the intervals of altitude were 100 feet; it would be as though wires followed the external surface of the feature to be mapped at 100-feet vertical intervals and then, the feature having desolved, all the wires dropped perpendicularly to the ground. The result would be a topographical delineation by contours.

Like some of his predecessors, Kains had studied systems in use elsewhere in the world. He was particularly attracted to the New Zealand model, as that country's physical features were so similar to British Columbia's topography. New Zealand had also already proved his theory that the existence of detailed topographical survey information lent itself positively to the development of an area. Kains clearly saw the comparison as a compelling way to persuade his political masters to open their pocketbooks and invest in a comprehensive topographical survey strategy for the province:

> New Zealand realized that, in going into the markets of the world to secure people and capital for the occupation of her lands and the development of her resources, it was necessary...to furnish good maps...showing the lands suitable for occupation and the routes by which they could be reached...It is probable that few countries would have been warranted in conducting a highly accurate trigonometrical and topographical survey in the early years....but the topography of New Zealand rendered it possible to make a portion of the great work serve alike as the best and cheapest base from which to survey her lands for settlement and construct good maps."

Kains went on to describe in some detail the process by which lands were first explored, then access routes located, preliminary maps and reports produced, and increasingly detailed triangulation surveys conducted to establish a framework upon which to create subdivision of individual properties and town sites. He reported that the average cost of a twenty-mile triangulation in New Zealand was between eighty-eight cents and one dollar per acre; a minor triangulation of up to five miles per side $1.86 per acre; if topography was included in the latter, it would go up to $2.62 per acre; and settlement or sectional surveys, requiring far more detailed work, came in at about $31.16 per acre. He believed that the same work could be achieved at considerably less cost in British Columbia—as little as fifteen cents per acre for sectional surveys, by comparison, and less than one cent per acre for triangulation or topographical work.

Kains firmly believed that establishing a permanent triangulation network over the entire province would save money in the long run. Certainly it would help cure what had become an increasingly vexatious problem: the expanding number of surveys of individual properties and townsites being completed without reference to each other, or indeed in some instances without reference to any fixed point at all. The effect was a little as if someone had stuck postage stamps at random over a map of British Columbia. Moreover, many of the postage stamps weren't even rectangular but of an irregular shape. While it hadn't mattered when there were only a few hundred settlers in the province, by 1892 the population was nearing 100,000 and the stamps were at risk of overlapping. In addition, customary dependence on wooden posts or bearing trees to delineate property boundaries was being undermined by the inevitable rotting of old posts and by indiscriminate logging. "By having all surveys joined to a well marked triangulation," wrote Kains, "costly and vexatious differences would be greatly avoided, since the evidence as to disputed boundaries would no longer depend on the durability of wood, or the casual recollection of locality, but on the mechanical application of trained scientific knowledge and skill." He thought that security of individual land titles would be greatly enhanced by the ability to check the boundaries against a permanent and detailed network of triangulation lines, rather than reliance on posts.

The total costs of annual topographical survey work over two million acres were estimated to be about $14,000, with a one-time, up-front investment of about $1,200 for equipment and a further $1,100 for horses (the latter would depreciate in value, but that was taken into account).

Tom Kains, surveyor general from 1891 to 1898.
ABCLS

It would not be quick work, Kains warned: a survey extending over all of British Columbia would be "the work of many years—even decades; but if faithfully carried out would stand as a lasting monument of work well done for the future peace, progress, and prosperity of the fairest Province of the Dominion."

His arguments must have convinced his superiors at least to some degree, for by 1893 Kains was issuing instructions to provincial land surveyors to conduct triangulation work in various parts of the province, including directions to W.S. Drewry to conduct photo-topographical work in the west Kootenays. Having completed his surveys in the railway belt for the dominion government, Drewry had applied for and received his PLS commission just the previous year. "Your own judgment and experience in this character of survey work will be your guide respecting the strength of your party and the best method to be adopted in carrying out the details of your survey," wrote Kains to Drewry on June 1, 1893. Drewry was also warned under no circumstances to speak to the "Press" without permission. For his efforts he was to be paid two hundred dollars per month, and his assistant James McGregor $125 per month. Drewry was permitted to hire three labourers and one cook, and to pay each of them between forty and fifty dollars per month, "depending on circumstances." A per diem ration allowance of sixty cents per day per man in the crew was allocated to his budget.

Kains had also been successful in obtaining a budget to pay for photo-topographical work, a method of mapping that he had enthusiastically

advocated in his 1892 report. Photography was an alternative method of producing topographical maps, utilizing images taken from a range of mountaintops to calculate elevations and contours. It was best employed, according to Kains, in conjunction with triangulation work, "especially as the additional expense incurred would be but the small cost of a camera and photographic plates." Andrew Birrell explained how this worked in 1981 in an article titled "Survey Photography in British Columbia, 1858–1900": "The surveyors occupied a number of stations whose positions had been carefully determined by triangulation. From each of these mountaintop stations panoramic views were made including several other triangulation stations in them. After the surveyor returned from the field, prints were made from the negatives and he could plot his map directly from the photographs using an instrument known as a perspectograph."

Even as early as 1893, photography was not a novel concept in terms of its use for surveying purposes. British Columbia's mountainous terrain was ideally suited for that use, and the province would become a world leader in the development of survey photography, and later, with the invention of mechanized flight, aerial surveying. In a 1966 article in *Canadian Geographic Journal* on the development of the survey camera, author Don Thomson explains: "When Dominion land surveyors reached the high Rockies they realized that survey methods used so successfully on the prairies were only partly applicable to mountainous regions...To lay out township and section lines would take considerable time; costs of operations would be high unless some new method was adopted."

Thomson also points out that temperamental mountain weather severely restricted the window of opportunity for conducting surveys to around three months. The simple act of climbing a mountain could take weeks alone, and even when the summit was reached, work could be halted by high winds, thunderstorms, or clouds: "In the limited time available for field work it was physically impossible to record by notes or by memory the immense variety of topographical detail to be found in the mountain country...The ability of surveyors

Land surveyor W.S. Drewry and his assistant J.J. McArthur, carrying heavy topographic and photographic survey equipment, 1887. CANADA DEPT. OF MINES AND TECHNICAL SURVEYS/LIBRARY AND ARCHIVES CANADA PA-023141

to cover any large tract of country in a short time became a matter of urgent importance." The camera, able to bridge large valleys in a series of images and record immense amounts of detailed and accurate information, was to provide the solution. An added time-saving advantage was the ability to bring the images back to a home base to undertake the work of measuring and plotting lines, rather than having to take time to do it in the field under the arduous conditions of camp life: "The map-maker," writes Thomson, "could study without haste the geography of the area as seen from two fairly widely separated vantage points."

The original concept of photo-topography, or photogrammetry as it would become known, became a reality in France. Although the principles involved had been considered elsewhere as early as the late eighteenth century, it was Colonel Aimé Laussedat of the French Military Survey who in the early 1850s developed a system for taking topographical measurements directly from a series of photographs. It was not widely used at the time because of the sheer bulk of the equipment required. By 1867 Auguste Chevalier had invented "La Planchette Photographique," which recorded a circular photograph from a theodolite-like device at a trigonometrical station. Captain R.H. Stotherd of the Royal Engineers observed the machine at the Paris Exhibition: "If a series of views were taken from prominent points," Stotherd immediately recognized, "a system of triangulation might be rapidly carried over any district or country."

The benefits of photography generally had been perceived already by the Royal Engineers. Training in photography for officers was established by the early 1850s, and a camera had been taken along on at least part of the 49th parallel surveys in British Columbia in 1858. The gear and equipment required remained of an "extreme cumbrousness," as not only the camera itself but also the glass plates and the entire laboratory of processing chemicals had to be taken into the field at the same time.

There were also, unfortunately, problems with the photographers themselves. The first photographer sent out in 1859 promptly deserted to the United States. That aberration aside, the young men who replaced him and who were operating the equipment were novices despite their training, and the usefulness of the final images proved limited. Lieutenant Colonel Hawkins complained fussily that he thought a competent artist would have been much more useful. Certainly, no attempt was made then to use the camera for the purpose of topographical mapping; its use was strictly limited to recording events for posterity.

In 1871 and for several years afterwards, two photographers named Benjamin Baltzley and Charles Horetzky were photographing with both the GSC and the CPR in British Columbia. By 1875, photographic technology had already started to improve, reducing the weight of the equipment, and cameras had started to become part of the standard gear carried with exploratory survey parties. It was still a burden, however: a standard camera in its wooden box, together with a dozen glass plates, weighed in at about twenty pounds.

Like their predecessors, Baltzley and Horetzky were still essentially making landscape images that were informative and interesting, but not suitable for mapping. Then along came Dr. Edouard Gaston Daniel Deville: surveyor general of Canada from 1885 until 1924. "In the truest sense," writes Thomson, "Deville may be said to be the father of photo-topographical surveying in Canada." Deville loved cameras and as soon as he had a chance to use one started experimenting with it. Well before Tom Kains made his ambitious proposals to the British Columbia government for funds to support photogrammetry, Deville was unsuccessfully lobbying A.M. Burgess, his deputy minister, for a photographic department in Ottawa. Undaunted by the lack of financial support, Deville personally set about adapting cameras for more specific application to surveying uses.

By 1887 he was sending various types of cameras out with surveyors like Drewry in order to test their usefulness in the field. The Eastman "Detective" camera, for example, which used a drop shutter and roll film, produced disappointing results in comparison with the glass plate versions used with heavier large-format cameras, but it was far lighter and easier to use. Drewry wasn't particularly satisfied with the camera, but the feasibility of using photography in the field was well established the following year, when Drewry's photo-topographical surveys in the Crowsnest Pass area came in at an average cost of $7.50 per mile, much less costly than a topographical survey conducted by the traditional

Brownlee Surveyors, Vancouver, with J.H. Brownlee, LS, on the left. This photograph was taken circa late 1880s. ARCHIVES OF BRITISH COLUMBIA I-46837

method, which cost $130 per mile. Deville needed no further encouragement to continue adapting cameras for use in the field; so good was his work that by 1895 at least one of his designs was in commercial production, and the instruments he developed remained in use until the early 1930s.

Deville continued to experiment with cameras and produced a manual on photographic surveying that was published commercially in 1895. With the help of Deville's advances, Drewry continued his photo-topographical work for the provincial government in the Kootenays. By 1896, according to a paper on mapmaking in British Columbia produced in 1939 by then chief geographer Major G.G. Aitken, Drewry had also produced a map of the Nelson region that Aitken claimed was the first contour map of a section of the province to show topographical colours: blue for water, black for "culture"—towns and railways, for example— and red for roads.

Over the next six or more decades, photogrammetry and its yet-to-be-conceived progeny, aerial surveying, would be the keys that would unlock the doors of a vast and as yet still largely unknown province. In the meantime, far from the towering peaks of the Rockies, most minds in Victoria and on the west coast of the mainland had turned to other matters for much of the 1890s. Ambitious and lofty plans for province-wide triangulation networks and detailed topographical maps were all very well, but of distant interest to politicians and businessmen with more immediately pressing concerns, which were quite literally at ground level. There might well be future benefits to the orderly agricultural settlement of the Cariboo and resource development in the Columbia Basin. But there was money to be made right now, and much closer to home: at the mouth of the Fraser River, in a boomtown called Vancouver.

10

The Wit to See and the Will to Do

Boats were used to access remote areas of the province in the days before cars and aircraft made life much easier for B.C. land surveyors. OFFICE OF THE SURVEYOR GENERAL

The city of Vancouver was incorporated on April 6, 1886. The new city's name had been chosen by William Van Horne, the future president of the CPR, which was fitting under the circumstances. Lumber mills had begun operations in the area well before 1886, and the downtown area known today as "Gastown" had existed since 1870. But it was the location of the CPR's western terminus on Burrard Inlet that really quickened the pace. Not even the massively destructive fire that levelled the city in June 1886 could slow things down. Wherever development was occurring in the province, surveyors were always close at hand, and Vancouver was no exception.

In 1918, William Powell, BCLS 88, presented a paper on city surveying to the members of the land surveying fraternity at their annual general meeting. According to Powell, Vancouver was incorporated with several existing district lots, each with its own original subdivision plans, of which there could be many—DL 192 alone, said Powell, had 117 registered plans, not including lots that had simply been created by legal description rather than by actual survey. "It is only by compilation of data obtained from many sources that anything like a City Map can be made up," complained Powell. "Moreover, each D.L. was planned without any reference to the subdivision of the adjoining lot: consequently jogs and deflections exist everywhere."

Prior to 1886, there had been sporadic bursts of speculative land acquisitions and a generally uncoordinated approach to the undertaking of surveys in the Vancouver area. Surveyor Walter Moberly had pre-empted a large area of land on False Creek in 1859, but sold it again almost as quickly to finance his expeditions east to search for a way through the Selkirk Mountains. Throughout the 1860s, members and former members of Colonel Moody's Royal Engineers took advantage of their location at New Westminster to apply for and receive choice lots of Crown land, "making deals which today would be considered highly unethical," wrote surveying history aficionado Barry Cotton in *The Link* magazine in September 2004.

Royal Engineer Corporal George Turner, on the other hand, appears to have been too busy undertaking numerous surveys in the area to have pre-empted land for himself. Turner's signature appears on many of the original plans and survey maps of Vancouver, including an 1863 plan of survey that incorporates Coal Harbour, Stanley Park (then a military reserve) and Deadman's Island in the harbour. The same year, according to writer Len Meyer, Turner also comprehensively surveyed "the entire west end of present-day Vancouver, from Burrard Inlet to English Bay, and from Burrard Street to what is now Stanley Park," entitling his map "City of Liverpool."

In 1870, the chief commissioner of lands and works, Joseph Trutch, instructed Frederick Walter Green to survey the Granville Townsite. Even then, the townsite was known as "Gastown," in honour of its best-loved resident, "Gassy" Jack Deighton, the owner of the saloon. For some reason, however, the survey plan was not registered until 1885—and in any event it was short-lived. After the devastating fire of 1886 a re-survey was undertaken by Ernest Hermon, who duly sent his survey notes and plan to city hall for registration. In what may amount to a record for bureaucratic delays, the new plan was not deposited for registration until 1917. Affidavits had to be completed by both Hermon and by William Powell, then employed by the city's survey department, "to identify and to aid in tracing the history and authoritativeness of the documents, which for thirty years had gathered dust in a pigeon-hole of the City Hall." All subsequent surveys of the downtown core, wrote Powell, are based on that 1886 plan, "so nearly lost to the community."

The oldest registered survey plan on record in Vancouver is not of the first survey done, but rather Plan 92, George Turner's subdivision of District Lot 155 labelled the "City of Liverpool" and registered on March 15, 1882. The town of Hastings, in the area of latter-day Hastings Park, had originally been surveyed in 1868, and was re-surveyed a few years later by William Ralph. An original plan of Hastings apparently created by Ralph is dated 1875. However, like the Gastown re-survey, the plan did not surface until 1917. When it did, it caused some consternation, for it showed both the CPR terminus and Hastings Park. This, Powell pointed out in his paper on city surveying, was puzzling, as neither of them "were located until 1886."

The city of Vancouver's first council was created in 1886, and one of its first aldermen was named Lauchlan Alexander Hamilton. Hamilton was a land surveyor with considerable experience farther east—he had signed, among others, the first survey plans for the towns of Regina, Moose Jaw, Swift Current, and Medicine Hat before moving in 1884 with the CPR to British Columbia, where he was to take charge of laying out the new townsite at the western terminus of the railway. Hamilton was a mover and shaker who designed the first coat of arms for the city of Vancouver and was a leading advocate for the creation of Stanley Park in 1887. He did not neglect his surveying duties, however, locating the first path around the new park—along much the same route as the existing road—and directing the laying out of city streets with a firm eye to the future needs of a rapidly growing city. He also took the initiative of adopting the "modern system" of using numbers for avenues and names for streets running at right angles to the avenues. It was Hamilton who selected tree names for many of the west end roads—Alder, Fir, Birch, and so on—although, according to Robert Allen, BCLS 487, in *The Link,* he "neglected to instruct [his draughtsman] to use them in alphabetical order."

Hamilton's primary task had been to prepare the way for the extension of the CPR line from Port Moody along the south shore of Burrard Inlet, requiring the clearing of many miles of forest. Hamilton's job was an undertaking, writes Don Thomson in *Men and Meridians,* "of considerable magnitude." One tree alone, standing on Georgia Street between Granville and Seymour, is an example of what Hamilton and his crew must have faced. Although it may have been one of the largest trees they encountered, it was just one of thousands upon thousands that had to be felled by hand, a colossus that Hamilton dubbed "Russell's Big Tree": "It was eleven feet, eight inches diameter on the stump, and 310 feet high," writes Barry Cotton. "When it fell along Georgia, it stretched almost to the next lane."

Six thousand acres had been granted to the CPR for rail yards, storage, docks, and hotel accommodation. It all had to be surveyed, as did the roads and streets that would form the key access routes into and out of the new city. "It was on the spot now marked as Victory Square," writes Thomson, "that Hamilton stood...as surveyor in charge of a party consisting of transitman, leveller, rodman, chainmen, picketman and axemen. They commenced the survey of an area five miles long and two miles wide, now constituting the central core of a metropolis extending for many miles on both sides of Burrard Inlet." Victory Square is at the corner of latter-day Hastings and Hamilton streets in downtown Vancouver. On April 20, 1953, sixty-eight years after Hamilton completed most of his work in surveying Vancouver, a plaque was unveiled on the southwest corner of the square to honour his achievements. The bronze plaque, attached to the building at 300 West Hastings, reads: "Here stood HAMILTON, First Land Commissioner Canadian Pacific Railway, 1885. In the silent solitude of the primeval forest, he drove a wooden stake in the earth and commenced to measure an empty land into the streets of VANCOUVER."

In 1884, the area around the mouth of the Fraser River must have indeed seemed an empty land to its European settlers. The population of the entire Burrard Inlet area then was around nine hundred. But by 1891, the population of Vancouver alone had skyrocketed to 13,709 people. The "boom and bust" cycle of the economy seemed not to affect the rapid growth of the city or speculation on its future riches, at least initially. Within ten years, the population would double; within twenty years, it would increase more than sevenfold. Initially, timber had been the core industry. But when the CPR trains started rolling into Port Moody in 1886, writes Norbert MacDonald in *CPR Town: The City-building Process in Vancouver, 1860–1914*, "survey crews, road gangs, home builders and real estate agents were busy." Real estate agents were certainly at the forefront of land speculation, with some thirty companies operating during the late 1880s and early 1890s, attempting to attract investors from all over the world. Perhaps the most famous land speculator to acquire property in Vancouver was author Rudyard Kipling, who in 1889 purchased his own "few thousand tons of granite...You order your agent to hold it until property rises," wrote Kipling, then sell out and buy more land further out of town...it is the essence of speculation." Sixty miles of roadway were surveyed and constructed by 1891, and a street rail system was in operation over thirteen miles of those roads. A bridge had been opened in 1889 over False Creek, more or less on line with present-day Granville Street.

Maps with glowing descriptions of the region were printed as part of the advertising campaign, and it seems that even Hamilton pragmatically used one such map, prepared by Ross and Ceperley, real estate and insurance agents, in 1887 to assist him in keeping track of clearing operations. His notes on that map were prosaic—"Cleared and piled, ready for burning"—but in other instances, Hamilton was given to making notes that were far more entertaining. In one of his field books, alongside the survey sketches, are notes of the price of galvanized pipe, the name of a young man who "went up to Hope to start a pack trail," and even a personal note that he may well have been scribbling to a friend to relieve the boredom of sitting in church: "Is it possible to have a Methodist revival without a pretty woman at one end and a dude at the other? Just look at the front bench in the choir! If she would only pray that God Almighty would give brains to some of that crowd in front, she would be praying for something."

New surveying firms were springing up in response to the demand for development. Ernest Hermon and James Garden set up shop together in 1886 on Cordova Street, opposite the CPR depot, later moving to Cambie Street (where, reminisced Hermon's son in the late 1930s, he could "dimly remember [the] office and the one or two bear cubs that for a while were kept, chained to a stump, in the back yard.") They were joined within a year by Herbert Mahlon Burwell, an Ontario land surveyor who, like so many others, had come west with the CPR.

Messrs. Garden, Hermon & Burwell would find their work cut out for them. From 1882 to 1885, according to Barry Cotton, the only survey firm that had been listed in the British Columbia directory was Woods, Turner, and Gamble, comprising George Turner in partnership with Charles Woods and Francis Gamble. Their business, writes Cotton, was varied—they advertised services extending beyond surveying to real estate, insurance, and refrigeration equipment sales. Partly to ease the speculation in land, and partly because there were still not enough competent surveyors available, many of the surveys in those early years were "paper surveys" only—plans drawn up on legal descriptions but not based on actual groundwork. Where surveys had been done, the fire of 1886 wiped out much of the evidence. Posts were reduced to ashes, and metal markers melted into obscurity. The result was often chaotic.

In 1929, Ernest Hermon reminisced about the chaos in a paper entitled "Surveying in the City of Vancouver." "Very few of the original posts survived" the fire, he writes, although a few were "referenced with gun barrels" immediately afterward. Hermon also describes how the portion of Georgia Street running through the Yale Town district (so named, according to Hermon, because of CPR workmen brought downriver from Yale and quartered there) had to be narrowed by five feet from ninety-nine feet to ninety-four feet. "On connecting the surveys at Georgia Street, we found a shortage of 6½ feet." It had been a difficult task to get this right on the original survey through the bush, says Hermon diplomatically, in very unfavourable conditions. A practical solution was devised: "To divide this shortage between the six blocks seemed excessive, so we were instructed by the Railway Company officials to take five feet off the width of Georgia Street and divide the 1½ feet between the six blocks, which explains the three inch shortage per block in this area." While the rest of Georgia Street is ninety-nine feet wide and even wider in some parts, the narrower stretch between Burrard and Beatty streets has remained unchanged.

Burrard Street, conversely, had to be widened by thirty-three feet to ninety-nine feet: "This was done by taking a 33-foot strip off Stanley Park and crowding all lots and streets in District Lot 185, 33 feet Westerly." All the lots in District Lot 185 between Georgia and Pacific streets had to be shortened by one foot, in order to make the streets in both DL 185 and DL 541 "come more nearly opposite." Even in the 1920s, when Vancouver was far less populated and frenzied than it is in the twenty-first century, Hermon apparently felt it necessary to excuse those initiatives that had taken place only a few decades earlier. "All of these incidents occurred when property was much less valuable than now, and as there were no definite rules for surveying such as we have today, it seemed the best thing to do in the public interest." As to the re-survey of the Granville Townsite, or Gastown, Hermon like Powell before him ruminated on the fact that the plan of the re-survey had gone missing for so long. His recollection was that by 1917 the plan was unregistrable, even though it had been the basis for all the detailed surveys that had taken place since that time. "We have been making surveys since 1888 to date, 40 years, in this area of six blocks, based on this survey," he wrote in perceptible wonder. "Buildings worth millions of dollars occupy the area, and probably not one lot is strictly in accordance with the registered plan."

Another small surveying firm, named Williams Bros. & Dawson, was formed in 1891. The Williams brothers, Sidney and "JTC," had hung out their shingle in 1886 and were joined by George Herbert Dawson in 1890. Williams Bros. & Dawson undertook the survey of the Keith Road when the District of North Vancouver was formed in 1891. There were only just enough resident landowners, writes Roy Pallant in a research paper on the early days of North Vancouver, to fill all the public offices. The polling booth on what is now Lonsdale Avenue was not easy to get to: "Without a ferry it was difficult at that time to reach the North Shore except by rowing boat or sailing boat."

The survey firm's job was to prove no easier. Its instruction was to locate the best route for a road stretching from the north arm of Burrard Inlet to "some point on Howe Sound"—some thirty miles or more across steep and thickly forested mountainsides and crossing numerous rivers, including the Capilano, the Lynn, and the Seymour, all major waterways. In addition, the best route proved to be through areas where numerous lots had already been pre-empted, although in numerous instances there was no evidence on the ground of that fact—no survey stakes or posts were to be found anywhere. Notwithstanding the lack of evidence, the owners of the lots took strong objection to the new road passing through or next to their properties. The new municipality was not the best employer, being not only effectively destitute for many years, but unable to legally operate. In 1897, according to Pallant, only one person was qualified as a resident landowner to run for council. As a consequence, there was no council for several months. Nonetheless, Keith Road was eventually built, although the jerky fashion in which it and its successor roads today dart through the north shore continues to tell the tale of the difficulties encountered in circumventing angry pre-emptors and difficult terrain.

Things slowed down in Vancouver during the depression of 1893, as they did throughout the province. In the annual reports of the Association of

Provincial Land Surveyors of British Columbia for 1894 and 1895, there were many matters troubling the members of the profession, not least of which was the amount of their own annual membership dues. It was duly resolved to lower them to three dollars. President John Kirk wrote in his 1894 address that the association had been unsuccessful in efforts to take over the management of the profession, despite sympathetic remarks from both the chief commissioner of lands and works and the premier. Legislation amending the Land Surveyors Act of 1891 had done nothing to achieve that objective, and Kirk's frustration was evident: "The fact remains that of all the Provinces of the Dominion, where Land Surveyors have a legal standing, British Columbia is the only one where the admission and discipline of practitioners is not, either in whole or in part, under the control of the authorized members of the profession." Moreover, reflective of the continuing tension between dominion and provincial surveyors, Kirk condemned the fact that the legislation governing British Columbia land surveyors was effectively a rehashed dominion Act. Kirk attempted to remain optimistic in the face of such treatment, however: "Although complete failure in this part of our work must be confessed," he wrote endearingly, "it will never do to give up."

Surveyors also felt they were suffering from an undue financial burden in the form of duty payable on surveying instruments imported from the United States. No such manufacturer existed in Canada, and the profession felt itself unfairly prejudiced in having to pay as much as 35 percent duty on some instruments. A memorandum had been sent early in 1894 to the minister of finance in Ottawa begging relief and pointing out that "the work of land surveying necessarily involves the ownership by each Surveyor of about One Thousand Dollars in instruments for the purpose of surveying...composed chiefly of Transits, Theodolites, Levels, Compasses, Sextants, Field Glasses, Telescopes, Levelling-Rods, Chains, Tapes, Draughting instruments, and material, including Drawing paper, Tracing linen, Cross Section Paper, and blue Process paper." Surveyors for the dominion government, the memorandum complained, had an unfair advantage—not only were the instruments imported free of duty, they were sold to those surveyors at cost. No pity was stirred in the heart of the minister, however, and the plea was rejected. But once again, the provincial surveyors were not prepared to give up. They resolved firmly to undertake "concerted action" with their brethren in other provinces.

The 1894 meeting ended, despite all these problems, with a banquet at the Hotel Victoria, where "speeches and songs were plenty," and "when the party broke up at a certain hour, there were none who did not vote the entertainment a first-class success." By January 1895, however, the depression was clearly making itself felt. President Ernest Hermon noted dolefully that 1894 had been "a very hard year for most of us to make ends meet financially." With melancholy he noted the death of fellow member D.T. Thomson "under most sad and distressing circumstances, far away from home and kindred...The general depression in business and the loneliness of his surroundings were probably the immediate causes of the rash act which terminated his existence."

One of the key issues for 1895, as described by Hermon, related to the extent to which the work of land surveyors was exclusive. Many surveyors were also civil engineers, and the line between the work of each profession had become blurry, to say the least. But increasing levels of definition were being accorded to the work of surveyors, and in particular, to legal surveys defining property boundaries. There were high stakes involved in getting work during the economic recession, and surveyors were starting to resent engineers muscling in on what they saw as their turf. The city engineer for New Westminster, for example, had made it clear he thought himself entitled to define street lines in his municipality. "In my humble opinion," fumed Hermon, "he is performing the duties of a Provincial Land Surveyor and some remedy should be provided." Hermon advocated an amendment to the Land Surveyors Act to define not just surveyors but "surveys." Once again the initiative would be unsuccessful, and the ground for a long-running battle between surveyors and engineers was laid. Hermon would never live to see his proposal put into place. Another century would pass until a statutory definition of "survey" was included in provincial legislation, in 2004.

Happily, at least a strong solidarity appeared to exist among the members of the survey profession. Even in the competitive economic times, they were holding true to an agreed tariff of set fees in order to ensure that clients would not "shop around" for cheaper options. "It is a great source of comfort to be able to refer a kicking client to 'the paper on the wall' and point out that all the other surveyors would charge him the same," noted Hermon. "It satisfies the client that he is being honestly dealt with, and relieves the surveyor of a lot of mental, if not audible profanity. The only thing wanting is some instrument of torture by which we can collect the fees after they are due."

Hermon's theory as to why fees were so difficult to collect went to the heart of a professional inferiority complex that appears always to have nagged land surveyors. "Our profession does not occupy the high position to which it is entitled," he complained. "We may reasonably claim that in no other profession is there a wider field for thought, and in no other is there such accuracy and certainty demanded in the prosecution of their duties." Despite that, the media indiscriminately and consistently called any member of a survey crew a "surveyor," and the public tended to follow suit. Hermon blamed the members themselves, as much as anything, for failing to be organized enough to ensure that only those qualified to practise be recognized publicly as surveyors. No one, he said, called anyone who worked in a lawyer's office a "lawyer" simply because of their place of work; likewise, a clerk or nurse in a doctor's office was never referred to as a "doctor." But surveyors had not achieved the same level of respect as doctors and lawyers, nor had they done anything to remedy the situation. "It is not surprising, therefore, that the public have fallen into the error of considering as a surveyor every person who can set up an instrument, read an angle, look wise, and drink whisky." On that note, Hermon berated his fellow members for their personal habits as well. "Do we at all times conduct ourselves with that dignity which is due our profession? I know that field practice tends to roughen our manners, and fasten upon us habits which are repugnant to polite society, yet our habits and customs have very much to do with the estimation in which we are held, therefore if we would wish to elevate the profession let us not neglect so important an item."

Although there is no mention in the 1895 report as to whether the evening's festivities were as greatly enjoyed as the previous year's, Charles Perry attempted to end the meeting on a lighter note with an essay on two of the fundamental tools of surveyors: originality and invention. The underlying objective of the essay was to convey the same message that Hermon proclaimed regarding the status of surveyors—"their accounts of the territories they explore should be as eagerly and impatiently expected as our morning paper or telegram when events of importance are occurring, and justly so." But Perry's tongue-in-cheek guide to writing such accounts poked unrestrained fun at his fellow surveyors who were tempted to pomposity in writing reports of their explorations, and raises a chuckle in anyone who has had to navigate through the lengthy and flowery surveyors' reports of the past. At the very least, the essay is likely to have caused some red faces in the audience of 1895. "A summary of an ordinary report would read as follows," writes Perry:

> Hired men, bought supplies (tell how many lbs. of each), embarked, arrived, took a latitude (here give name of maker, year and date, and opinion on instruments in general, with full description of how instrument was placed and general instructions on how to take latitude), camp (describe particularly what cook had for supper), embark again, see a bear, shoot at it and miss (explain why), see grouse (give Latin name to show you know it); ascend a mountain, stop to give a discursive sketch of the uses of barometers and yours in particular (state name of maker, etc), put in a table of heights— anywhere will do; throw in a little geology all over ("series" is a good word, also "formation," but "Palaeozoic" is a ripper), then camp (go into full details, principally what there was to eat), start again, find some "colours" (here give general account of placer mining, how to pan gold, flumes, rockers, etc., and general opinion as to gold-bearing ground and rocks), find a lake, sketch out railway routes (be sure and put in a few botanical studies or degress [sic] to discuss the proper meaning of an Indian name), wind up with a copious botanical, meteorological, or other table—failing these give your general view on things generally, and wind up with 'Your obedient servant,' and you will have a first-class Government Report.

The remaining years of the nineteenth century held both good and bad times for surveyors and for all British Columbians. Devastating floods on the Fraser River delta wiped out homes, farms, and settlements in

1894 and again in 1895. For surveyors, that meant work when there was precious little to be had elsewhere: a comprehensive diking program was initiated almost immediately by the provincial government. Government surveyors continued to work their way into increasingly remote parts of the province and to write their effusive reports for Victoria. Southeastern British Columbia continued to enjoy the benefits of mineral extraction and associated railway development, and such towns as Nelson and Cranbrook flourished despite the economic woes of the times.

Some work was to be found re-surveying original work first done in the late 1850s and the decades immediately following. In the 1935 annual report of the Corporation of British Columbia Land Surveyors, George Arbuthnot Smith, LS, spoke in his autobiography of retracing old lines near Sooke on southern Vancouver Island in 1888 that had been "originally surveyed by, I believe, a drunken sailor." As superintendent of public works for the provincial government, Smith went up to Port Alberni the following year, locating the first roads in the area, including much of what is now Highway 4 west to Long Beach. The latter event was a hugely important one for that region, Smith recalled, and a big party was held to celebrate the start of the work. "The government supplied the men and the grub and the inhabitants the Hudson Bay rum...we were told in no uncertain terms that unless we got a road through it would be good policy not to come back." The road was duly created, but it was a long and arduous journey for anyone brave enough to travel it. By 1935, Smith said, "instead of two days, you can go in two hours!—if you have good insurance on the car."

Conditions in the field did not advance in any way for surveyors in British Columbia during the 1890s. It remained tough physical work in remote settings, with poor technology and little, if any, of the comforts of modern camping equipment. Little wonder that surveyors returned from the field with the rough manners and hardened attitudes that Ernest Hermon bemoaned in his 1895 address to the profession. George Smith was involved in timber surveys on the west coast of Vancouver Island mid-decade: "It was the toughest work I believe I ever had. It was almost continuous salal anywhere from six to ten feet high, and the mosquitoes and sandflies awful. The salal nearly got us! When we boarded the

Skeena River survey party, including Mervyn Hewett, BCLS 66, and John Elliott, BCLS 7, likely circa 1912. CHAPMAN LAND SURVEYING

steamer at Ucluelet we were a tough-looking outfit. A very nice old lady in Victoria asked me why so many young surveyors take to drink, and I said I didn't know, but that there was a plant on the West Coast called salal that might easily account in part for it."

By the end of the decade provincial politics were in some disarray. Coal baron James Dunsmuir had been appointed premier after the 1898 election had resulted in complete chaos, with no single strong majority. It was hoped that Dunsmuir could pull together the parties and restore some badly needed order to British Columbian government. Notwithstanding the bedlam in Victoria, James Garden decided to withdraw from surveying in order to pursue politics, becoming mayor of Vancouver in 1898 and a member of the provincial legislature in 1900. Garden, Hermon & Burwell became simply Hermon & Burwell, Civil Engineers, Dominion and B.C. Land Surveyors, and Assayers.

PLS 60, Robert Smith, was registered as the last provincial land surveyor of 1899. PLS 61, Theodore Beauchamp, was the first to be registered in 1900. They were men in the same profession, from two different centuries. They were both about to witness the drama of a completely new age.

11

A Great Silent Country Waiting

Skeena River survey party, including Mervyn Hewett, BCLS 66, and John Elliott, BCLS 7, likely circa 1912. CHAPMAN LAND SURVEYING

The first decade of the twentieth century witnessed yet more leaps forward in development and technological progress in the province. Power from the Buntzen Lake project near Vancouver was being received in the city by December 1903. By 1911, it was producing fifteen thousand kilowatts. In 1903, in what the *Encyclopedia of British Columbia* describes as "an orgy of pre-war railway construction," the Grand Trunk Pacific Railway was incorporated with the goal of building a line from Winnipeg via Edmonton and through the Yellowhead Pass to Prince Rupert. Construction was completed on April 7, 1914. The Pacific Great Eastern Railway was incorporated in 1912, with the intention of running a line from Vancouver to Prince George. The Canadian Northern Pacific Railway was to run through the Yellowhead as well, but then head on a more southerly route via the Thompson and Fraser valleys to Vancouver. Construction began in Port Mann in June 1910, and the last spike was driven just south of Ashcroft on January 23, 1915.

Similar enthusiasm was being applied to road building. At the turn of the century, barely nine thousand kilometres of roadway existed in the province, much of it barely passable dirt track. But by 1907 the automobile had come into popular use in British Columbia, and the pressure was on to build proper roads. Premier Richard McBride created a new Department of Public Works in 1908 that was responsible, among other things, for highways and bridges. By the outbreak of war in 1914, the amount of roadway in the province doubled. Connell Higgins, BCLS 53, reported to Surveyor General George Dawson on December 12, 1913:

> My party left Vancouver on May 12th, to begin work in the vicinity of 100 Mile House, Cariboo Road, going into the district by motor over the old Cariboo Road from Ashcroft 87 Miles, this road being the great highway to interior British Columbia...the road is being improved to a greater and greater extent every year, by the Government...and while there are still some bad stretches where, in wet weather, wagons and automobiles get mired, these are being eliminated with good gravel and macadam. In dry weather the road can be said to be good throughout. The amount of automobile traffic, over this road, has increased prodigiously within the last

few years...I feel convinced that tourist traffic alone over this road will be a large factor in the development of the country."

The population of the province also more than doubled in the same period, standing at just under 400,000 people by 1911. Agricultural ventures expanded at an astounding rate: in the Okanagan Valley alone, the acreage under production soared from 7,430 acres in 1901 to 100,000 acres in 1909. Timber harvesting boomed. The mining of both copper and coal were solid industries, as was the coastal fishery. None of this was bad news for the surveying profession. In the year 1900, according to Robert Cail in *Land, Man, and the Law*, only seventy thousand acres of land were surveyed for a variety of purposes, including timber limits, mining claims, and pre-emptions. No government surveys of any kind took place in the years 1901, 1902, or 1906. But in the seven years from 1907 to 1913, close to four million acres were surveyed by the government, and more than eleven million acres were surveyed in total. By the end of 1913, writes Cail, "26,299,689 acres of provincial territory had been surveyed...roughly a ninth of the total land area" of British Columbia.

Photo-topographical surveys had kept a similar pace, led in many instances by renowned provincial land surveyor Arthur Oliver Wheeler. Wheeler recorded the early surveys of the Selkirk Mountains in detail in his 1905 publication *The Selkirk Range.* He was a man born to his time and to his profession; his surveys in the Selkirks and Rockies were his first alpine experiences, ones he enjoyed so greatly that mountaineering became his chief recreation. In 1907 he helped found the Alpine Club of Canada, and became its first president. His son Edward Wheeler would follow in his footsteps, joining the 1921 Everest expedition with George Mallory and engaging in photo-topographical surveys of the Tibetan side of the mountain.

Wheeler's experiences indicated that this kind of field work had not become any easier for surveyors, despite advances in road technology and the advent of the motor vehicle. Heavy cameras and instruments still had to be carried to high elevations, mountaineering skills were essential when crossing avalanche-ridden terrain, and the sheer physical challenge was overwhelming: in the 1902 season alone, Wheeler and his crew ascended sixty-four mountains, seventeen of them more than nine thousand feet high. It was time-consuming and expensive in the extreme, as former surveyor general Tom Kains had accurately forecast in 1892. In 1929, reminiscing about the physical hardships of photo-topographical surveying during the early part of the century, Wheeler hailed the dawn of aerial photography from airplanes as "a magnificent stride forward."

Despite that, Wheeler regarded his time and experiences in the mountains with a great deal of affection and humour, describing the joy he felt there as "so intense as to be almost a pain." He spoke of his work as being "of wonder and joy, filled with unique scenes and interesting people. There was the man standing by the switch at Rogers Pass," he wrote, tongue firmly in cheek. "To be friendly, I asked him, 'Are you a switchman?' He replied, 'No sir, I'm a Swede.'" Wheeler also described the dangers, in particular of clouds and electrical storms. Without the advantages of modern electronic positioning technology, clouds could completely destroy any sense of direction; it was sometimes necessary, said Wheeler, to shout and use the return echo to guess where he was. When highly charged electric clouds passed over, "the nearby rocks began to hum and ice-axes to buzz. If you remove your hat, your hair will stand straight up on end. Several times I have received a severe shock through touching a screw of a mountain transit while it was buzzing..." Wheeler once got caught on the summit of a mountain when an electrical storm blew up in the space of a few minutes. With no time to descend, he and his crew huddled thirty feet below the peak "and awaited developments." A thunderbolt struck forty feet away: "The whole top of the mountain had been electrified and we received a severe shock," he wrote tersely.

But it was all part of a day's work for surveyors. Frank Cyril Swannell, PLS 75, was undertaking exploratory triangulation surveys for the government in the Tweedsmuir-Omineca country in the years immediately preceding the First World War. Swannell and his crew also had to move supplies and equipment by hand, using canoes where possible and sheer muscle power where they could no longer navigate even the smallest vessel. Outboard motors were still not in common use; pack horses remained the most useful carriers of heavy gear, although not always the most efficient. "Old Bob has strayed off & only just caught," wrote

Thomas H. Taylor, PLS 51, extracting a tooth from one of his four-legged crew members. Groundhog District, 1913. OFFICE OF THE SURVEYOR GENERAL

Swannell in his diary on August 6, 1913, after nearly losing his horse. A few days later he noted: "The pass is execrable, being boulder-strewn trail alternates between rocks & muskeg. It took horses 4 hours to go 3 miles and Bob nearly kills himself." On September 12 Swannell wrote of running seventeen miles down the Mesalinka River, which he described as being a "very hazardous" waterway and littered with "sweepers"— trees that had fallen sideways into the current and beneath which the current could sweep the unwary paddler and trap in a moment's inattention. "Very swift & bad drift-piles. Run into one and a sweeper 3 times. When swept under sweeper we jump over as it passes but dog Dick is swept overboard makes for shore and will have no more rafting, thereby showing sound common sense."

Mosquitoes remained a menace, and late fall surveying had its own hazards: "Transit continually freezing up and have to build fires to thaw it," Swannell wrote on November 10, 1913. Ten days later, even a fire was of little use—even the meat in a frying pan would freeze on top, claimed Swannell, while the underneath was cooking. Food, of course, was all-

W.S. Drewry, PLS 14, surveyed in the Cariboo and Lillooet districts during 1912–1913. This image was taken on Deadman Road, near Rugged Rock. MRS. JOANNE DREWRY

important to the field crews. If the bill of goods issued to George Herbert Dawson, PLS 7, in July 1902 is any indication, in anticipation of their other hardships surveyors were determined not to go without certain luxuries if possible. Included in his provisions were not only the standard sacks of flour and sides of bacon, but six bottles of plum jam; five pounds of dried figs and apricots; Worcester sauce, pickles, and syrup; and eight pounds of cookies. The good food may also have compensated in some small part for the long separations—and silences—from loved ones.

Former surveyor general Gerry Andrews writes in a 1979 article in *British Columbia Historical News* about Swannell's 1904 summer season, immediately following his marriage. Among Swannell's crew was George Copley, a lifelong friend who had celebrated his own marriage in a double ceremony with Swannell early that spring. "The brides were left for long months 'incommunicado,'" says Andrews. "Mid-season, while occupying a wilderness station, an Indian chanced to pass, heading for a remote post office. Seizing opportunity by the forelock, they tore a blank sheet from the field-book, George writing to Mabel on one side

Members of the survey party of W.S. Drewry carrying supplies by raft on Bonaparte Lake, 1912–1913. MRS. JOANNE DREWRY

and Frank to Ada on the other…Months later on their return from the field, their welcome was tempered with poignant protest that had they torn the sheet in half, using both sides separately, each bride could have treasured her own 'billet doux' from her sweetie." Next season, Copley was determined not to get into similar hot water: "Copley, having a vivid imagination and a facile hand, spent a couple of hours writing a series of letters to Mabel, post-dated two weeks apart, sealed them in separate numbered envelopes and instructed the postmaster [at Fort St. James] to mail them at intervals accordingly. The latter, with other preoccupations of the trading post, forgot and dumped all of George's letters in the bag to go out next mail. Poor George had some very imaginative explaining to do at the season's end…"

Mapping continued to be a provincial priority in the early years of the twentieth century, spurred by the ambitions of Premier Richard McBride. In 1908 the Geological Survey of Canada created a topographic survey division, and it was determined that the most suitable place in Canada to train new topographers for the department was southeastern Vancouver

W.S. Drewry's camp. Camp was basic, often serving as an office to transcribe field notes as well as shelter. MRS. JOANNE DREWRY

Island. Not only was the climate moderate, but the area required a geological survey and topographical mapping. In 1909–1910 in this area, new methods of topographical surveying were given their first trials in Canada. In 1909 the federal Geodetic Survey of Canada was officially established, although geodetic work—a form of applied mathematics dealing with the shape, curvature, and dimensions of the earth—had begun in Canada in earnest several years previously.

In 1912, a geographic section was established in the provincial surveyor general's branch of the lands department. G.G. Aitken, who would later become chief geographer of Canada in the 1930s, was then working for the Geological Survey of Canada and took special leave from his federal role to organize the new provincial department. Aitken was taken to meet Premier McBride, who outlined his wishes in no uncertain terms:

> The Premier informed me that by his instruction an attempt had been made to draw and print a map of the southerly two-thirds of the Province on one sheet. Unhappily, this map effort, when

printed, was so disappointing in appearance that he had ordered the total printing destroyed. He said…he counted it most necessary to have a suitable large map of British Columbia…it was his further desire to have suitable printed maps prepared which would record the progress of geographical knowledge of the Province. It was with no little awe that I listened to the Premier as he outlined his wishes and, I confess, a certain sinking feeling even in my youthful stomach…I asked if he had in mind any particular time in which he expected this map to be compiled, drawn and printed. He said, "Yes—six months." All that I could think to say was that I would do my very best.

Aitken and his team did not achieve McBride's goal in six months, but in a still incredible time frame of eight months. The challenges that had been faced included the limited control surveys in existence in 1912: effectively, only the 49th parallel surveys and the dominion railway belt traverse were suitable to be used as base points for further mapping. In addition, next to nothing was known reliably at the time about much of northern and central British Columbia. "Even the geographic naming throughout the Province," mourned Aitken, "was nearly all in confusion and dispute." Nonetheless, the four-sheet wall map of British Columbia that was produced by Aitken and his staff stayed in use in the province for twenty-one years.

On June 1, 1905, the British Columbia Land Surveyors Act had been passed, creating the Corporation of Land Surveyors of the Province of British Columbia and instigating a new numbering system for surveyors registered after its enactment. The profession had finally achieved the goal it had been seeking since the early 1890s: control over the admission of new members. A board of management would oversee decisions as to who would be allowed to article and study land surveying in the province, the first step being an examination held under clause 41 of the statute on his "penmanship and orthography, and also as to his knowledge of arithmetic, algebra as far as quadratic equations, the first four books of Euclid, plane trigonometry and the use of logarithms."

To be admitted to practice, further examinations on a more detailed range of subjects were compulsory. Naturally, "satisfactory testimony as to his character for sobriety and probity" was a requisite condition for admission. In addition, the individual concerned had not only to be a British citizen but to be at least twenty-one years old. The latter requirement may not have seemed unreasonable. But the Corporation was quickly faced with a dilemma when in 1909 a precocious young man named Geoffrey Kirby Burnett sat and passed his exams, with the highest marks yet received by any candidate to date, at the tender age of nineteen. Before the error was realized, Burnett was issued a certificate as BCLS 51. It was promptly withdrawn, and it remains an unissued number in the records of the organization. In 1911, immediately after his twenty-first birthday, Burnett duly presented himself again to the Board and this time received BCLS commission 79.

With the new legislation in place, British Columbia land surveyors also obtained greater control over their domain, as thenceforth all registered plans had to be signed by a qualified member of the Corporation. At the same time, strict standards made themselves felt—chains, for example, now had to conform to a standard length, and no aberrations would be tolerated. So seriously was this being taken that failure to have a chain examined and certified as correct could result in the forfeiture of a land surveyor's commission. Six members were granted commissions in the first year of the Corporation's existence; in the years between 1907 and 1913, another 149 commissions would be issued. The year 1913, when the economic boom reached its height, remains unbeaten in the history of the organization: thirty-five new commissions were issued.

As the profession consolidated its stance in the province and there seemed to be no end in sight to the opportunities for work, more surveyors started to form themselves into firms. Several of these were family practices that would eventually become family dynasties, surviving into the twenty-first century on the strength of expansion and diversification. In 1913, brothers Frederic Clare Underhill and James Theodore Underhill received their BCLS commissions—143 and 146, respectively—and formed a partnership, Underhill & Underhill. The company now trades as Underhill Geomatics Ltd., working in the Yukon and the Northwest Territories as well as in British Columbia. In 1910, William Gordon

McElhanney received BCLS commission 38 and set up practice in Vancouver. In 1913, he was joined by his brother Thomas Andrew, BCLS 110, to form McElhanney Bros. McElhanney Land Surveying Associates now operates several branches around the province, as well as in Alberta and is colloquially known as "McElhanney."

In 1906 George Herbert Dawson, formerly of Williams Bros. & Dawson, took on John Elliott, BCLS 7, as a partner, setting up shop at 413 Granville Street in Vancouver. Elliott was by all accounts a charmer, considered one of Vancouver's most eligible bachelors in his time. Certainly his friend, Surveyor General Eric McKay, seemed to think so, jestingly writing in a business letter to Elliott on August 15, 1908: "Vancouver will look ever so much better when you come down and I am sure that the young ladies miss you very much." In 1911, when Dawson left to become surveyor general, Mervyn William Hewett, BCLS 66, joined the partnership to replace him. There was no end to the work that the firm and others like it experienced in the following two years. In 2005, William "Bill" Chapman, BCLS 526, head of the firm by then known as Chapman Land Surveying Ltd., said of the period: "In 1912, an average surveyor was probably creating in the magnitude of ten to twenty lots per working day, as opposed to us with four land surveyors, and a staff of fifteen people, creating possibly thirty lots this year. The number is just completely staggering and impossible for us to truly comprehend."

In April 1908, a treaty was concluded between Canada and the United States that agreed, among other things, that "in the intervals between the monuments along the parallel of latitude, it is agreed that the line has the curvature of a parallel of 49 degrees north latitude; and that such characteristic shall determine all questions that may hereafter arise with reference to the position of the boundary at any point between neighbouring monuments." The international boundary had been meticulously re-surveyed during the immediately preceding years. All the same, the agreement was a practical solution to any remaining uncertainties as to whether discrepancies existed between the line on the ground and the actual 49th parallel.

Another border between the two countries had also caused considerable strife. The question of the ambiguous description of the northern boundary line between Canada and the United States, following the latter's 1867 purchase of Alaska from Russia, had been of little moment—until, of course, gold reared its pretty head. In 1873, the yellow mineral was found on the Stikine River. Among Americans, a sudden interest flared in having the coastline surveyed, in particular the section separating the Alaska Panhandle from mainland Canada north of the junction between the 141st meridian and 54°40' N latitude. Essentially, the 1825 treaty between the Russians and the British had agreed that the border would follow a parallel line north of 54°40' along the mountain summits of the coast, more or less ten miles inland from the sea. The Americans had a strong interest in pushing the line as far east as possible, into the fjords and river mouths along the coast, in order to make access to the goldfields and to coastal waters fall squarely within their jurisdiction. The Canadians, naturally, had a diametrical interest in pushing the boundary west. Even if a line could be agreed, the coastline was so little known, and so tortuous in its outline, that any survey of the border was going to be arduous in the extreme.

A flurry of limited surveys along the south coast took place during the 1870s and 1880s. British Columbia land surveyor Joseph Hunter was instructed in 1877 to locate the boundary-line crossing of the Stikine River in order to set up a Canadian customs post. Similar surveys continued into the 1880s, but both countries continued to dispute where the border should actually go. In 1892, they finally set up a joint boundary commission to try to establish a permanent boundary. The initial survey, according to Andrew Birrell in "Survey Photography in British Columbia, 1858–1900," "was to be a rapid reconnaissance of the territory along the disputed border, from which it was hoped sufficient information could be gathered to resolve the debate over the boundary." Using photo-topographical methods, in just two seasons, "the first cut to only twenty good days because of abysmal weather, the Canadian surveyors managed to cover the entire territory allotted to them."

Unfortunately, while the surveys effectively established the heights of Mount St. Elias in Alaska at just over 18,000 feet and of Mount Logan in Canada at 19,850 feet, they did little to help resolve the dispute. To make things worse, the discovery in 1897 of gold in the Klondike swiftly elevated both ambition and tension. Access to coastal routes to the Yukon became a pressing matter for both countries. Discussions stalled, and the joint commission ceased to meet after 1899. Finally, a tribunal comprising representatives from Britain, Canada, and the United States was formed in 1902, and a settlement of the border reached in 1903. It was not one that Canada favoured, but at least certainty had been reached.

Certainty, that is, on paper. Following the settlement, surveys could begin in earnest to establish the settled boundary on the ground. Don Thomson describes the process in dry terms in *Men and Meridians:* "The original triangulation and photo-topography were revised and extended, monuments set at suitable sites to mark the boundary on the ground, and a 20-foot skyline vista was cut through most of the timbered areas." But such a terse summary of the work required does little justice to the men who carried out the surveys. The harshness of the region in which they were required to cut trail, climb mountains, ford rivers, carry heavy bronze monuments several feet in length, and simply survive, almost beggars imagination. More than eight hundred miles of border had to be marked along some of the most inhospitable country on the planet, sometimes by men who had never been in such a harsh environment.

In his memoir, *A Journey Through Life,* Alexander Gillespie, BCLS 13, of Victoria describes in detail the four seasons he spent working on the border surveys. Despite the sheer hardship, through the mists of many decades past, Gillespie clearly looked back on the adventure with relish and relates many cheerful anecdotes. "It was my first experience at mountain climbing, and I was thrilled…We used to have some wonderful slides on the hard snow when we were coming down the mountains…we got rather expert in the use of our alpine sticks." The cook, recalls Gillespie, was a young Englishman named Brewster, about his own age. "He had been employing all his spare time [at camp] making a tennis lawn, of all things…He was delighted when he heard I could play. He had balls and two racquets and a net. We rigged up the net and I think for the first time, lawn tennis was played in Alaska. That was in 1904."

All the same, his words also reveal the difficulties and challenges the men faced. Gillespie and his fellow surveyors had to repeatedly climb the same mountains to reset monuments. It was easy to become exhausted.

During the course of the boundary surveys, several lives were lost. Gillespie was more fortunate, but he describes one typical experience in which he and his companion, Scottie, had to leave camp before six in the morning. The pair had to first canoe several miles downriver to try to locate a trail that had been cut the previous season. From there, it was a five-mile hike up to about 4,300 feet. The snowpack was well below the timberline. Before exiting the trees, the men had to cut three large ones by hand axe, a laborious and time-consuming chore, and then carry the three heavy poles with them to the top. "The snow got deeper, as we approached the summit, and before we got there, it became a desperate struggle as we sank almost to our waists, and could only manage a few steps between each rest...We reached the summit at five in the afternoon. We found the top of the bronze monument, planted the previous year, and lashing our trees strongly together in the form of a tripod, we planted it over the monument, draping some bunting around it, and our job was done. It only remained," he writes, "to get back to camp."

Gillespie's companion Scottie, however, nearly gave up at that point. Gillespie was forced to cajole the exhausted man down the mountain and back to their canoe, and then had to single-handedly paddle back to camp—upstream. "It was about eleven when we finally got into camp," he writes. "It was a terribly hard trip to start the season on." Things got a little easier as the snow melted, although the scrubby alder and thorny devil's club plants that are typical of southern Alaska continued to pose problems in travel, as did the fast-flowing rivers, mosquitoes, and in place of the deep snows, the occasional avalanche. The melting snow had another disadvantage for the surveyors: a measurement taken on a snow-covered peak would have to be adjusted after the snow had gone and revealed the real summit. Setting up a tripod on the narrow space of a peak was occasionally impossible, causing deflections in the line. The air temperature was often below freezing, despite the summer season, making it difficult to work.

Despite all the challenges the surveyors faced in drawing a line across the northern coastal mountains, by 1914, the work was virtually complete: a twenty-foot-wide line running more than eight hundred miles north. In *Men and Meridians,* Don Thomson quotes one of the surveyors who worked on the boundary, Alexander George Stewart: "The survey line had to be 20 feet wide. Some of the trees we had to cut were six feet in diameter. We used double-bit axes and seven-foot crosscut saws. We worked ten hours daily, seven days a week...Markers had to be placed every three miles in solid rock. We couldn't find much solid rock in some river valleys so we had to pack in cement, gravel, and water and then build three-foot-square aprons for obelisk-type monuments. Smaller monuments weighed 56 pounds and stood 2½ feet high and these had much smaller concrete bases. These monuments were made of heavy bronze with *Canada* marked on one side and *United States* marked on the other."

Back in Victoria, George Herbert Dawson was named surveyor general of British Columbia in 1911 and moved into his new office to find it in disarray. The sheer burden of work arising out of the economic boom and land speculation had overwhelmed the limited number of staff in the branch, who were months behind in plotting and gazetting the work of government surveyors in the field. Things were, however, to rapidly change under Dawson's leadership. Among other achievements, he successfully lobbied for a considerable expansion of staff and resources, and within the space of only a few months the office had caught up completely. Dawson also sent out a flurry of circular letters with instructions to surveyors requesting them to take action on a number of matters, including guide-lines on the 1911 Crown lands survey regulations and requests to collect plant specimens for the province's chief botanist. In 1912 he admonished surveyors in the field who were unnecessarily killing game out of season. In 1913, he echoed Aitken's frustration at the mess of geographic names in the province, requesting surveyors to refrain from naming geographic features unless "a particular name appears to you to be eminently suitable." Land surveyors were most often the first to observe and map large areas of the province, and the temptation to name geographic features was great. Unfortunately, as Dawson pointed out sarcastically, they were frequently distinctly lacking in imagination in doing so: "There are on maps published by this Department, 6 Bear Lakes, 7 Salmon Rivers, 9 Beaver Creeks and 14 Boulder Creeks."

His particular desire was to see comprehensive surveyors' reports included in the annual report of the lands department, detailing all matters of observation in the districts surveyed: physical features, economic possibilities, and "generally, such information as will be of service to anyone proposing to settle or interesting themselves in the district." It is Dawson who is to be thanked for the fact that the reports of the lands department during that period and for several decades afterwards are not only comprehensive in their ambit but fascinating documents in their own right. The reports, instructed Dawson on October 22, 1913, "should be carefully written and in as interesting a style as possible, and should not contain technical details as to survey matters." By that date Dawson was also clearly losing patience with the fact that surveyors were not complying with his wishes. Having sent out numerous polite requests in the preceding eighteen months for co-operation in submitting timely reports of the nature he sought, in the same circular letter he took a sterner and somewhat sarcastic tone: "The Department anticipate that they will have the loyal support and co-operation of all surveyors in the matter of the preparation of this report and that same will be a distinct advance on that of last year. This result can only be arrived at if each and every surveyor supply interesting information on the country surveyed by him." Dawson also played the minister card. Having been so successful in obtaining additional funding for his department, Dawson was under some pressure to justify it to his political master: "The vote for survey purposes this year is, as you are aware," he continued, "an exceptionally large one, and the Department are especially desirous that the public have such a Report as will convince them of the efficiency of the Survey Branch. A report which will be read by the general public will accomplish the end in view." The implication was clear: it was in everyone's interest to keep the budget money rolling in by demonstrating to the minister responsible a high level of useful activity.

The reports of 1912 and 1913 show an erratic level of compliance with Dawson's detailed instructions. Some surveyors, such as William Drewry, made a distinct effort, while others clearly struggled with the notion of what constituted an "interesting" style. They make compelling reading nonetheless and illustrate the extensive level of activity in the province at the height of the boom times. During the course of 1912, five surveyors

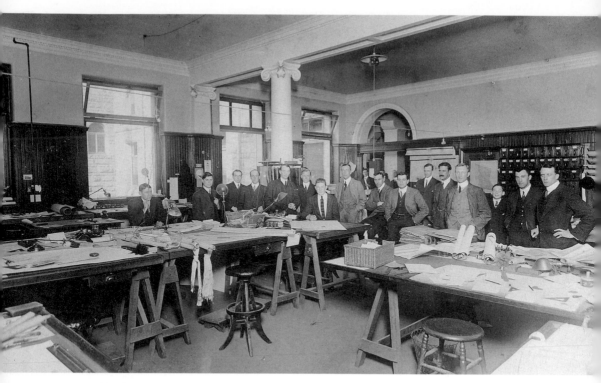

The Surveyor General's Branch, 1913. The ranks of surveyors in the province were about to be dramatically thinned by the outbreak of the First World War. OFFICE OF THE SURVEYOR GENERAL

were employed in land and coal and oil surveys in the Queen Charlotte Islands; more than half a dozen were spread out through the southern interior, the Bulkley Valley, the Cariboo, and the southern Peace River country; and continuing triangulation and exploratory work was taking place throughout the Kootenays. Drewry reported that his surveys in the Cariboo were "required for the rectification of maps which, in places, were so seriously in error as to render them useless as a guide to land-seekers, and of little utility for administrative or any other purpose."

By 1913, Drewry was in full flow, commenting extensively on all manner of aspects of his explorations, including problems with deforestation that were already showing themselves—an item that he included under the heading "Correlation of Things":

It has been noted that many years ago tremendous fires had swept

This image is simply entitled "The Boys." The location is the Skeena River, with Thomas H. Taylor, PLS 51, 1913. OFFICE OF THE SURVEYOR GENERAL

away the ancient forest, and that more recent ones had devastated large tracts. Complaints of lessening and variable stream-flow have been prevalent in areas watered by streams heading in this great interior plateau and adjoining mountains. A study of the question upon the ground has led to the conclusion that diminished stream-flow in summer is probably to a large extent the natural result of widespread destruction of the forest covering the earth, exposing winter snows and saturated earth to the direct rays of the sun.

Under the heading "View From the Peak," Drewry writes:

The view from this coign of vantage is magnificent. To the north are spread the basins of Red Creek and Canim Lake, with the high snow-capped mountains along Quesnel Lake and the Clearwater as a background. To the east lie the rugged multi-coloured mountain masses dividing the Bridge Creek basin from the valley of the North Thompson River. To the south are visible the backs of spurs of these mountain masses extending westerly and sloping down to the interior plateau. To the west is the great basin of Bridge Creek, some 600 square miles in area, containing innumerable lakes set like inlays of polished silver in broad valleys rimmed by fir-crowned hills; a great silent country waiting the advent of road and rail to bear the population whose footsteps are even now approaching it.

Within the space of a year, however, the feet of many British Columbians would be marching to a completely different drumbeat. On October 1, 1914, Frank Swannell and his survey party pulled into the bank of the Finlay River to investigate a red flag tied to a tree: "It had wrapped in canvas an August newspaper," writes Swannell, "with huge headlines announcing the Declaration of War." Around the province and the country, hundreds of surveyors downed their tools and immediately enlisted to fight. On November 17, 1914, Dawson issued yet another circular letter:

> It is unofficially reported to me that thirty [provincial] land survey-
> ors have gone to England, or propose to volunteer for service, and
> it is probable that at least as many articled pupils will be equally
> patriotic, while rumours that entire survey parties have enlisted,
> and are now training in the militia camps, point to the possibility
> of the land surveying fraternity being represented at the front by
> 200 or 300 men.

The glory days were over, at least for the time being. Land surveyors were marching to war, and into one of the darkest periods that members of the profession had yet experienced.

Survey camp, Silver Cup Mountain, Kootenay District, 1925. OFFICE OF THE SURVEYOR GENERAL

12

This Present Titanic Struggle

Monument on the British Columbia–Yukon border, 1908. The man pictured is
unidentified. OFFICE OF THE SURVEYOR GENERAL

"With the outbreak of the World War, in 1914," writes Don Duffy in *Cadastral Survey Practice, 1851–2004*, "the great boom turned, within a year, into an unprecedented bust."

William Stewart Drewry took over the presidency of the Corporation of British Columbia Land Surveyors from Frank Compton Green, PLS 45, in January 1915. Drewry had been president before, during 1909 and 1910. Unlike the tenure he had held in the heady days of the pre-war boom, Drewry's role for the next two years was to hold the members of the profession together through exceedingly difficult times, both economically and emotionally. Before Green handed over the reins, in his address to the members as the outgoing president he wrote:

> This is the tenth annual meeting of this Corporation and at our last meeting we little thought that the shadow of a great war would so soon cover our land in common with half the world. It is a time of great sacrifices and I know that most surveyors are doing all they can...Up to date forty B.C. Land Surveyors have attached themselves to the forces of Overseas service...the proportion of Articled Pupils who have enlisted is, I believe, even greater.

Green also wrote sombrely: "The bonanza years for surveyors have probably departed forever." Green meant financially, but his statement was equally true of a certain sense of innocence and of an unlimited future that had existed prior to the outbreak of the immense conflict. Such innocence would not return, for anyone; the world had changed fundamentally.

Each of the annual reports of the Corporation for the duration of the war quoted tragic statistics. By January 1916, some seventy surveyors were listed individually by name as being on active service. Two were known to be prisoners of war in Germany, and four had been killed in action, including PLS 1, James Herrick McGregor, who fell at Ypres on April 25, 1915. McGregor's loss was deeply felt beyond the ranks of the profession. At the time of his death, he had already served a term of office as reeve of the municipality of Oak Bay, near Victoria, and was president of the Union Club of British Columbia. The Geographic Board of Canada would subsequently recognize McGregor's contributions to the

Survey images from the British Columbia–Yukon border, 1908. These images appear to have been made by a dominion land surveyor named Wallace. OFFICE OF THE SURVEYOR GENERAL

country by naming the headwater tributaries of the Fraser River after him: Captain Creek, James Creek, Herrick Creek, and McGregor River.

"In consequence of the War and the general financial depression," reported Corporation secretary William Gore in the 1916 report in a subdued tone, "the past year has been an exceptionally quiet one professionally." Despite those words, a remarkable sense of optimism prevailed on the home front throughout the war years. In 1916, president Drewry was determined to maintain a positive tone in his address:

> Our profession has been adversely affected, in common with others, by the great struggle now going on; but hopeful signs for the future are not entirely lacking. It seems to be the general opinion that a great flow of immigration will take place at the close of the war; and if this impression is well-founded it should mean an increased demand for our services, since Surveyors are usually the scouting force of settlement, spying out the land and blazing trails along which occupation advances.

By 1917, one hundred and six members had joined the war effort and eleven had been killed. It was becoming harder to stay positive. The Corporation rallied to support the dependants of those who had gone overseas to serve and took measures to preserve the standing of articled students who had had to interrupt their three-year training period to enlist. Large sums were sent to Belgium out of the Corporation's accumulated funds to support the relief efforts in that country. With very little field work available for those still trying to carry on the profession in British Columbia, however, belts were tightened at home. Some surveyors who were working found themselves being paid in eggs and meat rather than cash. In the absence of sufficient income, others struggled just to pay their annual dues. "Private practice," reported President Neville Townsend, PLS 28, in 1918, "has been almost at a standstill."

Government attempts to stimulate agriculture and to support returning soldiers were at first greeted with relief, then anger at the consequences for surveyors. In 1916, the Soldiers Homestead Act was passed, with the objective of providing settlement land for veterans. The 1917 Land Settlement and Development Act established settlement areas in potentially productive agricultural areas along various rail routes in central British Columbia. The Land Settlement Board was authorized to purchase logged-off lands suitable for subdivision into farm units. It seemed that good work for surveyors would be available, and to a certain extent that was true. It was a mixed blessing, however: much of the land that the government acquired, in particular for the returned soldiers, consisted of cancelled pre-emptions for which Crown grants had never been issued. On many of the properties, surveys had been carried out but had not been paid for by the owner. The government was taking back the lands without dealing with the outstanding debts owed to the relevant surveyors, a point of much bitterness among the membership in 1917. A resolution was duly passed to demand that the government pay for the forfeited surveys. Whether it was successful is unclear; no mention of the issue makes it into the reports of subsequent annual meetings. It seems unlikely under the circumstances, however. The government was as short of funds as everyone else.

By the end of the war, more than 120 provincial land surveyors had served in the armed forces of either Canada or Britain—some 40 percent of the registered membership in British Columbia at the time the conflict commenced. Two dozen of them lost their lives in the service of their country, leaving an enormous professional gap that would be difficult to bridge for many years. The recession—one that would continue long after the end of the war—meant there was a great deal less work for the foreseeable future for those who remained. In his report for 1918 to the minister of lands, the Honourable T.D. Pattullo, Surveyor General Joshua Umbach wrote: "The appropriation for Crown land surveys for the current year was $70,000, being lower than that for any year since 1907. In consequence it has been necessary to further curtail field operations and to confine the work to only the most necessary surveys."

Since an amendment to the Land Act in 1917 had abolished the pre-emption of any unsurveyed lands, the priority was to complete surveys of outstanding pre-emptions, particularly those of properties of servicemen overseas. The survey branch also continued triangulation work along much of the coastline, spurred on by numerous applications for timber licences on the coast. Most existing charts were unreliable; one large inlet, reported Umbach, "was found this year to be about twelve miles out of place on the chart." The necessity of the work was self-evident, but it was the cause of another tragedy, this time back at home. John Laverock, BCLS 11, and his assistant, one J. Griffiths, drowned in Dean Channel near Ocean Falls when their small boat capsized in a sudden storm. "Mr. Laverock had been employed on Government work annually for several years, and his field-work and returns were always highly satisfactory," Umbach wrote sombrely. "It is felt that his unfortunate and untimely death has removed one of the most efficient men of his profession in the Province."

One of the few areas where a higher level of activity was maintained was at Cumshewa Inlet in the Queen Charlotte Islands. In that area the war had generated a significant industry in what was known as "aeroplane spruce," (now more commonly called airplane spruce) fostered by the Imperial Munitions Board. Sturdy, lightweight Sitka spruce wood had proved useful in the construction of aircraft and was in high demand during the war. While other types of wood have similar strength-to-weight ratios, they were not as easily harvested or as plentiful as the Sitka. Sitka spruce is also straight-grained, usually with few defects. All the same, a tree two hundred feet tall and eight feet in diameter—one that would have taken four hundred years or more to reach those dimensions—typically yielded only 5 percent or less of its mass in lumber of the quality necessary for aircraft construction, and as a result the use of Sitka spruce was an enormous drain on the coastal forests of British Columbia during this period. Alfred Wright, BCLS 90, was conducting triangulation surveys in the Queen Charlotte Islands in 1918. Reporting on the economic activity of the area, he described the industry:

> Some eight or ten camps are established on Cumshewa Inlet alone, and the industry should continue to flourish, even though the spruce may not now be needed for war purposes. The spruce is towed to the Northern Mainland sawmills at Prince Rupert, Ocean Falls, and Swanson Bay in Davis rafts. It is there sawed and shipped over the Grand Trunk Pacific to the factories in Toronto and Great Britain. The spruce timber in this inlet is particularly adapted for

the manufacture of aeroplanes, and so far 18,000,000 feet of Nos. 1 and 2 aeroplane spruce has been shipped from Cumshewa Inlet alone.

Provincial mapping efforts were, however, significantly reduced by the war. Enlistments almost entirely depleted the government geographic staff, leaving just two men available for mapping work for the duration of the war. Umbach reported that, since the demand for maps had fallen off, and as less field work was underway, "it has been possible to fill the most urgent requirements in this connection." The general collection of maps was, however, becoming not only out of date, but out of print, and Umbach forecast a need immediately after the war to ramp up resources and rectify the problem as quickly as possible. The one bright spot on the mapping horizon of the province during the war years was the opening, on May 27, 1918, of a Vancouver office of the Geological Survey of Canada. Geologist Charles Camsell accepted the directorship of the office, after first applying for a raise in pay to offset both the high cost of living on the west coast and "the more advanced social position" that he would be assuming. As a local distribution centre for maps and reports, the Vancouver office of the GSC was reported to be "an immediate success."

Among provincial land surveyors, despite the recession and the tragic effects of the war, a strong sense of fortitude prevailed. President Townsend wrote determinedly in 1918:

> There is a vast territory in this Province that has yet to be blazed out, and although it is doubtful if there will ever be the same demand for our services as there was five or six years ago, still I can see no reason why our profession should not share in the bright future which lies before this province, and which will most assuredly come when this present titanic struggle is ended.

In the meantime, matters of moment both large and small continued to occupy the minds of British Columbia land surveyors. By 1915 a practice of presenting papers on matters of interest to the profession at the annual general meetings of the Corporation was well established, and Stuart McDiarmid, BCLS 19, submitted a paper entitled simply:

The cover of the 1915 BCLS AGM program. A sense of humour prevailed, despite the shadow of war. CHAPMAN LAND SURVEYING

"Surveying." Despite what his colleague Townsend had just said about the vast uncharted portions of the province awaiting the gentle hand of a surveyor, McDiarmid's view was that, increasingly, the work of the profession was focused on what he referred to as "old" surveys. By "old" he simply meant "prior"—or anything that had occurred up until that date—writing that "the adjective 'old' is not used for the purpose of conveying a meaning of age, but may be used to include that definition which a land surveyor gives it on his land registry office plans when a post set by someone at 10 o'clock on Tuesday morning is found by him at 10:30 the same day." As the posts marking the corners rotted and the monuments crumbled, or they were illegally moved or removed by neighbours disputing each other's boundaries, surveyors were being called upon more and more to re-establish the original location of the post, the "corner." McDiarmid emphasized the need to re-establish corners with precision and to make the best possible effort at coordination among corners, so as to avoid gaps between boundaries, or worse, conflicting boundaries.

McDiarmid was to be congratulated for his thinking, wrote Don Duffy nearly a century later. "His point [was] to escape from the pioneer mindset, that of setting new corners without regard for the old, and to concentrate on replacement of corners in their original positions." This was not always easy, said McDiarmid, for in periods when "times were dull and money was scarce," corners were often cut, so to speak, to keep costs low and many original surveys were sloppy, leaving behind them "a heritage of troubles." Similar problems arose during the boom period of 1907 to 1913, when "there was more work than surveyors could do, which resulted in such carelessness on the part of some, that were it not for the provisions of a Special Surveys Act, most hopeless tangles would be before the Courts." Further complications arose from the fact that concrete sidewalks and pavements move with changes in temperature and gravity, and they thus cannot be relied upon as permanent reference points of any kind.

McDiarmid pointed out that a corner does not become "extinct" just because the post or monument marking it has gone astray. He recommended that surveyors engaged in re-establishing corners—finding the original posts and resetting them in position—would be better off looking for supporting evidence in the form of bearing trees or other indicators for the proper location of the corner. He quoted several anecdotes to support his view, including ones relating to the haphazard replacement of posts by road-building crews in various parts of the Vancouver region. One particularly enterprising rancher had even gone to the trouble of creating a duplicate post at the time an original survey of his land was done, in anticipation of the day many years later that he would wish to sell the property and could use it to make his boundary look much wider. "It might be made an axiom," advised McDiarmid, "that a post is an object for suspicion." In particular he warned his audience to watch out for the work of a "spiritual surveyor, i.e. one who goes upon the ground in the spirit rather than in the flesh." In that case, "too much care cannot be exercised."

The destruction of survey monuments during road construction was a matter exercising the minds of surveyors at the 1916 annual meeting. This was not a new issue; as early as the 1890s the problem had become pressing in Vancouver. Road builders were subject to the same penalty as anyone else for the illegal removal of posts—a fine of up to $250—but enforcement of the law was rare. In some cases it was almost impossible for road builders to avoid the posts or monuments—especially in Vancouver, where in some instances original monuments had been placed squarely in the centre of intersections. The discussion also turned to yet another difficulty that had started to surface as early as the 1890s— the professional line drawn between the work of surveyors and the work of civil engineers.

Connell Higgins raised the issue at the 1916 annual meeting of the Corporation. It was reported that Higgins "referred to the fact that road-making was in its infancy in the Province, and...he thought it necessary that it should be impressed upon the authorities that all roads should be accurately laid out and defined upon the ground; it seemed to him that surveyors should do that work." Stuart McDiarmid pointed out that a new bill had been introduced into the provincial legislature defining "engineers" in a number of significant public works statutes. If passed in its current form, said McDiarmid, the legislation would have the effect of debarring surveyors from a number of professional activities formerly within their purview. Many of his colleagues were engineers themselves, however. At that point, McDiarmid's remarks provoked little concern.

By 1918, alarm bells started to ring, albeit still quietly. Engineers in the province were actively seeking statutory authority over the licensing of their professional membership, in much the same way that surveyors already had. The concern was that the authority being sought seemed to include the licensing of surveyors as well, in conflict with the powers held by the Corporation. It still seemed unlikely to the members that this could happen; they felt it sufficient to form a committee with a brief to watch events unfold and, if necessary, to oppose any action detrimental to the Corporation.

Perhaps their emotions and senses had simply been dulled by the sheer enormity of world events over the preceding four years, and the impact those events had had on their profession and their comrades. As each new year had dawned they had certainly hoped for the best, as the few active surveyors in the province gathered together at their annual meetings to discuss their affairs and attempt to see into the future. It was perhaps just as well that they could not. The continuing cycle of boom and bust was to continue for both the province and surveyors for many years to come, and the bust phase was nowhere near over.

13

Good Fences Make Good Neighbours

British Columbia–Alberta boundary survey: monument 29F with Crowsnest Lake in background, circa 1915. OFFICE OF THE SURVEYOR GENERAL

The fourteenth annual general meeting of the Corporation of British Columbia Land Surveyors, held in Victoria on January 14, 1919, took place in a decidedly gloomy atmosphere. The war may have been over, but its aftermath was flapping raggedly in the winds of depression. Many soldiers remained embroiled in the post-conflict cleanup and had not yet returned home. In British Columbia, the economy was still under a heavy cloud. "Most of us found, I think," wrote President Neville Townsend, "that during the past year surveying was decidedly dull. I am afraid that from present indications, the prospects for the current year are none too bright."

All the same, the war had left a legacy of some advantage to the surveying profession. As is usually the case, military necessity spawned advances that were rapidly adopted in peacetime activities. The skills of surveyors were put to use during the fighting to improve the shooting accuracy of gunners using maps that showed the locations of targets rather than visual observation. The technique was called "map shooting." Surveyors plotted enemy locations utilizing "sound ranging"—a form of triangulation using sound resonance—and "flash spotting," a system of taking bearings on the "flash" of an enemy gun and plotting the location on a map. Cecil Simonds, BCLS 162, wrote in 1920: "At the front we experimented in many ways trying to get a closer liaison between the map and the gun, and we did a tremendous lot latterly of map shooting...we have [sic] to use our tables and calculations had to be worked out, on plans, and really a good deal of it came within the surveyor's art." The techniques experimented with were adapted for use in general surveying after the war was over.

The other immediate benefit of the conflict to surveyors was a rapid increase in mechanical and technological advancement. Prior to the war, about the only mechanical aid available to surveyors—other than the compass and the theodolite—was the outboard motor, and that had been in use only very shortly before the outbreak of war in 1914. Following the war, however, radio found its way into mainstream use in North America as early as 1920, and it held promise of vastly improved communication options for surveyors in the field. More sophisticated forms of the surveyor's transit were introduced in Canada in 1925, and by 1930 they would be in use in the British Columbia government service. But perhaps the most exciting development coming out of the war—one that would have life-changing implications for surveyors in the mountainous terrain of British Columbia—was a massive leap forward in aerial technology.

Richard Farrow, BCLS 181, came home from Europe and immediately reported on the subject to his colleagues:

> Aerial photography as a development of photo-topography was, of course, unknown before the war. It was the demand of our Intelligence Corps in France for more and minute information about the enemy which initiated it, and it was still in its infancy in the spring of 1915. Since that time it has gone ahead in leaps and bounds, until by the summer of 1916 it had become our chief source of information as to enemy activity and works. All maps were kept up to date purely from the plotting in of the details shown on aerial photos.
>
> Photographs taken from as high as 8,000 feet showed even the smallest and least distinguishable of enemy works, such as barbed wire, tracks made by patrols going out through the wire, telephone lines, [and] buried cables. Where great detail was not necessary photos were taken from as high as 20,000 feet…

Being at such a height in a tiny two-seated structure made of canvas and spruce must have been daunting. Nonetheless, Farrow continued, "under peace conditions, the operation becomes simple in the extreme and deserves serious consideration as a development of surveying." The airplanes were most stable, he argued, were capable of travelling up to one hundred miles per hour, and indeed were "practically flying themselves." The pilot was thus able to give his almost undivided attention to the photography rather than the controls. What was required was simply a steady hand, an even keel, and a series of overlapping images that could then be mounted together in a virtual mosaic and reduced to any scale desired.

The advantages in a province such as British Columbia were enormous, Farrow enthused. The ease with which huge and previously

An example of a typical oblique aerial photograph, Mount Waddington, circa 1959.
ABCLS/G.S. ANDREWS

uncharted regions could be mapped was beyond compare, and existing maps could be rapidly improved by the completion of any number of missing details that aerial photographs would supply. There were really only two downsides: the inability to calculate elevations from vertical images, and cost. Farrow felt sure, however, that the government would support an aerial survey initiative, with all its "wonderful possibilities."

The provincial government, at least, was not so immediately enthusiastic. In a 1973 article entitled "British Columbia's Air Survey Story," retired surveyor general Gerry Andrews writes that "undisputed credit for the first air survey in British Columbia" must go to Arthur Musgrave, BCLS 212, in 1919. Helped by a volunteer pilot named Lieutenant W.H. Brown from the Aerial League of Canada, Victoria Branch, Musgrave was able to produce a detailed plan of a section of land at the intersection of East Saanich and Martindale roads on the Saanich Peninsula, north of Victoria. Surveyor General Joshua Umbach provided a small sum toward the costs of the plan, and his department handled the processing of the images. However, when the Aerial League immediately wrote to the premier to ask for substantially more money, Umbach made his views clear in a firmly worded memorandum to the premier's office: "It is the opinion of the writer that any serious work with a view to developing aerial photographic methods for practical mapping of unmapped territory is quite beyond the scope of the provincial government."

It would be left to the federal government to begin developing aerial surveying in British Columbia. In 1921 the Air Board of Canada, the body responsible for the control of commercial and non-military flying in Canadian airspace, opened a station at Jericho Beach in Vancouver. Some experimental aerial photography was begun using Canadian air force planes and personnel. In the first two years of operation, the Jericho station, as it became known, supplied photographs of the upper Nicola region and the Fraser River to provincial government surveyors for their use. The merits of the technique were becoming obvious, and it was a topic of ardent discussion at the 1927 annual general meeting. Dalby Morkill, BCLS 57, felt strongly that members of the profession interested in aerial surveying should be able to secure training in flying in order to pursue that line of work. His interest was more than just professional; it was a pragmatic one. Like many of his colleagues, in the seventeen years since his registration as a provincial surveyor Morkill had suffered financially and professionally from the classic boom and bust economy of British Columbia. Morkill explained his reasons for wanting surveyors to learn to fly:

> Aerial surveys are bound to play an increasingly important part in the development of this province. Now it appears to me that with the Royal Air Force preparing to make extensive surveys and explorations, and some of them more or less on a commercial basis, and with private firms springing up rapidly, either the surveyors must take to the air or the airmen will pick up sufficient surveying

technique to knock us out forever from a branch of our work which will expand rapidly from now on. This cannot be considered entirely a selfish fear, for it would presumably take much longer to make a good surveyor out of an airman than vice versa.

Morkill recommended the formation of a committee of members of the Corporation, to promote training in flying for surveyors and the assignment of aerial surveying work to licensed provincial surveyors. The recommendation was strongly supported by his colleagues. Arthur Musgrave reported that immediately after the war he had been offered a post with the dominion government as a photographic officer in charge of the Jericho station. Musgrave had declined, on the basis of what he sarcastically called the "enormous salary of $175 a month." A commercial photographer from Vancouver with no knowledge of surveying was appointed instead, said Musgrave, emphasizing that Morkill's concerns had some substance.

The newly formed aerial surveying committee spent much of 1927 lobbying for pilot training at the Jericho station for the members of the Corporation, writing to the Department of National Defence, the Royal Canadian Air Force, and the topographical survey branch in Ottawa. They were disappointed to learn that no aerial mapping was taking place that year, and no facility to train surveyors as pilots was under consideration by the air force. The air force administration in fact saw what the surveyors themselves apparently could not: it made much more sense for them to learn to use the cameras rather than the airplanes, and leave the flying to the experts. A diplomatically worded letter dated June 22, 1927, seems to have helped the surveyors see reason in that regard: "We should be very glad to arrange for any of your members interested who can call at the station to have the camera and its use fully explained to them personally," wrote air force secretary J.A. Wilson. Wilson also reassured the Corporation: "All technical instructions issued to our flying staff for photographic operations are received from the office of the Surveyor General, who is responsible for that part of the work." The air force, Wilson emphasized gently but pointedly, "only takes the responsibility for flying." The point was taken; the committee decided that perhaps, after all, a surveyor's natural inclination should be toward receiving training in aerial mapping techniques rather than flying itself.

On August 29, 1928, Surveyor General of Canada F.H. Peters wrote a letter to the Corporation of British Columbia Land Surveyors that would arrive in an unprecedented fashion. "Dear Mr. Musgrave," wrote Peters, "The first Air Mail to ever cross Canada is expected to leave Ottawa today, and I am taking the opportunity of sending you this note." The airplane left Ottawa on September 5, 1928, at 7:00 a.m., and arrived in Vancouver at 6:00 p.m. on September 8, 1928. By 1929, regular passenger service flights were well established between North America and Europe, as well as within Canada. The Boeing aircraft company in Seattle had close to one thousand employees engaged in building airplanes; and three private air companies were operating out of Vancouver and Victoria, including a small company called Pacific Airways. The economic state of affairs was sound for the time being, and the time was ripe for engaging in extensive aerial surveying. That year, the first widespread aerial survey took place in British Columbia.

The goal was a survey of about 25,000 square miles of land in the Peace River region, in conjunction with surveys of land related to the Pacific Great Eastern Railway (PGE), intended to reach from Vancouver to Prince George. Still under construction, the rail line had been plagued by ill fortune from its inception and was half-jokingly referred to as the "Please Go Easy" or the "Prince George Eventually." Since its incorporation in 1912, the PGE had not reached anywhere near to Prince George, but nonetheless a survey was planned. Moreover, it was to be paid for in large part by both the Canadian Pacific Railway and Canadian National Railways, leaving a still cautious provincial government with only a small portion of the expense.

Aerial surveying is, of course, reliant on good weather, and the 1929 survey was typical of years to come: there were only twenty-one days of good flying weather in the whole season. Despite that, more than twenty thousand photographs were taken, necessitating a whole new line of training for mapping staff. "Although theoretically simple, the plotting of 21,000 photos is rather a complicated matter," wrote Norman Stewart, BCLS 120, afterwards. "An entirely new staff had to be trained in

A rock cairn on a peak between the southeastern arm of Quatsino Sound and
Kokshittle Arm, in 1928. Harold E. Whyte, BCLS 83, is one of the men pictured.
OFFICE OF THE SURVEYOR GENERAL

handling the photographs and plotting the flight strips." Some of this
had to be done in the field while the work was going on, in order to
direct the pilots to cover gaps or repeat poor images. "We also had to
devise new instruments," wrote Stewart. "To increase the output with the
scant accommodation and equipment at our command, a night shift was
employed. The reductions were made on two pantographs working night
and day." There were many gaps in the final eight-thousand-square-mile
map, writes Gerry Andrews in "British Columbia's Air Survey Story,"
"due to primitive navigation aids and no doubt a modicum of inexperience...The mapping was crude, by modern standards, but evidently met
requirements. The job was a convincing demonstration of air surveying
for the authorities...all this was to bear fruit in government policy and
application in the years to follow."

More primitive techniques had been employed in what was still a fundamental piece of work for provincial surveyors over the years 1913 to 1924: the survey of the British Columbia–Alberta provincial boundary. The border had been defined in the 1866 statute creating British Columbia as a line "extending from the boundary of the United States northwards by the Rocky Mountains and the 120th meridian of west longitude." But Alberta had not become a province until 1905. Major coal discoveries and the value of timber rights only became prominent in the boundary region during the early years of the twentieth century. Even then, not until 1913 was a boundary commission established by dominion and provincial authorities, with Arthur Wheeler representing the British Columbia government. Richard Cautley, PLS 35, who was qualified as a land surveyor in Alberta as well as in British Columbia, was appointed to represent the government of Alberta. The third commissioner was dominion representative John Wallace.

Compared with the experience of other boundary commissions, the work of the British Columbia–Alberta commissioners was implemented with relative ease. The definition "northwards by the Rocky Mountains" was less than clear-cut, but the commissioners readily agreed that the watershed line dividing the waters flowing toward the Pacific Ocean from those flowing elsewhere would form the line until it intersected with the 120th meridian. That meridian would then form the line north to the border with the Yukon Territory at the 60th parallel. The commissioners also agreed that the Surveyor General of Canada, Edouard Deville, would supervise the border project, which would primarily utilize photo-topographical methods. The survey itself began on June 23, 1913, in Kicking Horse Pass.

The field work required was, however, less simple. Although the watershed line was a straightforward means to define the boundary, in practice finding that line was not always simple, and frequent refinements had to be negotiated literally on the ground. Whether or not the watershed line crossed actual peaks, those peaks still had to be climbed to take photographs and erect trigonometrical stations. Many summits in the Rocky Mountains exceed ten thousand feet in height and are challenging even to experienced mountaineers. Alpinist Arthur Wheeler was, of course, in his element, but the twelve years of surveying work—most of it in the mountains, and the rest in mosquito-ridden muskeg—took its toll on the survey teams. As with the surveys of the Alaska border a few years previously, the men were required to repeatedly climb the mountains and cross glaciers with heavy equipment and monuments, in conditions nothing short of extremely hazardous. On one occasion all of Cautley's instruments were lost when a horse was swept away in a river; Cautley was forced to break off his work and return to Edmonton for replacements. Head packer Jacob Koller lost his life in a similar incident. Avalanches and hidden crevasses were a constant danger. Inexperience also took its toll. Field notes with a week's worth of work were lost when a crew member carelessly placed the knapsack containing them on a ledge too narrow to hold them properly. A moment's inattention meant the knapsack was irretrievably lost to the ice below. Nothing else could be done but to return and repeat the work of the previous week—an immensely depressing task.

But a week of repeated effort was minor, considering that a total of twelve years were invested in the original surveys. By the end of the 1924 season, more than eleven hundred kilometres of the watershed line had been surveyed. In addition, more than four hundred kilometres of the 120th meridian had been marked with monuments. The surveys were approved by the provincial governments in 1931, and the delineation of the border declared official by an Act of Parliament in 1932. Even then, it was not complete: not until 1949 was a new commission appointed to finish the work of surveying the 120th meridian between 57°26'41" and the 60th parallel.

Despite ongoing work on the boundary surveys after the First World War and a steady flow of subdivision work in the more populated parts of the province where the government was encouraging settlement, the severe recession that hung over British Columbia and Canada until the mid-1920s made it tough going for provincial land surveyors. As Surveyor General Umbach had indicated in the early 1920s, there was little or no money available for any ambitious mapping projects. Compared with 1911, when 3,226,610 acres of provincial land were surveyed, in 1924 a mere 100,374 acres of surveys were completed. The railway belt surveys

British Columbia–Alberta boundary surveys were completed over the years 1913 to 1924. These images were all made in the summer and fall of 1914 around Crowsnest Pass, and carefully pasted into a black-paper album in the surveyor general's office date-stamped 1915. The number of each monument is noted—for example: "Monument 8F with Sentinel Mountain in background." OFFICE OF THE SURVEYOR GENERAL

Monument 3F on the British Columbia–Alberta boundary, circa 1915. OFFICE OF THE SURVEYOR GENERAL

Monument 7F. OFFICE OF THE SURVEYOR GENERAL

Looking toward Monument 39F.
This monument and Monument 41F
are 2,180 feet above the railway at
Crowsnest, from which 5,400 pounds of
cement, gravel, and water were packed
up to make these two monuments.
OFFICE OF THE SURVEYOR GENERAL

Looking toward Monument 45F. OFFICE
OF THE SURVEYOR GENERAL

Monument 57F. Alberta Boundary Commissioner R.W. Cautley is pictured. Cautley
was also a British Columbia provincial land surveyor, with commission PLS 35.
OFFICE OF THE SURVEYOR GENERAL

Heavy dry timber between 71F and 73F. OFFICE OF THE SURVEYOR GENERAL

Cautley at Monument 95F. OFFICE OF THE SURVEYOR GENERAL

Monument 99F. OFFICE OF THE SURVEYOR GENERAL

Akamina Pass, Mr. Wheeler's camp. Arthur Wheeler was the British Columbia boundary commissioner and a land surveyor for the province. Wheeler was also the founder of the Alpine Club of Canada in 1907. OFFICE OF THE SURVEYOR GENERAL

Cache built in Akamina Pass, October 11, 1914. OFFICE OF THE SURVEYOR GENERAL

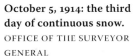

October 5, 1914: the third day of continuous snow. OFFICE OF THE SURVEYOR GENERAL

that continued for much of the 1920s were of little help; dominion land surveyors continued steadfastly to hold on to their monopoly over federal lands. Thwarted in their half-hearted efforts to make much headway into the railway belt, members of the Corporation focused instead on protecting what professional turf they did have from the increasingly alarming threat—as they saw it—posed by professional engineers.

The draft "Professional Engineers Bill," reported William Drewry to his fellow Corporation members in 1920, appeared to "cover every part of the economic and industrial life of the country, and under its provisions it would force you to become a member of the Professional Engineers Society before you could carry on many of the usual branches of a Surveyor's practice; such as surveying mines underground, locating ditches or flume lines, etc." Outraged that the provisions of the proposed bill "may constitute a serious menace to the Corporation of B.C. Land Surveyors," a resolution was passed to endeavour to remove objectionable portions of the statute.

The surveyors also felt forced to circle the wagons around the issue of municipal taxes. In 1919 the city of Vancouver began a practice of charging a ten dollar licence fee to carry on business as a land surveyor in the municipality. One surveyor had refused and had been hauled into court. Arguing that the city had no powers to authorize him to practise under the provincial legislation, the surveyor won. In Victoria, the fee was forty dollars. While Victoria too had lost the initial court case, the city was appealing. By the time of the Corporation's January 1921 annual general meeting, the issue had lost strength. Many surveyors were simply paying municipal licensing fees, reasoning it was cheaper than fighting it out in court. The Corporation decided to keep the matter under consideration and perhaps to combine forces with other professions to take a test case. After that, the matter appears to have died a natural death. By 1922, the surveyors were fully occupied with the fact that 1921 had been the seventh consecutive lean year for the profession. President John Elliott reported: "The year 1921, I am afraid, was not a very bright one for most of the Land Surveyors in British Columbia; the depression in general business throughout the country as usual magnified itself many times when applied to Land Surveying."

The province's Engineering Act was passed the same year; if not contributing to the financial depression, it certainly added to the pall overhanging the surveyors. The Corporation had at least succeeded in negotiating a "saving" clause in the legislation, preserving its members from any effect except a prohibition on referring to themselves as "professional engineers." But by the beginning of 1923, they still felt compelled to take a watching brief over any attempt to prosecute surveyors for activities deemed under the engineers' legislation to be outside their authority. That may have been the toughest year yet, for there is little mention of anything other than financial hardship in the proceedings of the annual general meeting. While endeavouring to maintain a tone of optimism, president Stuart McDiarmid was forced to acknowledge "the economic problems of the day." With settlers struggling to keep a grip on their land, surveyors were not experiencing any rush of new immigrants demanding plans for new properties. McDiarmid tried to paint a hopeful picture of better days to come, in which British Columbia's coal and oil resources would be extracted and large power developments would be created— all projects ripe for exploitation by eager surveyors—but he also had to admit: "In the meantime, many will find it difficult to hold on for the brighter day."

The chief concern that year was a failing sense of security in the loyalty of members of the profession to each other in financial matters. "The prospective client," warned McDiarmid in ringing tones, "will, if possible, play one surveyor against another to the detriment of all." A practice of clients calling for tenders from surveyors was alarming some members of the Corporation who preferred that their colleagues respect a set spectrum of agreed fees, in order to avoid undue competition that would force already low rates even lower. Resolutions were passed to amend the Corporation's bylaws to forbid tendering or competing for contracts as "unprofessional conduct," and instructing the directors to formulate a code of professional ethics for consideration.

In 1925, signs of hope for a better future had started to show, but the president, William McElhanney, declined to show too much enthusiasm: "Conditions in the profession are possibly gradually improving...but conditions outside are not very favourable yet." McElhanney pointed

Breaking camp at the U and I mineral claim, Silver Cup Mountain tie traverse, Kootenay District, 1925. OFFICE OF THE SURVEYOR GENERAL

the finger at excessive levels of national and provincial debt, and correspondingly high taxation at all levels of government. Immigrants were being attracted to the more prosperous and cheaper United States rather than to Canada. "I don't want to paint a gloomy outlook at all," protested McElhanney. All the same, he did: "With our own Society we have had our ups and downs, and possibly they have been largely down these last few years…A few years ago we had a large surplus and wondered what we would do with it, and it has been gradually shrinking, and now its shrinkage has become almost alarming. We used to have about 260 members, we are down now to about 170 paying members." The theme continued into 1926. President William Powell bemoaned the situation: "Our present authorized roll contains 186 names, sufficient to handle three times the amount of work offering." Powell even went as far as to suggest considering amalgamation with the professional engineers as a means to solve their financial woes. Even in these times, it was a shocking notion.

But by 1927, everything had changed. "A survey of the progress during the past year of almost every aspect of industrial endeavour in British Columbia leads one to the conclusion that this Province has ploughed through its period of 'lean years' and that 1927 will establish a record beyond comparison with any year previous," crowed the president, Percy Gregory, BCLS 37. "It is clear that confidence in our Province is again

Frederick Clements conducted a triangulation survey in the Kettle Valley in 1927. This image, taken on August 16 of that year, shows the crew loading up for a trip to Big White Mountain, about thirteen kilometres west of the Kettle River. Motor vehicles were already in enthusiastic use by survey parties who were all too used to slogging in heavy equipment on foot. OFFICE OF THE SURVEYOR GENERAL

fully restored and capital is seeking out investments in many directions. One of the first to feel the influence of this," he stated gleefully, "is the surveyors." Any thoughts of amalgamation with the engineers or anyone else were scornfully rejected. "We should regard ourselves as specialists in our walk of life and endeavour to promote that 'esprit de Corps' which bound together the 'old-timers' of our Corporation and not seek to endanger our position or traditions with any more than a friendly alliance with any other professional association."

Matters were not that simple. Many of the surveyors were themselves professional engineers and felt the separation of the two occupations to be artificial, if not downright silly. While the issue had been tentatively raised in previous meetings, in 1927 the engineers among the gathering finally made themselves clear in no uncertain terms. The committee that had been formed to liaise with the association of professional engineers stated unequivocally that both bodies were of the opinion that "In future a surveyor to carry on his profession successfully would of necessity have to be a professional engineer as well. That is to be an engineer and a surveyor. It is not so much necessary for an engineer to be a surveyor, as for a surveyor to be an engineer." Surprisingly, that notion met with little resistance, at least for the time being.

Pack train at Peters Lake Camp looking east, October 7, 1929. Frederick S. Clements, PLS 53, had been instructed to conduct triangulation surveys in the divide between the Shuswap Valley and Arrow Lakes. Clements was diligent in numbering and dating every photograph that he submitted to the Surveyor General's Office at the end of the season. OFFICE OF THE SURVEYOR GENERAL

The last order of business at the 1927 annual general meeting of the Corporation was a discussion regarding a letter written to Premier John Oliver the previous year. With a multitude of supporting arguments to back him up—access to information, the better economic development of the province, and so on—Corporation secretary Thomas Gore advised the premier that "it is the opinion of this Corporation that the administration of the Railway Belt Lands can be more advantageously and more economically managed by the Province than by the Dominion." Instead of fruitlessly arguing with the dominion government over the right of provincial land surveyors to work in the dominion-controlled railway belt, they had clearly decided on a different tactic: persuade the provincial government to take back control. The premier wrote back to say that he was "favourably impressed" and would look into the matter.

British Columbia land surveyors were now enjoying the glory days of yet another surge in the economic fortunes of the province. By 1927 comparatively large numbers of them were once again making forays on behalf of the government into more remote parts of the province, and at the 1928 annual general meeting, Frank Swannell reported: "There has of late been a great revival of interest in Mackenzie and his wonderful journey. This interest, it is gratifying to surveyors to note, has been powerfully inspired by the location by one of ourselves, [BCLS 73] Capt. R.P. Bishop, of the actual spot marking the westerly termination of Mackenzie's journey. This is the famous rock upon which, as every Canadian schoolboy knows, or should know, Mackenzie wrote with a mixture of vermilion and melted grease his memorable inscription: Alexander Mackenzie, from Canada, by land, the twenty-second of July, one thousand seven hundred and ninety-three."

At the 1929 annual general meeting, much hilarity greeted the creation of a new and permanent tradition when outgoing president Dalby Morkill wore smart new spats to the meeting and formally placed them on the feet of the incoming president, Donald McGugan, BCLS 136. "All signs point to a new period of prosperity in British Columbia, in which we, professionally, may expect to participate," Morkill announced triumphantly. He related with great satisfaction the fact that the dominion government had finally agreed to return to British Columbia the railway belt and Peace River block lands. Frederick Burden, BCLS 9, had been appointed the provincial minister of lands, to the gratification of his former colleagues.

Things were looking good. So good, in fact, that Morkill felt confident enough to state self-importantly:

> It seems quite natural that, as we pass through the Province from one end to the other, in the carrying out of our duties, we should get an insight into conditions and developments that is hardly possible to anyone else, and be able more readily to form correct opinions as to the trend of affairs. In other words, I think we can see things coming a little sooner than most...and what we see now to be imminent—a general return of prosperous times—is something that is very pleasing to declare.

Morkill had no idea how soon—and how bitterly—he would regret those words.

To Hold On for the Brighter Day

Alan Campbell, BCLS 101, led the topographical survey under way in Garibaldi Park, 1928. Many surveyors in British Columbia have had to acquire mountaineering skills rapidly in order to do their job – and to survive the trip. OFFICE OF THE SURVEYOR GENERAL

In 1932, Harry Hughes Browne, PLS 84, died. Among his notes was found a hand-penned epitaph, typical of the humorous surveyor's approach to his work and life in general:

> Beneath this cairn and witness post
> 　　A land surveyor's bones are laid:
> The bearing trees inform his ghost
> 　　When hubs from azimuth have strayed.
>
> Along the front, where moved his tent,
> 　　Departure grew with latitude,
> But still he never saved a cent:
> 　　His recompense on high he views.
>
> He seldom grumbled at his lot
> 　　(Surveyors are not built that way),
> But made the best of what he got
> 　　And called the fraction "Parcel A."
>
> Methinks I hear this message short
> 　　As from Polaris he looks down,
> "Sir, I've the honour to report,"
> 　　Your most obedient servant—Browne.

Browne was seventy years old when he died; he had worked in the province for thirty-odd years. During the course of his career, he had certainly seen the good times come and go. It may have been with a wry smile that he wrote this farewell message to his fellow land surveyors, hoping to give them encouragement in what may have been the worst economic times they had ever experienced in British Columbia. In 1928, the province had enjoyed the highest per capita income in Canada. Within the space of five years, the economy had shrunk by two-thirds, and the pain of rank poverty was felt by many for the first time in their lives.

Barely two months had passed after global stock markets took a crashing nosedive on October 29, 1929, when the president of the Corporation

This image by Frederick Clements, PLS 53, is dated July 20, 1930: "Making flags at Sweet Grass Ranch, Crawford Bay" (Kootenay Lake). OFFICE OF THE SURVEYOR GENERAL

of British Columbia Land Surveyors, Donald McGugan, BCLS 136, delivered his retirement address to his colleagues in Vancouver. The date was January 9, 1930, and as yet McGugan saw no reason for concern:

> During the year just passed I think that practically every Surveyor on our Active List has had an exceptionally good year. The prosperity of the Surveyor is an excellent index of the prosperity of the Province, and this year has been no exception. The Province as a whole, excluding perhaps some unfortunate activities in the oil and mining stock markets, has had one of the best years in its history.

All the same, in 1929 not one new surveyor was admitted to the profession in British Columbia. In 1930, dominion land surveyor Wilfred Humphreys became BCLS 252. He was the only one to join the ranks that year, and over the next ten years that would be typical. Government work during the Great Depression years fell to almost nothing as funding quickly became curtailed, and the hope of finding private work was a joke, albeit a bitter one. The realization of what was facing them had not yet sunk in at the 1930 annual general meeting, however. Much of that meeting was spent fiddling while Rome burned, arguing about the

Station "Best Yet," looking east: July 7, 1930. OFFICE OF THE SURVEYOR GENERAL

most appropriate manner of ensuring rigorous adherence by survey-ors to an agreed scale of minimum professional fees. A resolution was eventually passed to amend the bylaws of the Corporation, setting the minimum annual salary at which surveyors could accept employment at $3,600. It was beyond their comprehension that within the space of two years, many of them would be happy to work free of charge if they were provided food and lodging in compensation.

Equally importantly—if not more so to men whose occupation also represented a fundamental way of life—even unpaid work at least would keep them actively occupied, and might mean a job waiting for them when the hard times were finally over. In 1932 the provincial government topographical division laid off all but one staff member, Alan Campbell, BCLS 101. By the following year, even he had no work. In a biography of Campbell written in 1957, the author observes that "Campbell, [BCLS 95, Robert] McCaw, and [BCLS 120, Norman] Stewart, rather than see their life work cut off offered to take the field without pay...the field work would provide office work if and when the Topographic Division was re-established...It was better by far than twiddling thumbs at home for other survey work in 1933 did not exist." Adam Burhoe, BCLS 279, was more fortunate. When Burhoe started work as a rodman for the city of Vancouver in 1930, his days as a qualified land surveyor were still nine-teen years ahead of him. He might never have made it had he been laid

Coffee Creek Camp, looking west: June 27, 1930. OFFICE OF THE SURVEYOR GENERAL

off like many other city employees, as the municipality struggled desperately to cut costs. Burhoe's good fortune rested in his junior status: the city would have had to pay him more on welfare than it had to pay him to work as a rodman.

Arthur Musgrave presented a gloomy analysis of the profession at the January 1932 annual general meeting: "The field of activities of the B.C. Land Surveyor appears nowadays to be as narrow as the eye of a needle. Not alone has his normal cadastral surveying work been cut to the bone, but Government topographical and cadastral work has been pared so fine it is difficult to see…The number of new B.C. Land Surveyors created annually is, fortunately, only a shadow of what it was…" Musgrave also asked despondently: "Am I justified in giving the best years of my life to the study and mastery of land surveying, only? Is the remuneration over a period of years, even to a successful Surveyor, worth the energies of a first-class man?" Retiring president James Underhill concurred with Musgrave's pessimism: "The past year has been a severe trial to most of us."

Unfortunately, 1932 would prove worse still. The registered number of surveyors had dropped from a high of 259 during the boom years of 1911–1913 to a low of 147—perhaps, as Musgrave noted, a blessing under

On the back of this image, taken on August 9, 1930, Frederick Clements noted the following: "Office cabin on trail west fork St. Mary River looking northerly." OFFICE OF THE SURVEYOR GENERAL

the circumstances. Of that number, only nine were employed in government service for the full season that year, and four part-time. Surveyor General Frank Green reported sombrely on January 14, 1933, that provincial revenues had continued to decline: "The 1932 appropriation for surveys...was the lowest in over twenty-five years...Expenditure in 1932 on all types of surveys was under $15,000...No work was done on the triangulation nets...the photo-topographical staff were all on short time." Corporation president Frank Swannell struggled to find any positive note in his annual address to members:

> There is no disputing the fact that conditions in B.C. are very bad. The depression from which we have suffered so long has intensified during the past year and, more unfortunately, it seems probable that during the Winter we may sound a lower level still. A dubious ray of hope lies in the thought that, things being at their worst, there is only one way for the pendulum to swing, slowly upwards towards betterment...
> Land surveying, both private and government, being at such a low ebb that the majority of our members could not last year

eke out even a bare living, some of our younger members tried their hands at other trades, only to find that the labour market was glutted. Everywhere, no matter in what field of industry, there were far more men than jobs.

Government work was not completely non-existent during those difficult years. In 1930, the provincial government finally succeeded, to the gratification of the surveyors, in reacquiring the remaining undisposed parts of the railway belt and Peace River Block lands, a little over six million acres of the original eleven million transferred to the dominion in 1871. The path to the successful return of the former CPR lands had had to be carefully negotiated, as the memorandum of agreement between the provincial and dominion governments indicates in its recitals: "the Province could not by reason of its own agreements and statutes advance any legal claim, but…its request should be considered from the standpoint of fairness and justice rather than from the strictly legal and contractual position." Provincially qualified land surveyors were able to move into the former railway lands at last and get to work, limited as it was for the time being. Various government land settlement and relief programs were implemented, and the ongoing settlement of the 2,700-acre University Endowment Lands in western Vancouver that had begun in 1923 continued, albeit slowly.

In addition, by 1928—the same year that the city of Vancouver enjoyed the novelty of its very first set of traffic lights—right-of-way surveys for highways had commenced under the auspices of the surveyor general's department. The number of cars on the roads had increased dramatically—from 630 in Vancouver in 1920 to somewhere around 36,500 by 1930—and the demand for road-building, at least, was unabated. Surveyor General Joseph Umbach issued detailed instructions on highway surveys on May 22, 1929: "The survey of a highway is made preferably along the centre line," wrote Umbach. "In cases where there is heavy traffic," he acknowledged, "the survey may be made on a convenient offset." The general improvement to the provincial road network was felt by land surveyors in other ways than the availability of work: John Elliott, for example, drove to Fort St. John from Vancouver for the 1931 Peace River

Block surveys. In his 1930 report to the surveyor general, Elliott had already noted presciently: "Of late years, [the numerous pack trails into the mountains] have nearly all fallen into disrepair, and on the completion of the highway will probably disappear and the pack-horse and the boatman will become extinct in the land." Elliott's regret is patent, but the existence of the highway meant that, at least for the time being, there was less danger of the surveyor becoming extinct.

The government even found money for some new equipment before the worst of the financial impact hit: in 1930, the province acquired some brand new Swiss Wild T2 theodolites and put them to immediate use in government surveys. The lighter gear was not only easier to carry, it saved considerable time, and the accuracy levels were noticeably better. But the most significant financial government priority during the 1930s was a continuation of the ambitious photo-topographical mapping work so dear to the heart of every surveyor general since Tom Kains's day. Frank Green was no exception, despite his financial woes, writing in his 1933 report that

> British Columbia, being a young and rapidly developing country, must crowd an undue part of such work into a few years... Expenditure on this basic and permanent work could rightly be classed as capital expenditure and financed out of loans, as is done in other countries, thus easing the unfair load on current revenues...
>
> In our photo-topographical staff we have an efficient working field force unsurpassed anywhere. They are giving us the best maps we have ever had at much the lowest cost yet reached in this difficult country. It costs about $38,000 per year to keep them and their survey crews working at full efficiency, but for this...we can add 2,000 square miles per annum to our contoured mapped areas...
>
> It would be true economy to expand this type of work rather than to curtail it, even in the face of present financial difficulties.

Among the many concerns expressed at the 1933 annual general meeting was the fact that the provincial forestry department appeared to be "slowly and gradually usurping the practice of the Land Surveyor," employing men who were not registered with the Corporation to conduct large-scale timber surveys. One such man was Gerald Smedley Andrews, whom the Forest Surveys Division had employed in 1930. Andrews had studied both forestry and surveying, and had some practical surveying experience: he seemed ideally suited to the task. He was also entirely fascinated with the possibilities that aerial surveying offered.

It may have been just as well that events conspired to place Andrews in the forestry arena to pursue his obsession, rather than in the surveyor general's department. In 1929, hopes had been high that aerial photography was the way of the future. So confident was Surveyor General Umbach that arrangements had been made to set aside a whole room in the basement of the legislative buildings to house the tens of thousands of vertical images already provided to the province by the Royal Canadian Air Force (RCAF). But in his 1934 report to the minister of lands, Frank Green simply stated tersely: "No salaries having been voted for the topographical staff and the appropriation for surveys having been almost wiped out, little could be done in the field." The forestry department, on the other hand, still had money, and Andrews was to prove instrumental in laying the groundwork for success of the aerial survey program in British Columbia, with a stubborn determination to demonstrate its value notwithstanding difficult economic times. In writing about the development of aerial surveying many years later, he entitled the section that covered his early years in the forest service "The Air Photo Bug Beats the Depression."

During the 1930 season, Andrews was assigned to working on the inclusion of several former dominion forest reserves within the old railway belt into the provincial reserve system. He discovered "by chance" that some 380 miles of the Niskonlith Forest had been covered by RCAF vertical photographs, which were still stored in the legislative buildings, "supervised by an old time surveyor who was a friend," Alistair Robertson, BCLS 24. "Without permission," writes Andrews, "these were 'borrowed' for the season...A stereoscope, for observing the photos in three dimensions, was also scrounged." Once in the field, Andrews laid the misappropriated images out on the floor of the ranger station which he was using as a base camp for the surveys. In order to correlate the photographs with the existing maps, Andrews and his team plotted the strips of images onto waxed lunch paper: "Far from ideal, [but] they showed infinitely more detail for best access to and arrangement of our cruise strips," writes Andrews. In the midst of the chaos, Andrews's boss, Fred Mulholland, unexpectedly arrived. Mulholland had not been in favour of anything other than traditional methods of surveying; Andrews had essentially been caught red-handed disobeying orders. "The place was a shambles, with most of the floor space littered with air photos, preliminary to plotting. Explanation was demanded." Unfazed, Andrews launched into a defence of his method: "My explanation had the courage of conviction, and [Mulholland] approved, with reservations."

However, Mulholland also told Andrews and his team to complete the surveys as originally instructed, using orthodox methods. The photographs could be used to supplement that work in their "spare time," of which, of course, there was next to none. Andrews still refused to give up. Once back from the field, in addition to the traditional maps, Andrews "made a special sheet for the area covered by air photos, which showed…the information as obtained with the photos and that which would have accrued without them, by ground methods alone. The result was convincing proof of the virtues of air photos…Mulholland was satisfied, and thereafter became a staunch and influential supporter of air survey."

Similar success was achieved in the 1932 season in the Shuswap forest area, with far greater areas of ground mapped and at much lower cost per square mile than with traditional photo-topography. But even the forest service was suffering by 1933; Andrews and his teammates were placed on indefinite leave without pay. Andrews wasted no time in heading to Europe to pursue his passion, studying aerial photographical mapping with experts at Oxford University in England and in Germany. He learned to speak German, learned how to operate a Zeiss Stereoplanigraph and other plotting apparatus, and even had his very first flight in an aircraft, from Leipzig to Dresden: "I was scared stiff!" Armed with substantial new knowledge but precious little else—Andrews's funds had all but dried up by the spring of 1934—he leaped at the opportunity for re-employment in the British Columbia forest service when it was offered that May.

Andrews was assigned to northern Vancouver Island for the 1934 season, where his biggest challenge was keeping dry the fifty pounds of aerial photographs the survey crew was carrying. The notorious west coast rain was constant: "A routine round our evening campfires was to spread out the photos to dry, some becoming 'toasted' to a light golden brown." The year 1935 proved easier: there was so little money that not much in the way of field work was undertaken, and Andrews headed to the United States to learn more in his chosen field. In Victoria, efforts were concentrated on experimentation: "Design and construction of improved stereoscopes; work on a simple, but intriguing stereo-plotter, based on fundamentals conceived and proposed by Deville in 1895; obtaining and cataloguing technical data...in the Survey Branch air photo library."

Experimental flights were also undertaken, despite the cost, to test techniques using different types of filters and infrared equipment. Those tests proved abortive; more successful was the determination of tree heights over a tract of forest near Sooke Lake, west of Victoria. The fundamental flaw in vertical photography had been the inability to determine relative elevations of geographic features for the purpose of topographical mapping. But using "a simple parallax micrometer bar designed and beautifully made by a local instrument machinist, Louis Omundsen," it was possible to accurately gauge the tree heights, and another important breakthrough was made. Andrews himself also experimented with adaptation of camera equipment and theodolites to create survey cameras suitable for use from forestry lookout towers. "To orient the camera in a precise direction, it was mounted on the base of an old 'muzzle-loader' theodolite, in place of the original telescope superstructure...this enabled it to be levelled and turned to any desired angle on the horizontal circle," wrote Andrews later. On the instrument he had adapted, Andrews also found an inscription that read: "Repaired by Schmolz, San Francisco, 18 February 1858." Despite its age, it served his purpose admirably. Andrews later found a home for it in the Royal British Columbia Museum in Victoria.

Progress continued to be made on aerial surveying techniques and mapping in the province, in spite of the depression. By 1935 Grant McConachie, who would later manage Canadian Pacific Airlines, was busy taking surveyors into the interior in his fleet of three United Air Transport floatplanes. In 1936, Andrews was able to rent an aircraft, borrow a camera, and get into the air himself: "We used a Waco on floats and an old War I camera, mounted over a hole in the floor," he reminisces. "The photos were horrible, but served the purpose...I emphasized that with good camera equipment, we could get good photos." The following year, he got the good camera equipment; in 1938, more pilots and additional contract funding for aircraft time. By then Andrews had passed his preliminary survey exams and articled to Frank Swannell, but he continued his work for the forestry department. Despite all the technical improvements, things did not always go smoothly. Of the 1939 season in the Arrow and Kootenay lakes region, he writes:

> The Fairchild 71 aircraft on floats could operate effectively at 16,000 feet altitude, adequate to cover the rugged mountain terrain, but we had learned at altitudes above 10,000 feet oxygen was necessary against physical fatigue and to sustain mental acuity, both vital in this demanding work. The equipment for this was primitive, a large steel bottle for the oxygen, such as hospitals use, with rubber tubes to each of the crew, Clare Dobbin, pilot, Bill Hall and myself who shared navigation and camera duties. The routine on the long climb to altitude was to get the camera ready, and at about 10,000 feet activate the oxygen supply. On one occasion when we began to inhale the sustaining vapours we were at once overcome with violent seizures of choking, coughing, tears and sneezing—our bottle contained ammonia, not oxygen! Immediate return to base was necessary to rectify the booboo by the supply people.

While aerial surveying continued to progress, land surveying generally continued to rest in the doldrums. Despite some mineral strikes in the early 1930s that led to minor mining booms, and a gold rush in Zeballos in 1936, surveyors remained in more or less dire financial straits. By 1934, anxiety had reached such levels that the Corporation struck a committee

A photo-topographic survey party on top of Mount Tolmie, Victoria area, spring 1936. Among those pictured are N.C. Stewart, BCLS 120; and Alan Campbell, BCLS 101.
ABCLS/G.S. ANDREWS

to consult with the provincial minister of lands regarding the possibility of amalgamating all land surveyors into the civil service. As government employees they would be paid only a fraction of what private practitioners were used to charging, but at least they might have work. It was a scheme that smacked of desperation rather than any real desire, despite a long list of justifying reasons attached to the resolution creating the committee. Nor realistically did the government have the kind of money required to support such a grandiose scheme; nothing would come of the proposal.

Little changed through the closing years of the decade as the realization dawned on the country's citizens that yet another global conflict was looming. While technology continued to advance, other things did not, including cultural attitudes. Lots in some new subdivisions of the city of Vancouver, for example, continued to contain covenants prohibiting the owner from selling or renting to or permitting any form of occupancy of the land and house in question to "any person of the Chinese, Japanese or other Asiatic race, or Indian race or Negro." In other instances, approval in writing by a representative of the CPR was still required for the architectural design of the proposed house on the lot.

In Victoria, Surveyor General Frank Green continued to complain in his annual reports about lack of funding to complete triangulation

The *B.C. Forester*, a government vessel used to transport forestry survey crews, in
Cooper Bay, Queen Charlotte Islands, near "Allison's logging camp," August 20, 1937.
ABCLS/G.S. ANDREWS

surveys of the province, which by the end of 1938 he estimated to have
been only one-seventh covered by satisfactory topographic maps. "At the
present rate of progress it will take 150 years to cover the entire area,"
grumbled Green. Proper triangulation work was required, he argued,
in order to prevent mistakes in planning transportation and development. He cited the impending Alaska Highway construction project as
an example: "There is an old and proven railway construction maxim,
'The cheapest tool with which to do grading is the transit.'" Green's argument was compelling: "That a speeding up of this [triangulation] work
would be justified may be indicated by the fact that one mile of mountain
highway thereby saved would pay for 1,000 square miles of topographic
mapping."

While senior government surveyors remained preoccupied with
funding, by January 1939 the professional body occupied itself with
administrative matters, including the creation of yet more committees.
As well as local chapters of the Corporation from the Okanagan and
the Kootenays, eight standing committees existed, including a public-
ity committee, the long-lived but relatively idle professional engineers'
contact committee, and the cadastral maps and restoration of old survey
corners committee. A new Land Surveyors Act passed in 1936 had done

Communication by radio was still a novelty and a blessing in June 1937, when this photograph of party member Fred Petersen was taken by Gerry Andrews on a forestry survey. ABCLS/G.S. ANDREWS

little to change any of the fundamental principles by which they were required to conduct their occupation, simply adding detail and clarity to some of the administrative procedures attached to membership of the Corporation and qualification as a surveyor.

The Corporation's members were also unquestionably concerned about the possibility of impending conflict. President Arthur Musgrave contemplated the fact that surveyors had just experienced "one of the worst depressions of our lives, out of which we are just now slowly crawling, perhaps to be only rudely pushed back into the abyss by the greed of Dictators." This time the membership was determined to be prepared for eventualities, calling for the immediate gathering of data about the skills and military experience of the group in order to prevent "too many square pegs [being] awkwardly plugged into round holes," as had occurred during the previous war.

Other matters that concerned the members included one unforeseen consequence of the Great Depression: a lack of younger members "coming up the ranks." "As we near the end of our trail," wrote Musgrave

Gerry Andrews's 1939 air survey field party. Andrews's aerial survey expertise would help take the province to the forefront of world aerial surveying technique development. From left to right: Bob Frye; Bill McPhee; Mort Teare, mechanic; Claire Dobbin, pilot; Bill Hall; Gerry Andrews. ABCLS/G.S. ANDREWS

of the older surveyors among the group, "there may be none to ease the pack off our backs or carry the tripod." No immediate solution was forthcoming. But the meeting ended on a light note, with the delivery by Rupert Haggen, BCLS 69, of a paper about the New Zealand land surveyors legislation. Frank Swannell commented afterward that, while on a trip to New Zealand, he had marvelled at "the great accuracy of the Surveyors." With tongue held firmly in cheek, he continued: "They even made an allowance for 'kinkage' due to the chain passing amongst a herd of sheep. The sheep interfering with the chain were counted, and knowing the 'kinkage' for one sheep the total was then calculated."

Much darker hours were ahead for the world, even darker than those of the Great Depression, difficult as that may have been to believe at the time. But in many ways, the days of the Second World War would prove to be the return of the glory days of British Columbia land surveyors. War has always been good for the economy; without question, it is good for employment. Within a short time, no land surveyor in the province would find himself lacking for opportunities to be fully occupied.

15

As Steel from the Furnace

The peaceful days of surveying in the remote regions of the province were shattered by the beginning of the Second World War. The loss to the conflict of young surveyors like this unidentified man was deeply felt by the profession. OFFICE OF THE SURVEYOR GENERAL

In his address to members of the Corporation of British Columbia Land Surveyors on January 12, 1940, retiring president Geoffrey Burnett told his colleagues:

> Since our last annual meeting...the war clouds, which were then gathering over our Empire and practically the whole world, steadily thickened. After using every diplomatic and honourable means in an endeavour to avert armed conflict, the Empire was finally forced to declare war on Germany owing to acts culminating in the latter's brutal and unprovoked invasion of Poland. Canada has taken her place at the side of the Motherland, as befits her position as the leading Dominion, and already her contingents are in camp in England, fit and ready to maintain the traditions of valour and efficiency established by our soldiers in the 1914–1918 struggle.

The onslaught of war following on the footsteps of the preceding terrible decade was, naturally, a difficult blow for all to absorb. Once again, dozens of BCLS men devoted themselves to the war effort. More than eighty of them had enthusiastically returned the questionnaire that had been sent to them in 1939, asking for a summary of their abilities and skills in the event of conflict. Alas, the problem that president Musgrave had identified at much the same time—the steadily aging ranks of the profession—meant that relatively few were actually accepted for service. Naturally, those few were younger men. The dilemma of how to fill the footsteps of retiring surveyors worsened.

In 1941 Rupert Haggen, BCLS 69, who had been practising his occupation in British Columbia since 1911, reported with great concern that "in the Kootenay and Boundary areas there are no Surveyors under 50 years of age and several over 70." The situation was so serious, thought Haggen, that he even suggested bringing it to the attention of the prime minister. He pointed out that, of the four surveyors in the Kootenays actively engaged in full-time surveying, none were "overworked," nor could any of them afford to take on a student surveyor under the circumstances. Haggen blamed much of the problem on the unpalatable fact that a great deal of work falling within the purview of land surveyors was being done by unqualified individuals in many situations, leaving insufficient work for properly qualified men. Under such circumstances, it was difficult for surveyors to encourage new practitioners into the field. He cited housing loans being granted without certified plans that showed buildings to be within property lines: "Any kind of individual with any kind of measuring device is apparently considered capable of delineating the boundaries of his lot."

The provincial forestry department, he said, was using "minor officials...armed solely with compass, axe and self-assurance" to undertake boundary surveys for timber licences. Haggen also went on to describe right-of-way surveys and explanatory plans that were in a complete state of disarray. "Mine plans are posted by individuals whose ignorance is so abysmal that they do not realize how easy it is to lose direction when in the bowels of the earth. There is the famous case in Bridge River where the tunnel, shown on the plan as straight, turned practically a complete circle." Haggen clearly felt hard done by, for the conclusion to his report reached a crescendo of indignation:

> Surveying has been the charge which all parties, Ministers, engineers, lawyers, contractors, miners and owners, have sought to eliminate. Many Government officials have made good fellows of themselves by working out some method by which requisite surveys might be avoided. As a result of this, some lovely messes have developed and are developing today.
>
> Surveyors have played an important part in Provincial exploration and development, and it is recognized throughout the British Empire to be in the public interest that they should continue to function. Conditions in British Columbia have now reached the point where serious consideration must be given to the perpetuation of the profession. It must be made sufficiently attractive to secure new personnel.

The problem was one that would not quickly disappear. Not until 1949 would the numbers of new surveyors start to creep back up, and then only a handful at a time: six that year, eleven the following, nine in 1951.

Because of the lack of younger men available in the 1940s, what tasks there were for qualified surveyors were sometimes difficult to complete. In his report for the 1944 season, Surveyor General Frank Green complained: "All topographical survey-work is still suffering from the absence of our younger partly trained assistants in the armed forces, and by the difficulty in getting helpers of the best age-group. The work involves much hard mountain-climbing and projects are being selected where the men available can be used with the best results." Alan Campbell, BCLS 101, stated in his 1943 presidential address, in anticipation of post-war reconstruction work: "The older men will find their place, but there will, in all probability, be a call for more young men than the Corporation can supply. The danger then arises is that work which we have been accustomed to consider belonged to Surveyors will be given into other hands to the detriment of the profession...it could almost be called a patriotic duty on the part of Surveyors...to encourage young men to become Surveyors."

In the meantime a number of BCLS men were doing their patriotic duty in Europe, young Gerry Andrews among them. Given his background in aerial surveying, Andrews had opted to join the British army's Royal Engineers air survey team. Disappointingly, his first assignment was as mess secretary—from Andrews's point of view, an unwarranted waste of his skills. But by 1943, Andrews succeeded in putting his experience to good use. That year he was transferred to the Canadian aerial survey liaison section and put in charge of the installation of sophisticated aerial cameras into long-range Mosquito aircraft, work for which he was later officially recognized with an MBE. The work for which Andrews is less known was, however, distinctly more pivotal in the war effort: an aerial surveying mission dubbed "Operation Overlord."

In late 1943, the Allied forces were already considering how to approach the beaches at Normandy, France, with a view to a potential landing. In particular, knowledge was required of how the surf affected the beaches and the depth of the water at various tide levels, in order to plan a landing with the maximum element of surprise. According to Andrews's daughter Mary and author Doreen Hunter, in their joint biography of Andrews entitled *A Man and His Century*, a royal engineer named Major W.W. Williams had devised a technique to compare the velocity of the waves approaching the beach with water depth by using timed overlapping aerial photographs. The idea was to assess whether a landing at low tide might be feasible in order to catch the enemy by surprise. Andrews and his team were selected to make measurements and do the comparative work from the aerial photographs of the beaches. They were not, of course, told of the significance of the work, nor whether the beaches they were looking at would be the ones actually used. Andrews wrote: "Security was paramount. We plotted our work on detailed charts of the actual beaches. I tried to bluff my crew, each of whom had been fully vetted, that our work might be just a decoy for Hitler." His crew played along, but may well have known what was in store. "Morale was excellent. On D-Day when the radio announced the exact location, my crew shouted in unison, *OUR* BEACHES!"

Such cause for celebration paled, however, against the tragedy of loss. As they had in the First World War, many surveyors had joined the fray. By 1945, 27 out of 138 members of the Corporation were on active service abroad, and several more had been killed or remained missing in action. On the home front, the war meant an increase in industrial activity that had many benefits for surveyors in the province. While the Geological Survey of Canada (GSC) put off its centennial celebrations in 1941—the celebration would eventually belatedly take place in 1947—it would have had little time to devote to such an affair in any event. Prior to the war Canada had purchased much of its metals, minerals, and energy resources from outside its borders. The global conflict spurred a huge effort to locate and extract domestic sources instead, and the staff of the GSC were immediately diverted from their usual work to concentrate on the search for metals such as chromium, manganese, and tin. According to Christy Vodden's brief history of the GSC, *No Stone Unturned*, vast deposits of mercury were discovered by the GSC in British Columbia and "rushed into production, [becoming] the largest source of mercury in the British Commonwealth."

War resources on all sides had also been concentrated on the speedy advancement of technology that would later prove invaluable to surveying worldwide. Major advances were made in the development of radio for navigational purposes. "Gee," or "G" (shorthand for "Grid")—a radio navigation and distance measurement system utilized by the British during the war—was adapted by the American defence department into what was known as the LORAN or *long range navigation* system. Originally known as "Loomis radio navigation" or "LRN" after its inventor, physicist Alfred Lee Loomis, both LORAN and Gee worked on a system of radio signal transmissions to measure distance and locate the positions or intersections of two converging vessels or aircraft. LORAN was adopted after the war as a measuring device for non-military purposes, but it would eventually be made almost redundant by the even more effective satellite-based global positioning system, or GPS. *Radio angle detection and ranging*—a system using radio signals to map moving objects such as aircraft that quickly became known simply as radar—also saw vast leaps forward in technological efficiency thanks to the war, especially in Britain. The German forces were less successful in developing radar efficiently, or at least developing it quickly enough to provide them with any level of superiority over the smaller British forces.

On the other hand, the Germans were more successful with regard to flight itself, designing and manufacturing one of only two types of helicopter put into operational service during the war, the F1282 Kolibri (Hummingbird). (The first manned helicopter to stay aloft had carried a Frenchman into the air at Roubaix on August 24, 1907.) While the First World War had seen huge advances in fixed-wing aircraft, very little had been achieved with respect to rotary-winged vehicles. Painstaking experimentation had continued in various parts of the world, however, and by the time the Second World War began a Russian immigrant to America named Igor Sikorsky had taken the helicopter to a stage where it could be relied on to "hop" short distances. In the summer of 1943, another American helicopter was taken on a test flight in Gardenville, New York: the Bell Model 30. It was the precursor of a series of Bell machines that would be put into commercial use as early as 1946. By the beginning of that year, Surveyor General Frank Green was already stating in his annual report to the minister of lands and forests: "The war has brought about great improvements in aerial photography equipment…with these improvements aerial coverage can be secured with fewer pictures, and the intensity of ground control can be reduced, all of which means mapping at lower cost." Green added wistfully: "A practical helicopter would also help." By 1947, a small British Columbian company called Okanagan Air Services had purchased a Bell 47-B3. Working life for land surveyors in remote locations would soon change dramatically.

In 1929, however, as Canadian and American authorities pondered the desirability of road access—let alone aerial access—to northern British Columbia and to Alaska, such thrilling technological advances were scarcely to be dreamed of, let alone implemented. Military necessity was not yet a primary driver for a highway to the north. With the increasingly common use of motor vehicles during the 1920s, tourism had become a realistic goal, and governments throughout North America were interested in expanding their road networks. The Yukon Territory and Alaska were also well known to be rich in mineral and timber resources, and a cost-effective means of transportation was critical. The Pacific–Yukon Highway Association was formed in the late 1920s to promote the building of a highway to Alaska, a goal that also saw British Columbia premier S.F. Tolmie organize an "On to Alaska" caravan in 1929, taking fifty cars from Vancouver to Hazelton. At much the same time U.S. president Herbert Hoover was seeking co-operation from Canada to conduct a feasibility study for a highway connecting Alaska to the south through British Columbia. The dominion government showed little interest, deferring to the province. The province, on the other hand, was extremely interested.

In 1930, John Rolston, BCLS 141, and John Hamilton Gray, LS (Gray was qualified prior to 1891 and therefore had no associated BCLS number), were instructed by the government to begin reconnaissance surveys for potential highway routes. There were several potential routes the highway could take. Two led from Prince George—one following a more westerly route up the Stikine Valley toward Whitehorse, the other following the Rocky Mountain Trench to the east. Another potential route, quickly dismissed because of its remoteness and therefore its impracticality, was via the Mackenzie River. A prairie route through Fort Nelson and Dawson Creek was attractive because it traversed relatively level terrain and was far enough inland to be secure from coastal attack in the event of war.

The onset of the Great Depression left no capacity to pursue the initiative, and little was done in pursuit of the feasibility studies for nearly ten years. However, the threat of war soon revived interest. By early 1939, writes Gerry Andrews, who was still then working with the provincial forestry department, "the Province gave top priority to locating a road to the Yukon and Alaska via the Rocky Mountain Trench." Suddenly all the resources possible were available to throw at the reconnaissance surveys: "The Surveyor General deployed four topo and three trig parties for standard mapping and Highways fielded an engineering party. Arrangements were made with the chief forester for me to provide air photo cover." The survey of the trench route took three full seasons to complete, and apart from its military priority it was, in a surveying sense, ground-breaking. A biography of former surveyor general Frank Green notes: "This survey…was for that time an ultra modern show in technical respects, and entirely a provincial effort. It included special air photography, field radio communication, optical reading instruments, and advanced methods of terrestrial photogrammetric control originally developed in the [Survey] Branch."

All the same, the surveys were not easily undertaken. According to Gerry Andrews in an article published in *The Geographical Journal* in 1942, ten separate survey parties were strung out through the trench during the 1939 season. Both communication and consistent supply were problematic. Despite all the modern conveniences of motor and air transport, the crews still had to resort to boats and pack horses for much of the work. "It will be seen that the movement of men, equipment, and supplies was arduous, expensive, and except for the outboard motor, little less primitive than conditions one hundred years ago," he wrote. Even the use of floatplanes for aerial survey was a mixed blessing: "Take-off conditions for the heavily loaded aircraft on the river were none too good, as the straight run was barely long enough and air conditions were often turbulent due to a prevalent wind from the Peace River gorge through the Rockies meeting with strong air currents moving up and down the Trench…Take-off conditions at Fort Ware were even worse…owing to the rapid current, a rather short run, and an obstruction at the lower end in the form of a high timbered bluff."

It was huddled around the aircraft radio that Andrews and his teammates heard news of the outbreak of war in Europe. The building of a highway to Alaska now seemed inevitable, although the route was still undetermined, despite the detailed exploratory work done by the Canadians. In his January 1940 report to the deputy minister of lands, Surveyor General Green wrote:

> The construction of a highway through British Columbia to Alaska seems to be a certainty of the near future. There are about four possible routes, each offering some advantages over the others; but owing to the small population of, and difficult access to, the northerly 300 miles in latitude, survey-work in the Province has been, until now, largely confined to the regions south of latitude 56°.
>
> The selection of a wrong highway route could easily cost the public millions of dollars, and the best insurance against a wrong selection is obviously complete contour information over all promising routes. In 1939 the Survey Branch started on one of the routes, diverting all available funds to the purpose. What is generally known as the Rocky Mountain Trench was chosen for mapping. This route offered the shortest distance from United States points to Dawson and Fairbanks...

Green, like all bureaucrats eager for funding and spotting an opportunity to make a case, hadn't hesitated when he saw the obvious chance to get government backing for detailed survey work in the north. He clearly favoured the Rocky Mountain route, reporting that its merits included the relative ease of engineering compared with other possible routes and, from a tourism perspective, "the shortest over-all distance, the longest season, the best grades and alignment, and scenery not far short of the best." Green also thought it offered excellent access for resource extraction and a route "comparatively safe from bombing, and with many sites for airfields."

As events transpired, however, Green's clear preference would not end up as the chosen path for the Alaska Highway. On March 18, 1942, the Canadian government signed a deal with the Americans for the building of a highway through the Rockies from Edmonton to Fort St.

John on the Peace River and thence north to the Yukon and Alaska via Whitehorse—a completely different route from any previously considered. "The route chosen under the new agreement," wrote Andrews dryly, "came as a distinct surprise." Andrews was naturally disappointed that the work of the British Columbian survey crews seemed about to go to waste. He dismissed the final route convincingly, citing numerous disadvantages including distance, construction problems, flooding risks, and the fact that virtually nothing was yet known about the terrain that the road was to pass through. Surveyors would literally have to work steps ahead of construction engineers to complete the highway in one season. But in the end, the Americans had selected the route as being obvious: it followed the line of a series of airports built in 1941 to support air crews engaged in the war in Asia. The United States was also building and paying for the road. Canada supplied gravel and timber, and some labour—including long-time British Columbia resident and dominion land surveyor Knox "Mac" McCusker, famed in the north for his robust storytelling—but the Americans had the cash, the equipment, and more than five thousand men dedicated to the project. The route went where they said it would, despite protests from the British Columbia government and its surveyors.

Within a few months in 1942, the American army had worked day and night to push nearly two thousand miles of mind-numbingly rough road through Alaskan permafrost and British Columbia's mosquito-ridden muskeg to Fairbanks, Alaska. According to J. Kingston Pierce in *American History* magazine, one sergeant was moved to write of the depressing and exhausting experience: "The Alaska Highway winding in and winding out, fills my mind with serious doubt; as to whether the 'lout' who planned this route was going to hell—or coming out!" The highway—now more commonly known as the Alaska–Canada Highway, or the "Alcan"—was officially opened on November 20, 1942, and almost immediately, upgrading work began. Grumbling aside, work for surveyors on the improvements was plentiful. In fact, its location on permafrost that heaves and breaks up the paving means that the upgrading of the road continues to be required on an annual basis. It is as easy to spot a surveyor along the Alcan in the summer as it is to see bears and moose.

This monument, erected around 1940 on the British Columbia–Yukon border, replaced a monument originally placed by George Mercer Dawson in 1887. Pictured, from left: Norman C. Stewart, BCLS 120; unidentified man; Claire Dobbin, pilot. ABCLS/G.S. ANDREWS

The construction of the Alaska Highway necessitated another series of surveys, this time concluding the delineation of the British Columbia–Yukon border along the 60th parallel. Significant sections of the border required re-surveys—the previous surveys had taken place prior to 1910—and at least sixty-five miles, or more than one hundred kilometres, had not yet been surveyed at all. In 1943 the dominion and provincial governments created a new British Columbia–Yukon boundary commission, agreeing that "the route of the Alaska Highway, now under construction, crosses and recrosses the sixtieth parallel of latitude...[and] that the resulting activity, in the vicinity of the boundary area, makes it necessary that the boundary line be surveyed and marked on the ground." The commissioners were the surveyors general respectively for the dominion government—F.H. Peters and B.W. Waugh—and for British Columbia, Frank Green, and after 1946, Norman Stewart. For the next seven years, provincial survey teams led by Alan Campbell and dominion surveyors employed by the Geodetic Survey of Canada worked each summer on finalizing the boundary, reporting to the commissioners at the end of each season on the extent of their work.

Although the necessity of having clear boundary markers at the places where the road intersected the border was obvious, a pragmatic approach was taken to the survey of what remained a fairly remote area through rugged terrain. The instructions issued to the surveyors required them to take astronomical observations spaced anywhere between fifteen and twenty-five miles apart as the basis for drawing the boundary along the 60th parallel. Surveyors being as wedded to accuracy as they are, Campbell and his colleagues still were diligent in obtaining measurements that were as precise as possible, paying rigorous attention to creating permanent marker posts and, wherever practical, establishing three bearing trees at each monument or post.

The line was run west, explained Campbell in his 1946 report, "in a series of chords 486 chains long, with a fractional chord adjoining the next westerly point on the parallel." In other words, the boundary line running west was not a straight line but a series of straight lines each running at a fractional angle to each other as they headed west. Campbell observed that the local impression was that the surveyors had made some fundamental error in the line and were forced to make constant adjustments to "bend" it in the right direction. In case his superiors—or perhaps indeed future historians—got the wrong impression, Campbell decided to explain why such a constant series of deviations was required: "Any lines run or surveyed on the surface of the earth follow what is called a great circle... If a line were started running west at any point on the 60th parallel and carried round the earth and back to the starting-point, when halfway around it would be at the 60th parallel *south* of the Equator." Because of the shape of the earth, Campbell said, any endeavour to run a straight line would always "cut" the earth into two equal halves: "The Equator is the only parallel of latitude on which a straight line can be run west or east" and meet along the same parallel. Any other line is curved by definition, rather than straight. "The further away from the Equator, the greater the curvature. Hence a method of following this curve closely must be used. There are several ways of doing this, but the method used on the British Columbia–Yukon boundary is by short lengths of straight lines, the ends of which are on the parallel. At the end of such a straight line or chord, the line is deflected or bent a certain amount so that the end of the next chord will also be on the parallel."

As to the survey work itself, the trials and tribulations of remote northern work were nothing new to the crews. All the same, there were some surprises in store. In his 1944 report, C.H. Ney, DLS, reported with some apparent astonishment that hiring a camp cook in Edmonton had proved impossible: "Selective Service officials in that city informed me that, at that time, they had applications for 43 cooks with none available." Given the war, perhaps Ney should not have been so surprised. Ultimately, he succeeded in employing a cook from Saskatchewan and an eighteen-year-old university student to work as a labourer.

Ney also provided his observations on a range of interesting matters, none of which would make it into a dry, twenty-first-century government report. On June 12, Ney and his team had arrived in Dawson Creek, where it promptly started to rain. "In two or three hours the clay streets of the town were worked up by the traffic into a porridge-like batter about a foot and a half deep…The walls of the hotel rotunda, where we stayed, were fringed at the bottom with a row of muddy footwear, while the owners paraded nonchalantly about the building in their socks or stocking feet. The deplorable street condition seemed to be accepted with cool unconcern by the local residents but caused most newcomers to wonder why prompt and energetic measures were not taken to correct the situation." The DLS surveyor commented on the fact that bears, fox, and moose might occasionally be seen by the roadside, and he was particularly taken with the hot springs at the Liard River. "Before bathing there," he warned, "it was necessary to agitate the water violently with a paddle to get a uniform mixture at a lower temperature."

Tempting as it evidently was to pepper the reports with anecdotes about the hardship of their working conditions, broken-down trucks in axle-deep mud, and obstreperous packers and labourers, Ney and his various counterparts over the years also provided detailed reports on the surveys themselves, including reports concerning the technical methods employed, various aspects of the equipment used, and their final results.

As their predecessors had been doing for decades, the surveyors also described the conditions and climate of the country they were traversing, commenting on its utility for timber extraction, mining, tourism, and agriculture. The construction of the Alaska Highway had added an unprecedented layer of significance to such reconnaissance work. In 1946, Alan Campbell reported: "There were many survey parties along the highway this year, showing what an interest is being taken in the country." Those parties were still largely engaged in geodetic triangulation, topographical work, and mining surveys. By 1948, Campbell had this to say about the development of the area:

> The highway is beginning to lose the appearance of a new road through wild country, and if the present rate of progress is maintained, it will not be long before it will be entirely safe for motorists to travel along it without the necessity of carrying extra gas. Accommodation such as hotels, camps, and restaurants is increasing, and there are rumours of more. Contrary to reports heard from the outside that the road was being let go to wrack and ruin, the maintenance crews are keeping it up and making improvements at many places. In the opinion of many it is better now than ever it was.
>
> This year two buses a week, each way, from Dawson Creek to Whitehorse, were run by the British Yukon Navigation Company, as well as regular freight trucks. Many other trucks travel up and down the road, but the number of private cars, though they were considerable, was not as great as expected.

The implications of extended development throughout the province had been of concern to land surveyors for some time already. While on the one hand the amount of associated work was highly desirable, the lack of a coordinated approach to mapping and triangulation, let alone detailed surveys, had been exercising the minds of Corporation members since before the war. During the 1940 annual general meeting, it was a subject of such interest that lengthy discussions ensued over a detailed report by Hugh Verrall, BCLS 103, in which he waxed lyrically and with some disgust over the state of British Columbia's mapping and survey efforts.

James T. Underhill, BCLS 146, with survey party members, 1947. H.B. "BARRY" COTTON

"Is it any wonder that some people are decidedly gun-shy of the cost of surveys and maps?" he asked. Verrall cited a list of more than twenty-five kinds of surveys then under way in the province. Of that list, some coordination existed between dominion and provincial geodetic and photographic surveys. "But there is virtually no co-operation outside of this," complained Verrall, "because there is no system to which all surveys could be tied."

In this complaint lay the heart of the problem: no integrated and coordinated system of reference points had yet been established with which all surveys could be compared and which could be used to resolve conflicts concerning boundary lines. "The system of land surveys in B.C. has almost always been a piecemeal one... [this] leaves us with a truly crazy-quilt which the Land Registry system of separate plans cannot accurately fit together. Owing to there being no control survey, it happens that adjoining lands have conflicting surveys which involve the owners in great expense and create much ill-will against Surveyors." The rapidly expanding road system added to the problems: "The Public Works Department has inherited from the early days a burden of roads as winding as a drunkard's way home, which are mostly unsurveyed, and not shown on maps."

Verrall was the first of his colleagues to so strongly and clearly advocate an integrated survey network of some kind to solve the problems

In 1949–1950, H.B. "Barry" Cotton, BCLS 290, worked as crew on the Columbia Cellulose surveys near Prince Rupert. Cotton is pictured on the far left of this shot he captioned "A bunch of the boys—Mark, Harry, Keith, and HBC." H.B. "BARRY" COTTON

he outlined. He suggested at first a simple grid system, "fudging up" the larger inaccuracies to make them fit, until a precise system of control could be implemented. Illegible, ambiguous, or outright incorrect plans should be redone and fitted within the grid. It was an ambitious proposal, one Verrall considered perhaps "a ridiculous vision too vast for words," and which would "involve an immense amount of work and money to complete. It is unlikely that any but the youngest Surveyors will live to see such a system any way near completion."

Verrall hoped all the same that progress on his visionary plan could be made a step at a time. He could not possibly have foreseen the astounding leaps forward in technology over the next few decades that would enable the implementation of an integrated system much sooner than he had anticipated. In the meantime, he and his colleagues focused on a more immediately pressing issue: unionization. In 1943 the Civic Employees Union, which was affiliated with employees of the provincial government's Department of Public Works, had begun demanding that all civic employees, including "professional men," join the union. The

Leaps forward in technological advancement after the Second World War did not mean that it was any easier for surveyors to get around on the ground. Here survey party members on the Columbia Cellulose project are forced to ford a river to continue the line. H.B. "BARRY" COTTON

surveyors were horrified, immediately beginning an intense campaign for exclusion.

By 1945, for unclear reasons, the threat was over. Nevertheless, surveyors were entering a different time, and a different world, as the last days of the Second World War dragged to their conclusion. Reactions to unionism and technological growth, and an increasing understanding of

James W. Hermon, BCLS 213, with Barry Cotton on the Skeena River near Prince Rupert, 1950. H.B. "BARRY" COTTON

the need for improved systems—all were merely symptoms of a trend toward an exploding growth of knowledge and awareness of what had always previously been thought to be impossible. The sense of liberation went beyond freedom from conflict and fear. The province was about to ride yet another economic boom, and surveyors as always would ride the coattails of any economic direction the province took. From the dust and gloom of the war, a golden period was about to emerge.

16

A Most Fortunate Twist

John Matthews, BCLS 356, and party members on a topographical survey, circa 1950. Matthews recalled still using pack horses on the survey. JOHN MATTHEWS

The first one hundred years of European settlement in British Columbia witnessed a rapid growth in population, industry, and development, all within a vast area previously unknown to the rest of the world. But the two decades following the Second World War saw an exponential acceleration in that growth, on a previously unimaginable scale.

There was optimism in 1946: the province's deputy minister of lands reported happily that year that "the backlog of demands for land, built up during the war, began to make itself felt, and the year's business showed a big increase over 1945." At the same time, a general recovery phase in provincial administration occurred in the second half of the 1940s—there were numerous departmental reorganizations, including the separation of surveying from mapping duties. Human and financial resources were regrouped, both within the government and in private-sector surveying companies. Although business for government lands personnel was booming, it was still a mixed blessing. Gerry Andrews, who had been appointed as the chief engineer of the new air surveys division, bemoaned that "the outlook in the spring of 1946 for accomplishing very much in the way of air photography on a Provincial basis during the year was most discouraging." Andrews's chief complaint was a lack of resources—outdated and poorly maintained camera equipment, no spare parts, no charter aircraft available, and "due to war casualties and disabilities, the only experienced person available for air crew," Andrews claimed, was himself. Labour, all the same, was cheap. Barry Cotton, still an articling student at the time, spent six weeks in 1947 working at the land registry office in New Westminster, copying plans by hand for his employer. To purchase copies of the three-hundred-odd plans from the government would have cost one dollar apiece: at Cotton's low wages, it was far more economical for him to copy the plans.

Government reports from 1946 to 1949 are laced with shadowy and optimistic forecasts of what was to come in the next twenty years. In 1946 the Coal, Petroleum, and Natural Gas Control was set up within the Department of Lands to monitor and support oil and gas exploration; while oil drilling had not produced any results to that date, it seemed most promising. Nor did Andrews have to wait unduly long for his updated equipment and resources. Aerial mapping techniques

Atlin, 1953: Kenneth "Ken" Bridge, BCLS 350, and an unidentified man with a typical stone cairn.

Atlin, 1953: Arthur "Art" Swannell, BCLS 288, on left, with Ken Bridge at right, sawing firewood with a crosscut saw. According to Stirling Knudsen, Henry Junke was holding the log in place while playing "German woodcutting music" on his guitar.

Atlin, 1953: Henry Junke cooks supper while George Miller, BCLS 383, looks on.
STIRLING KNUDSEN

Atlin, 1953: Ken Bridge and George Miller, with crewman Henry Junke at camp.
STIRLING KNUDSEN

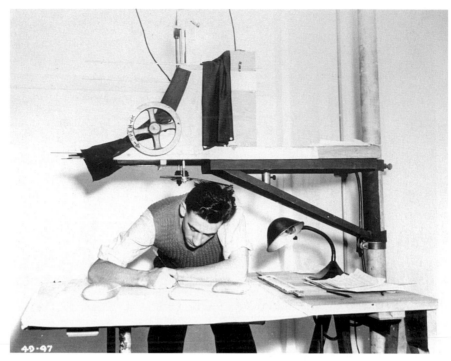

Working with overhead projection methodology: British Columbia Topographical Division, possibly around 1948. JOHN MATTHEWS

proved extraordinarily useful during the disastrous 1948 Fraser River floods. Airplanes were mobilized instantly to survey the flood plain, and the resulting images, produced within a matter of hours, were used to develop and implement emergency measures. In the longer term, the photographs were used to plan for diking and other preventive measures. Notwithstanding the disaster, government surveyors were delighted, because provincial financial support for aerial photography rapidly reasserted itself. There was, however, a corresponding difficulty: a sheer lack of physical space to file the tens of thousands of printed photographs that had already accumulated. It was a problem that became more pressing as each season progressed.

In comparison with the relative quiet of the late 1940s, British Columbia's industrial and urban development during the 1950s and 1960s exploded on a scale that was the envy of Canada's other provinces and territories. The province appeared to be the golden child of investment

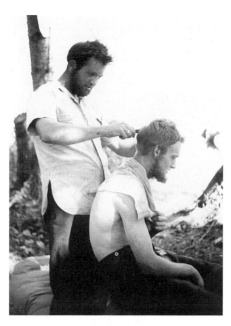

They decided to start all over again because the haircuts were so bad. JOHN MATTHEWS

Bridge River Valley headwaters, 1947 or 1948: Jim Cambrey cutting the hair of John Matthews (who received his commission BCLS 356 in 1956). JOHN MATTHEWS

opportunity. In 1951, assistant superintendent of lands R. Torrance wrote in his annual report:

> After decades of steady but slow development, British Columbia has been 'discovered' by big business and it has been proclaimed by some leading industrialists that this Province contains the continent's last great store of undeveloped natural resources. Be that as it may, new industry, backed by a seemingly unlimited supply of capital, has moved in to give British Columbia its most startling push since the gold rush days of the 1860s…It would appear that the gates to British Columbia's almost untapped hinterland have been swung wide open.

The demand for land was massive. Roads, power plants, and new company towns seemed to spring up overnight. With the urgency of potential resource wealth resonating in the hallways of government

Sandifer Mountain mineral claim, 1953. Douglas "Doug" Meredith (who received his BCLS commission 368 in 1957), Rupert Seel, and George Smith, BCLS 311, who were all working for McElhanney. DOUG MEREDITH

finance departments, work continued well into the 1950s to complete outstanding boundary surveys. Alternative highway routes to the north were explored and abandoned. The Alaska Highway was improved instead, and expanded. In 1948, the Columbia Cellulose Company started construction of its new $27 million plant near Prince Rupert. The provincial government created a $100 million expansion program in the pulp and paper industry. Also in 1948, the Aluminum Company of Canada had engineers and surveyors exploring the British Columbia coast for potential power schemes; by 1953, the $550 million Kemano power project near Kitimat came on stream to fuel aluminum production. After years of fruitless exploration, oil was finally discovered in 1951 in the Peace River country. The Trans-Canada Highway was officially opened at Rogers Pass on September 3, 1962. The Columbia River treaty, signed in 1964 between Canada and the United States of America, was the basis for the construction of three huge hydroelectric dams in eastern British Columbia during the second half of the 1960s and the early 1970s. Dozens, if not hundreds, of other enterprises and infrastructure schemes on every scale of size and along the entire spectrum of potential profit were being explored and implemented across the province. Surveyors were run off their feet, and government departments were hard put to keep up.

In 1950 the British Columbia Lands Service had responsibility, among other things, for the continuing development of the University Endowment Lands in Vancouver, diking construction and maintenance, the administration of the Land Settlement Board, oil and gas and water rights, and the Southern Okanagan Lands Project, aimed at supporting agricultural production. In addition, its two main branches were the Lands Branch (with land surveyors among the staff) and the Survey and Mapping Branch, which covered legal surveys. The surveyor general was Frank Morris (who was never registered as a BCLS). His branch contained an air surveys division under Gerry Andrews, who by 1950 had not yet received his BCLS commission; a topographic division under Alfred Slocomb, BCLS 267; and a geographic division under W.H. Hutchinson. In his 1950 annual report, the deputy minister of lands, G.P. Melrose, wrote lyrically and in an elegant style long gone from government reports:

> Exploration and investigation are carried on over, above, and under the surface of the Province of British Columbia, from foreshore to mountain-tops, in the valleys and along the ridges, in arid areas, and on snowfields, up to the tiny tributaries of headwaters, across lakes and muskegs, and down rivers to the sea. Reports are made on our heritage of resources, including soil, water, grass and forests, fisheries, mines, and the sources of power for industry, homes, and farms, and the recreational opportunities for our citizens and visitors.

Almost all of that work continued to be undertaken by land surveyors. According to Melrose, however, it was slow going. Work may have been plentiful, but the ranks of surveyors remained thin, and at the beginning of the golden era the technology available to help surveyors had not yet caught up with the economic ambitions of government and private enterprise. When it did start to catch up in the 1950s, technological progress would proceed at a speed almost impossible to comprehend, overtaking

Barry Cotton spent the summer of 1950 working on an extension of the British Columbia–Alberta boundary northward from the point to which it had last been surveyed in 1924, some sixty miles north of Fort St. John. The twenty-one-man crew included boss packer Angus Beaton and his thirty-two horses. H.B. "BARRY" COTTON

A helicopter used in mid-1950s surveys in the north. ROBIN KNUDSEN

Taking work back into the city to process it was impractical on remote projects up until as late as the 1970s and even the 1980s. In 1951 at Piebiter Creek, a tent office had to suffice for Barry Cotton. H.B. "BARRY" COTTON

the ability of some to keep pace with it. At the beginning of the decade, however, such developments were still several years in the future. Topographic mapping of the Sechelt coastline had begun in 1950, using the *BC Surveyor*, a lands department boat acquired in 1947. To cover the entire coast from Vancouver to Stewart, an area of some 64,000 square miles, Melrose estimated that "at the present rate of standard mapping for one party, using the motor vessel *B.C. Surveyor* it will take about ninety years to complete this task." Helicopter work had "eliminated a lot of very hard foot-slogging and arduous climbing," but "owing to the limitation of its effective load and its cost of operation, it has not as yet decreased the cost of mapping."

Raft-making for a helicopter pad, northeastern British Columbia, 1954. ABCLS/G.S. ANDREWS

Helicopters had started to come into survey use in British Columbia in 1948, when the provincial lands department became the first survey agency in Canada to use this transportation method to carry surveyors and equipment to high altitudes for triangulation work. According to Peter Corley-Smith in his book *Helicopters: The British Columbia Story*, Ernest "Ernie" McMinn, BCLS 325, recalled how the first use of helicopters had come about:

> In 1947, on my first survey job up in Terrace, we had a university student on the crew, and we'd gone out to do a little practice mountain climbing to see how the crew could handle it...this kid looked around. He said, "Why don't you use one of these new-fangled things, a helicopter?" We all laughed about that; but... instead of laughing, [party chief Gerry Emerson, BCLS 272] took to the idea, and followed it up.

The following year, McMinn was with Emerson and Surveyor General Norman Stewart on the first surveying contract using a helicopter,

Triangulation survey for the Kemano tunnel, 1951. This was one of the earliest uses of a helicopter specifically for surveying purposes in British Columbia; the first use was in 1948, in the Fraser Valley. Doug Meredith commented: "It had an open cockpit and it was underpowered and dangerous, but we didn't know it at the time. It sure beat walking!" DOUG MEREDITH

a mapping project in the Chilliwack area. Okanagan Air Services was hired, and owner-pilots Carl Agar and Alf Stringer ferried the three men one at a time to the top of Cheam Peak in their Bell 47-B3. The landing site, said McMinn, "was far from ideal for a helicopter landing. It was at the foot of a glacial cirque...and the cold air was coming down off this ice like a waterfall." All the same, "we thought it was a great thrill—sailing over this ground at 60 miles an hour." The helicopter work was so spectacularly successful in saving time that helicopters were widely employed from then on in survey work.

While time savings were substantial, as Melrose had pointed out, cost savings at that stage were not. A major mind shift was also required to manage logistics on field trips entirely differently. No longer were massive amounts of gear and food being loaded onto horseback or into trucks. In 1952 Emerson wrote in *The Canadian Surveyor* that a helicopter taking off at sea level and flying to seven thousand feet could carry a payload of only 150 pounds in addition to the pilot and fuel. Greater efficiency was required not only for packing the payload, but in undertaking the high-altitude work of setting up triangulation stations. "Instrument crews on a helicopter survey have a far greater responsibility than in former years," writes Emerson. Previously, survey crews had largely used maps and sweat to explore possible options for setting up stations. Now, with the limitations on payload and the hourly cost of the helicopter, it was critical to take great care that the right points for setting up a station had been selected from the beginning and that it was a location where a helicopter could land. Once there, it was entirely possible that the helicopter would not be able to return at the end of the day if the weather changed. It was thus necessary to carry emergency rations and to be prepared to descend the mountain unassisted. "Emergency rations were carried by the pilot at all times; these consisted mostly of Dot chocolate, a few matches, and mosquito repellent, the latter being the most important for survival. We always planned for the worst…"

Pilot fatigue was a concern: the weather sensitivity of surveyors trying to conduct triangulation surveys in typically poor mountain weather was increased exponentially for pilots manhandling what was still remarkably unsophisticated equipment in crosswinds, storms, and fog. Emerson concludes his report with three key pieces of advice to his fellow surveyors, with an admonition to ensure the maintenance of the helicopter (which required a day-long overhaul after every thirty hours of flying). First, says Emerson, never consider any landing or take off "routine." Don't leap from a hovering helicopter: "At first, some of the men jumped thus upsetting the balance of the craft and adding grey hairs to the pilot. Also the stabilizer bar revolves about seven feet above the floor of the cockpit, and a slight upward trend in the jump might remove a head." Finally, he advises against "bump jumping"—moving lightly equipped crews over multiple peaks in a day—in case the weather closed in and stranded the crews without food or shelter.

Emerson also reports that radios were essential for helicopter operations. In 1952, he writes, thirty-pound radios were used, with a full-time operator at the main camp maintaining a ten-minute standby hourly. Notwithstanding the advances in helicopter and radio technology, advances in other areas remained modest. In Victoria, Surveyor General Frank Morris reported in 1950 with evident pride that his branch was

Frederick Henry Nash, BCLS 281, who received his commission in 1949. DOUG MEREDITH

providing services to other departments and to the public "through the operation of a Photostat machine." Morris was also pleased that "by a new process of the Canadian Kodak Company it is now possible to have these Photostats produced on tracing film." On the mapping front, Alfred Slocomb reported the same year that survey field work had been completed on "one-ninth" of the province. Slocomb was happy with the progress of production of colour maps, which he found aesthetically pleasing: "A few daubs of colour and a rounded figure can usually attract a man's eye no matter what the subject," he muses in his section of the annual report. But Slocomb also anticipated slow progress in completing the mapping of the province at the scale of one mile to one inch: "At our present rate of production, this represents sixty years' work."

Chaining continued to be employed as a standard method of measurement. Robert Thistlethwaite, BCLS 276 (who would shortly afterwards become surveyor general of Canada), described the 1950 work on the British Columbia–Alberta boundary survey in great detail: "Chaining is the most exacting phase of the present work, and it may be said that only

Robert "Bob" Thistlethwaite, BCLS 276, was party chief on the British Columbia–
Alberta boundary survey north of Fort St. John, 1950. Thistlethwaite would later
become surveyor general of Canada. H.B. "BARRY" COTTON

By the end of the summer of 1950, the British Columbia–Alberta boundary survey crew had reached the south bend of the Hay River, where they set their last monument. They had run about 107 kilometres of boundary line, but Barry Cotton estimated they had each walked more than eight hundred kilometres to do it.
H.B. "BARRY" COTTON

by the exercise of a high order of ingenuity, care, systematic procedure, and industry can worth-while results be obtained...both the chaining and levelling parties normally devoted part of each day to cutting line." Thistlethwaite's party included Barry Cotton, who had just received his BCLS 290 and was working as the transitman. In many respects, the survey party would have looked little different from one several decades earlier: with gear loaded onto horses, hand axes tucked into saddle bags, and shotguns toted to supplement food supplies. By the end of the season, delayed by weather, Cotton said that "food had dwindled to nothing more than a little rice and macaroni, with occasional flavouring of spruce-hen, rabbit, or jackfish."

Far to the west, in the rugged Nechako River Valley, similarly primitive methods, if more sophisticated technology, were being put to use on an entirely different project. Boatloads of supplies, equipment, and men had to be transported across Tahtsa Lake to the western end, where work was to begin, but the lake was frozen solid. Timing was critical in this particular project, which involved vast sums of venture capital. Waiting for the ice to melt was simply not an option. Spraying equipment was

Kitimat–Kemano, West Tahtsa Lake baseline, 1951. Left to right: party chief Morley Horton, Henry Krol van der Hoek, and Doug Meredith. DOUG MEREDITH

hooked up to a helicopter, and a mixture of soot and coal oil sprayed for eighteen miles along a suitable navigation channel in the lake. It worked well: the ice along the sprayed strip melted two weeks before the rest of the lake. If any thought was given at the time to the environmental impact, it was not mentioned.

The project was the construction of a major hydroelectrical installation at Kemano to power the Aluminum Company of Canada's new plant at Kitimat, fifty miles away. Combined with the construction of the smelter and a new "company town" at Kitimat, the Alcan project would be the largest technical engineering and surveying feat the province had yet witnessed, in the middle of almost unbelievably rugged wilderness. Thousands of workers were employed on the four-year construction project. At the time, the Kemano dam was the third-largest of its kind in the world. The goal was for Kitimat to produce 550,000 tons of aluminum annually—the power needed to achieve that, based on the smelting process at that time, was estimated to be the equivalent required to light more than eight million homes over the same period.

Surveyors, including the legendary Frank Swannell, PLS 75, had been assigned to the area well before the 1940s for early reconnaissance and triangulation work. Now, however, they were employed to produce much

Rest stop on the Kitimat River, CNR line location survey, 1951. Left to right: Rupert Seel, Bob Clift, Doug Meredith. DOUG MEREDITH

more detailed information to support the project. On June 1, 1949, party chief Ernie McMinn "landed at Kitimat Village after a 75-mile trip by Indian boat from Butedale...It was realized that movement in the Kitimat Valley must be planned like a military invasion." McMinn's assignment was to conduct ground control surveys, but it was an operation plagued with ill fortune. The journey upstream on the Kitimat River took eight hours, whereas downstream it was fifty-five minutes. River travel was so dangerous, reported McMinn, that "a trail was commenced through the green hell of swamp, bush, and muskeg of the west bank." Three weeks later, a twenty-year-old axeman named Raymond Bowbyes drowned; his body was lost in the rapids. Fine weather was wasted in having to move camp laboriously on foot. By the time the new camp was established, low cloud and heavy rain had set in, causing a two-week delay in the work. Then "three men became mysteriously and violently ill; one developed an infected foot; the cook quit...J. Wade, the assistant, was injured in the climb to 'Raven' triangulation station, and had to be flown to hospital at Prince Rupert. His helper, who was carrying the theodolite, had a bad fall, and the resultant jar rendered the instrument completely useless."

McMinn kept his cool, and the field surveys were completed despite

Horetzky Creek Survey Camp, Kemano, 1951: relocating the old CNR line. Party members Bob Clift on left, and Rupert Seel (of Ootsa Lake) at right, on boat-building duty. Even as late as the mid-twentieth century this kind of task was sometimes a necessary part of survey work. Doug Meredith was a member of the survey party.
DOUG MEREDITH

all these setbacks. The crew ended the season at the mouth of the Kitimat River: "There are no roads, no trails, and no people," he reported. McMinn also visited what he referred to as "Kitimat Indian village," two miles upriver and "one of the more modern Indian communities on the Coast." Unlike some of his early predecessors in the region, McMinn sang the praises of the people he met, finding them "invariably good-natured," and their community "a credit to any small town." Presciently, he also commented on issues that were becoming a pressing concern for First Nations in the province, but which would remain well below the radar screen of general public awareness for decades: "There is a new Government school and dispensary, both inadequate for the need. The trappings of white culture are superficial; for instance, while religion is nominally Protestant, the gravestones, which are planted in the front lawns, quite casually combine the cross and totem. The problem of their education lies in the disagreement in home life between the old superstitions and the ways of modern living."

Indeed, the late 1940s and the 1950s were a transitional period for many people in Canada. Promotional literature for the Kitimat–

Surveying near Atlin, 1953, with Art Swannell, BCLS 288; Ken Bridge, BCLS 350; and George Miller, BCLS 383. The survey took place along the old telegraph line route from the east side of Atlin Lake. "The best boss and crew you could ever want," is how party member Stirling Knudsen, a teenage student at the time, remembers the team. Knudsen is on the left, with his horse "Queen," and Henry Junke, another crew member, is here with "Croppy." STIRLING KNUDSEN

Atlin, 1953, the Swannell party: Elmer Curtis is observing and Stirling Knudsen is making field notes. Knudsen articled to Doug Roy, BCLS 295, but did not complete his commission in British Columbia. STIRLING KNUDSEN

Elmer Curtis on instrument, and George Miller, BCLS 383, making field notes. STIRLING KNUDSEN

Party member Harry Wicks catches a ride with George Miller on a steep climb near Atlin, 1953. STIRLING KNUDSEN

Kemano project was styled in the typically effusive, booming language of the period: "Kitimat: Tomorrow's City Today!" The mood was to think big—nothing was impossible. Certainly, for the surveyors involved, the work of building the massive dam and power plant, the associated infrastructure, and the new town of Kitimat involved unprecedented challenges and opportunities. In 1951 Frank Swannell's son Arthur, newly commissioned in 1950 as BCLS 288, was working on his first major job, a triangulation project in Tweedsmuir Park connecting to the Kemano tunnel. Swannell's work was cause for personal as well as professional celebration: as part of the triangulation, he tied into some of the points established by his father during the 1926–1927 season. But for one young Chinese-Canadian surveyor named Kenneth Wong, the Kitimat project was a mixed blessing.

Wong succeeded in obtaining his BCLS commission 334 in 1953, against the odds. A general anti-Chinese sentiment persevered in Canada despite the law change in 1947 providing Chinese Canadians with equal rights to vote, be educated, and to work. Wong was the first Chinese Canadian in British Columbia to receive a BCLS commission, and one of the first in the country to become a registered surveyor. He was both fortunate and wise in his choice of occupation: the demand for his skills outweighed other considerations during that period. He was also in a profession where loyalty to one's colleagues was paramount. Initially employed by the Underhill partnership, Wong was employed by Alcan in 1954 to assist James Gordon Hirtle, BCLS 299, the chief surveyor for the Kitimat–Kemano project. Wong's assignment was to focus on the new Kitimat townsite, an entirely planned community, overseeing legal surveys of town lots as well as both road layout and lot locations, dimensions, and measurements. "It was an interesting and challenging task, though an onerous one," Wong mused fifty years later. Wong's diligence demonstrated itself in the faultless results that he and all his colleagues produced in the townsite location work. But clearly, all was not ideal for Wong in the remote coastal location. While it may not have been the cause of his decision to move back to private practice in Vancouver three years later, Wong later wrote: "It was Alcan policy to have all survey parties to be a three members' crew...to glean hopefully from some of

Horetzky Creek Survey Camp, Kemano, 1951. DOUG MEREDITH

the survey parties members who may decide Alcan was a good Company to work for and thus bring their families to reside permanently in Kitimat. Unfortunately, [I] found it otherwise."

For two of the larger surveying partnerships in the province, though, the Kitimat–Kemano project was nothing but good news. After the hardships of the Great Depression and the Second World War, both McElhanney and Underhills (as they were and remain colloquially known) enjoyed an expansion of their work in and well beyond the Nechako Valley. The sheer amount of work involved for surveyors around the province, not just Kitimat, provided a basis for the bigger partnerships to take leaps into previously uncharted territory. McElhanney staff would within the next few years go as far afield as the Mekong River delta and Saudi Arabia on work contracts for the company. Underhills consolidated an unshakeable position across the province, establishing an engineering division in the 1950s to complement its surveying and mapping work, and focusing its energies heavily on emerging technological developments.

Many eyes also turned to the northeast corner of the province as it became increasingly clear that oil discoveries were both likely and imminent. The search for oil had of course been going on for decades, and pressure increased as the use of the automobile became more and

Doug Meredith, 23, at work on the Kitimat–Kemano project, 1952, on the location line survey for a new road above the Alcan floodline, Ootsa Lake. DOUG MEREDITH

more widespread. In British Columbia, the search extended widely. In 1928, for example, Leroy Cokely, BCLS 36, reported in his field notes from the Queen Charlotte Islands, where he had been undertaking timber surveys: "On this lot is a very old graveyard, with the dead buried in trees. From the growth of the trees it would appear that most of the bodies had been there upwards of a hundred years. Right in the midst of this graveyard an oil-well was drilled, although I know of no explanation for the choice of this site. Apparently no oil was found, and the derrick has collapsed."

By 1930, oil had been discovered in the Flathead Valley in Alberta. Gerry Andrews recalled: "The B.C. Oil Co. and Crowsnest Glacier Oil Co. had small crews at the so-called Sage Creek oil wells. Natural oil seepages on Sage Creek were a convincing sales pitch for local oil stocks...the oil was a light viscous amber. Bears were said to immerse themselves in the pools as a repellent for fleas and mosquitoes." Farther to the west, the Peace River region of British Columbia had been under close scrutiny for years. In 1946, the newly appointed commissioner of petroleum and natural gas, Thomas Williams, wrote in his first annual report: "The wealth of the Peace River area has long been recognized." Oil surveys had been conducted as early as 1918. Between 1940 and 1942, drilling operations had taken place in the Pine River Valley but with no conclusive results. All the same, noted Williams: "There are plenty of signs that there will be much petroleum activity in British Columbia during 1947."

Williams was correct, in part because a North American oil shortage had occurred by early 1947. Drilling activity increased; optimism and speculative land trading activity grew; but still no oil was to be found. Then, on October 31, 1951, reported Williams with little emotion, "The Peace River Allied Fort St. John No. 1 well encountered oil and gas." The British Columbia portion of the field was estimated to contain reserves of 1,585 billion cubic feet of gas, the largest to that date in Canada. The rush was on. The Trans-Mountain Oil Pipeline Company was granted rights to construct a pipeline from Edmonton to Vancouver, requiring right-of-way surveys that were the first of their kind in the province. Interest surged in seeing the Pacific Great Eastern Railway line completed from Quesnel to Prince George. The West Coast Transmission Company's gas line from Fort St. John to Vancouver was approved. Arthur "Bert"

Ralfs, BCLS 275, described what happened next for surveyors in a paper prepared for the 1954 BCLS annual general meeting:

> In the spring of 1953 the whole of northeast B.C. was blanketed with oil permits and a few licences issued under the Petroleum and Natural Gas Act...Permits are not intended to be surveyed. When the drilling stage is reached, the areas required are re-issued as licences and these may be surveyed...Even though survey has not been intended for permits, enough inquiries had been received by the Surveyor General which indicated that there could well be some cases where the location on the ground of one or more boundaries of permits would be required...

In other words, with so much at stake, permit holders wanted to be able to protect their turf. It was clear that control surveys of the region were essential and that they needed to be completed as quickly as possible. "It was therefore decided to divert the majority of effort of our topographic division to this project and accordingly Mr. E.R. McMinn was assigned to this task and took to the field in May, 1953," wrote Ralfs. McMinn's advice was that in order to cover the entire area of ten thousand square miles in the all-too-short hundred-day season, triangulation was the only method that would work. Triangulation techniques are tricky, however, in flat, muskeg-covered terrain that is spattered thickly with scrubby black spruce: it is impossible to connect two points from ground level because of the lack of visibility.

The solution, wrote Ralfs, was "the erection of double observing towers, the interior for the instrument base, the unconnected exterior for the observing team...a lot of credit is due to [Mr. McMinn and his team] for their ingenuity and resourcefulness." That was a remarkable understatement. The idea of tower-building was indeed creative; the task itself was challenging in the extreme. "Those Peace River towers were made with kids, Swede saws and spikes," said George Miller, BCLS 383, in 2004. "It was a stupendous enterprise, one of the greatest achievements that B.C. land surveyors ever did." Miller was a student at the time working on the towers, as was a young American named Stirling Knudsen.

Surveying the region north of Fort
St. John with Ernie McMinn, BCLS
325, and Duff Wight, BCLS 327,
in 1955. The Peace River district is
bounded by the Alberta boundary,
the Alaska Highway and the 60th
parallel, and the Nelson River—an
area of some 22,000 square miles.
The government Beaver floatplane
(CF-FHF), pictured here, was flown
by Cliff Matson, BCLS 324, here seen
standing on the float at front while
the plane is being unloaded at Fort
Nelson. STIRLING KNUDSEN

Joe Cully and Bill McKay, survey
party members on the 1955 Peace
River district surveys with Ernie
McMinn. STIRLING KNUDSEN

"Most members of the crews were university students on summer jobs," wrote former helicopter pilot Lock Madill. Madill described the process of tower construction:

> The towers were started by selecting three trees of suitable size about ten or twelve feet apart at the base, limbs were removed as the crew climbed up and spiked diagonal bracing drawing the trees closer together until they ran out of tree and then spike extensions on them until sufficient height was obtained to see over the tops of surrounding trees. [Then] another tower had to be built inside the first one on which the transit instrument was mounted…this was not to disturb the transit while walking around 360 degrees taking the reading on other towers around the horizon.

The towers averaged more than sixty feet in height, and went as high as one hundred and twenty-six feet at platform level, according to Jon Magwood, BCLS 504. Building the towers was hazardous work, but so was using the finished towers. Former surveyor general Don Duffy, BCLS 385, observed in 2003 that some of the towers were built "to extremely scary heights." Duffy worked in the region on oil and gas surveys for exploration companies between 1956 and 1962, and used many of the tower points in establishing well locations. But he was happy never to have to climb one himself. "There was never a serious accident on those towers," said Knudsen, "[although] all we wore was shorts and caulk boots. We climbed around up there like squirrels. It felt like I was flying in the clouds." Despite Knudsen's claim, Magwood recalled that Arthur Bridge, BCLS 386, did fall from a tower, sustaining injuries severe enough to require his evacuation from the camp. In addition, accidents with axes occasionally occurred, and forest fires threatened the towers, especially during the 1955 season. Two towers blew right over in strong winds.

There were unexpected hazards as well as the usual ones. A food drop from a Beaver floatplane went awry, and forty pounds of supplies literally exploded in the branches of a poplar tree near the camp. "Have you ever climbed a tree just to get a lick of crushed pineapple?" asked Knudsen in mournful recollection. And of course, the ubiquitous mosquitoes made their presence felt.

As a teenager Robin Knudsen, like his brother Stirling, crewed on survey teams north of Fort St. John in the summers of 1953 and 1954. It was a life he enjoyed greatly, but it had its dangers. Here Knudsen (who now lives in Alberta) is constructing a triangulation tower, which would be sixty or more feet in height when completed. ROBIN KNUDSEN

A completed triangulation tower in the Peace River country north of Fort St. John. Use of these man-made structures was an innovation that made it possible to survey efficiently in the flat, treed country of the north. Towers like this one could be completed in four or five days. ROBIN KNUDSEN

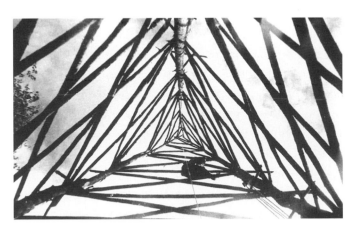

A triangulation tower under construction. Another structure would be built inside the main tower to house the survey instruments. That way, the instrument man could use the outside structure as a platform without disturbing the instrument. ROBIN KNUDSEN

Fort Nelson region, 1955. Ernie McMinn, BCLS 325, posing with instrument (Wilde-T-2) atop a triangulation tower. STIRLING KNUDSEN

"We were plagued by mosquitoes at the base camp," recalled Madill. The solution was simple enough at the time: a Beaver floatplane and a couple of barrels of DDT. "A large refuelling funnel was fastened to the float spreader bar and connected to a bung hole in the barrel which was inside the cabin. With the barrel on its side and a signal from the pilot during a low pass over the camp the other bung was removed to let in the air and a very effective spray spewed out." This was so successful, Madill said, "we could even go around with our shirts off and no mosquito oil or spray required." That perhaps explains another Knudsen anecdote. It was a day off work, and "the weather was really nice, so McMinn decided going nude [at Sandy Lake] was OK. I came in on the chopper with [pilot] Tommy Gurr and there was McMinn, as nude as the log he was sitting on, cooking up a deal with our neighbour, an Indian man camping across the lake." Notwithstanding his state but in complete accordance with his reputation, McMinn remained unflappable and successfully negotiated the trade of a barrel of gas for replacement moccasins for all his crew.

A grid system for locating oil and gas permits and leases was introduced in 1954, making the work of surveyors much simpler in the future. Difficulties remained in dealing with existing permit and licence surveys, many of which conflicted with the new grid system. McMinn and the other surveyors who had worked on the locations to that point had faced problems in determining what reference points to use for drawing the boundaries. Part of the Alberta–British Columbia border had not yet been completed. Despite the fact that the transfer of the railway belt and Peace River block to the province by the dominion government had taken place more than twenty years earlier, many of the survey field notes for the area remained in Ottawa. The Alaska Highway right-of-way survey was of little help: many of the posts were missing or had been moved. Considerable discrepancies, conflicts, and gaps were the confusing result. In the end, after the new grid system was established, it was decided simply to adjust all existing permit boundaries to the nearest grid line and to compensate anyone adversely affected if necessary. "It has presented a major task," wrote Arthur Ralfs in 1956. "But it is felt to be well justified in the promise of easier administration for the government and the oil industry."

In June 1956, Miss Katherine Janet Wilson retired as secretary to the surveyor general after thirty-seven years of working in the lands department, and she died shortly afterwards. She was remembered kindly by Surveyor General Gerry Andrews for her friendliness to members of the land surveying profession. "She will also be remembered by those of the department who served overseas," wrote Andrews, "for her loyal and energetic support in the form of knitted socks and other comforts during the war years." It was an honest and well-intentioned salute to a treasured employee, but the times, all the same, were a-changin'.

The role of women in surveying remained largely one of support

"Cloud Nine" triangulation tower in the Peace River country, 1954. OFFICE OF THE SURVEYOR GENERAL

from the home front, although not exclusively. No women were commissioned as surveyors, or articled to surveyors. Women had been involved in camp work occasionally, and many field parties had benefited over the years from being located near a ranch or town where good, home-cooked food and beer were supplied on demand. But Barry Cotton's wife, Kittie, was the first woman on the official payroll of a field crew. In 1952, she joined her husband as cook and bookkeeper at a camp on Piebiter Creek, near the Bridge River, where Cotton was undertaking mineral claim surveys. Like many other wives then and since, she had assisted her husband in the office and on in-town surveys. But this was her first time in the field:

> The large tent, which my husband and I shared, was also the office, while the two assistants shared another smaller tent. I quite naively said to my husband, "What do I do out here if it rains?" He said, "It never rains up here in June; blue skies and sunshine every day." They left camp early next day. When they returned, there I was completely covered in a hooded parka, with rain and hailstones beating down mercilessly on everything in sight.

Undeterred, Cotton carried on to Kitkatla with her husband later that summer, returning to Vancouver at the end of the season for the birth of their first child.

If that year had been a season of adjustment for Cotton, for the men in the profession, the advent of women into their working lives was, for the most part, welcome. Some discipline in the matter was evidently thought appropriate by Surveyor General Gerry Andrews, however. In 1956 he issued a circular letter regarding government staff on field assignments, remarking on both the hardships and the privileges. With respect to "wives in the field," Andrews, considered that "due to the innumerable variables, no broad ruling can be made on this privilege"—the pun was probably intentional—"beyond warning that generally wives do not fit in with field operations. However, where special circumstances warrant, where not prejudicial to the work or party morale...the presence of wives in the vicinity of the work camp will not be discountenanced."

In 1952, Barry Cotton worked on mineral surveys at Piebiter Creek in the Bridge River country for Mrs. D.C. Noel, a well-known pioneer of the time. H.B. "BARRY" COTTON

Barry Cotton's wife, Kittie, served as party cook on the survey. Cotton thinks Kittie may have been the first woman to serve officially on a survey crew in British Columbia. H.B. "BARRY" COTTON

In 1955 the Corporation of British Columbia Land Surveyors decided to celebrate the fiftieth anniversary of incorporation in a novel fashion: "It was decided, in the face of a very stiff minority opposition, to invite ladies to be present at our annual dinner and to participate in a dance afterwards." Numerous wives accepted the invitation with alacrity and attended the occasion, which by all accounts was a huge success, at the Crystal Ballroom in the Empress Hotel in Victoria. So successful was the affair that the following morning, at the annual general meeting, Gerald Christie, BCLS 175, proposed a motion that "Ladies" be present at all general meetings from then on. Clare Underhill—quite possibly encouraged by his wife, Helen—enthusiastically seconded the motion. One member expressed outrage at the break from tradition and threatened resignation. The meeting minutes record diplomatically: "A discussion followed in which it was suggested that a mixed affair be held every fifty years. Much talk pro and con."

The motion was not carried then, but deferred to the board of directors when considering the next annual meeting; they duly decided to invite women from then on. It was a break from tradition for which the members of the profession, at least in British Columbia, were more than ready. Other changes were also in the air: to tradition, to technology, and to many aspects of the administration and implementation of surveying methods. British Columbian surveyors were ready for those changes, too, but it was with considerable sadness that they watched the past, and the grand traditions associated with a pioneering way of life, slip further and further into history.

Location line survey, Stewart–Cassiar Highway, 1956, showing the line-cutting crew from Telegraph Creek. Doug Meredith recalls the names of Merle Marin and Dennis Dennis, on right. DOUG MEREDITH

A pack train leaving Dease Lake for a reconnaissance survey of the future Stewart–Cassiar Highway, 1955. The building on the right is the old Hudson's Bay Co. post. The road was put in initially for the Cassiar asbestos mine and has since become a scenic route to the north for the hardy traveller. Doug Meredith walked the entire reconnaissance line, accompanied by two First Nations crewmen from Telegraph Creek. He recalled their names as being Jimmy Gleason and Richard Dick-Dick. DOUG MEREDITH

17

The Instrument Was the Heart

Frank Cyril Swannell, PLS 75, at Dease Lake, 1955. The Department of Lands had sponsored a retirement visit for the famous surveyor to one of his old haunts. Swannell instead chose Dease Lake, a spot he had never visited. Doug Meredith was at Dease Lake doing survey work for McElhanney on the future Stewart–Cassiar Highway. DOUG MEREDITH

That surveying was moving through a state of great change is evident throughout the pages of the 1956 annual report of the lands department. While Arthur Swannell's re-survey of the British Columbia–Yukon boundary had used a combination of floatplane and pack horses, "this could well be one of the last sizeable survey operations to use horse transport," wrote Surveyor General Gerry Andrews wistfully. "The surveys and mapping business appears to be entering a period of metamorphosis." At the 1955 BCLS annual general meeting, Andrews mourned: "Much of the rugged romance of wilderness work with slow access to remote areas has gone forever."

He described, with a strong sense of loss overshadowing his words, a general acceptance of progress in surveying and working life in general that had barely been considered three decades previously: aerial photography, optical reading theodolites, the internal combustion engine, the portable radio, and "mechanical computing machines." "The 20-second 70-pound theodolite bristling with micrometer screws has been replaced with the streamlined 1-second optical reading instrument weighing less than 20 pounds in [its] case. The staple menu of beans, bannock, sowbelly and treacle has retired into oblivion before the modern breakfast of grapefruit, milk-sodden cereals, fresh eggs et al. The legendary T&B pipe tobacco in half-pound plugs is beyond the ken of most modern, brown fingered addicts to tailor-mades," he sighed.

But progress is progress. Between 1952 and 1958, the Geological Survey of Canada mapped half as much of Canada as they had in the previous 110 years, all thanks to the use of helicopters. On the ground, bulldozers were in use by grateful survey parties clearing line through heavy underbrush on re-surveys along the British Columbia–Alberta boundary. Conversely, urban and rural surveyors alike were finding that bulldozers were destroying long-standing corner posts and right-of-way markers and cursing the machines roundly as they laboured to relocate and replace the posts and markers. "When I lived in Fort St. John, I used to tell all the cat skinners (bulldozer operators) that if I got lost, all I ever had to do was tie a small piece of flagging on a survey post and it wouldn't take long for one of them to find it and bulldoze it out. I could then get a ride home with them," said surveyor Robert Allen.

Construction in general changed irrevocably, following the Kitimat–Kemano scheme, with a focus on ever bigger infrastructure projects, more and more hydroelectric dams, recreational facilities such as ski resorts, and central urban development. "The day of the simple theodolite, the chain, and pack-horse is over, just as the day of the spade, pick, and wheelbarrow is over for road construction," wrote Gerry Andrews. On August 7, 1954, Englishman Roger Bannister and Australian John Landy both broke the four-minute-mile barrier at Vancouver's brand new 32,000-seat, $1.5 million Empire Stadium, which had been completed for the Empire Games that year in Vancouver. By 1956, that city was enjoying its first modern skyscraper, the Burrard building. In the surveying world, a brand new form of electronic distance-measuring device, or EDM, was perfected that year in South Africa, capable of measuring to within a few inches distances of up to twenty miles. The machine was revolutionary in the extreme: it might save a survey party twenty miles of travelling between two points.

The cost of all this new technology was a major issue, however. The EDM cost $5,000. Airborne profile recorders, capable of measuring elevations for contour mapping at one-hundred-foot intervals, cost more than $20,000. Stereo plotting equipment ran to over $50,000; air survey cameras, $15,000; and electronic computers were simply too expensive for most individuals to consider owning. Those who were using the new machines were taking cards carefully inscribed with data to a co-operative computing centre to be transformed into hole-punched cards, and eventually into printouts from which they could draw up a plan. They would wait for hours—and sometimes days—for the results. The new way wasn't always necessarily the faster way.

Not everything had changed, of course. Plans were still being produced by hand on linen using India ink. Although suggestions were being aired that would permit tracings of standard plan data to be mass-produced using lithographic methods, with the specifics of an individual survey to be entered subsequently by hand on the standard form plan, in 1958 the deputy minister of lands, E.W. Bassett, reported that the blueprint and photostat section "consumed the staggering total of 63½ miles of paper and linen in the production of more than 200,000 prints for use by

Student Peter Leidtke assists Richard "Dick" Wright. Some things haven't changed: "The mosquitoes were bad that day," recalled Wright. RICHARD WRIGHT

A typical survey camp setup at Bear Lake, circa 1966. RICHARD WRIGHT

government departments and the general public." The notion of profes-sional and financial solidarity with fellow members of the Corporation was still as robust as ever, as was taking the self-effacing high ground in matters of finance and competition. The 1955 version of the BCLS code of ethics required members never to gouge extra margins on their fees from clients, use "self-laudatory language" in advertising, or associate with enterprises of "doubtful character." Given that the practice of land surveying was "a learned and arduous profession involving much respon-sibility" and that charging a low rate of pay "invariably caused inferior work," surveyors were also required to conform to a set schedule of mini-mum fees, the daily rate at the time being forty dollars plus expenses.

Life in the field had greater perks in terms of communication and transport, but the hardships of camping far from home for months at a time and in inclement weather and harsh terrain remained the same. Some of the perils were new, as Barry Cotton found in downtown Vancouver when "a drunk walked right through my transit, set up at Hastings and Abbot Street, then disappeared in the traffic before even any sound had any time to emanate from my open, outraged mouth." In 1956, Donald Whyte, BCLS 318, surveyed the Canadian National Rail-ways' right-of-way along the new Trans-Canada Highway near Spences Bridge. "The traffic was quite heavy but generally paid heed to the 'Survey

A government Otter after an engine change at Parker Lake in Fort Nelson, circa 1968. The pilot was Glen Lamont. Floatplanes were an invaluable way to get into remote country, although limited by weather and, occasionally, unsuspected rocks in rivers and lakes. RICHARD WRIGHT

Crew—SLOW' signs. However, for some motorists it would not matter how many signs were put on the road. This was proven when one gentleman ran into a new 'Cooke' 20-second instrument, despite the fact that the tripod was painted red and white like a barber-pole and was set up between SLOW signs. The instrument was a total loss."

Fortunately, no one was injured. The same could not be said of air travel. The hazards of river journeys had been largely replaced by the risks associated with relatively unsophisticated helicopter and airplane equipment. Aircraft routinely came to grief landing or attempting to take off on rivers in which lurking rocks hid just below the surface or where the sun blinded an accelerating pilot. Helicopters were unstable and delicate vehicles. In July 1969, four employees of Vancouver's D.H. Burnett and Associates were killed in a helicopter crash on a survey job in Ontario. The profession came to a shocked standstill as members contemplated the loss of their colleagues, as well as the implications for their own safety.

The *Redcoat* at anchor, June 1960. Gordon McKay Thomson, BCLS 425, mid-deck, second from bow. The *Redcoat* was used extensively by Thomson's survey firm on work along the mainland coast. GORD THOMSON

Overall, however, the new technology on all fronts was seized upon with enthusiasm. According to the Canadian Institute of Geomatics, the first EDM to be used in Canada, in 1952, was the geodimeter. At that stage the instrument, which used light waves for measurement, weighed "hundreds of pounds" and was impractical for any field use other than baseline measurement for triangulation work. The more practical tellurometer, which measured distance by timing the transmission of radio waves, was first used in Canada in 1957 for topographical surveys by the Surveys and Mapping Branch of the Department of Mines and Technical Surveys in Ottawa. Chief topographical engineer S.G. Gamble was unequivocal about the results: "It can be stated, without fear of contradiction, that no single piece of survey equipment has had a greater impact on the Topographical Survey than the tellurometer." Even so, recalled former surveyor general Don Duffy, the instrument was "slow to set up, and with car batteries as a power supply, brutally heavy to carry." Although it was ineffective for the short-distance measurements required for most cadastral surveys, said Duffy, the tellurometer "revolutionized the measurement of long lines in oilfield and right-of-way surveys and in mapping control." Indeed Duffy, according to Charles "Chuck" Salmon, BCLS 535, was the first land surveyor to carry out oil well surveys using EDMs in British Columbia.

Claims are numerous as to who was first to use the EDM in the province—or indeed in Canada—and when. A 1995 biography of George James Smith, BCLS 311, who had been a partner with the McElhanney group, states that in 1955 Smith "was instrumental in purchasing the first EDM unit in the province for use in control surveys." Gerry Andrews claimed that, when in 1957 a tellurometer was acquired for the topographic division of the provincial government, British Columbia became "the first Province in Canada to adopt this revolutionary aid to survey." Andrews may have been distinguishing between provincial and federal government use. John Matthews, BCLS 356, gave credit to another well-known McElhanney surveyor, Frederick Henry Nash, BCLS 281, who "pioneered the use of electronic distance measuring equipment in British Columbia." In a tribute to Earl Little, BCLS 340, Jeffrey Robertson (himself BCLS 699) claimed it was Little's firm—Little, Longstaff & Associates—that was a leader in using the "first EDMs in the 1970's." Robert Allen was working for that firm at the time: "It is true that we were the first to use modern EDM's for oilfield work. They also had a set of tellurometers."

There is no doubt that the provincial government purchased its first EDM in 1957, as chief of the topographic division Alfred Slocomb recorded in the department's annual report that year. Although it arrived too late in the season to be put to any substantial use, some experimentation was done by Albert Wight in the Clinton area. Wight reported: "The shortage of time prevented any appreciable amount of control being completed with this instrument. However, sufficient was accomplished to give an insight into the revolutionary aspects this instrument will have on future mapping control jobs. One small crew in a very short season of good weather could do sufficient work to overtax the present plotting and draughting facilities of the entire Division."

By 1965, the use of both tellurometers and geodimeters was increasingly common. The technology was improving in leaps and bounds. Andrews reported that year that the model 6B geodimeter was capable

Rocky Mountain Trench, 1964. Vertical control station "Tutu." The instrument being used is a tellurometer MA100. This image of Dick Wright was taken by student Peter Liedtke. RICHARD WRIGHT

Topographic survey for provincial mapping purposes north and west of Bear Lake. Rudy Stoessel is using a tellurometer at Station "Klay," 1966. RICHARD WRIGHT

of measuring distances "to within a few millimetres" (one of the first uses of metric terminology in government reporting in the province). By the mid-1960s, the discussion had shifted from an awestruck celebration of the arrival of the new technology to a more practical consideration of its best use: "The geodimeter is ideal for close work in congested urban areas. The tellurometer is still unchallenged for measurement of longer lines." The latter instrument had the same limitations, all the same, that its predecessor the theodolite suffered; due to "uncontrollable factors such as visibility, atmospherics, and the human element (as in adjusting and reading a theodolite micrometer on a frigid wind-blown mountaintop, eyes watering, fingers numb, instrument possibly vibrating, etc.)."

By 1969, Hewlett-Packard had got the weight of its HP 3800A down to thirty pounds, including the power pack. "The introduction of the EDM brought us into the real world," Duffy reminisced in 2005. Use

Mount Selwyn, 1964: topographic survey to establish control for mapping of the Rocky Mountain Trench, prior to completing the construction of the Bennett Dam near Hudson's Hope. This image of Dick Wright was taken by Peter Liedtke, a university student hired for the summer by the Topographic Division of the Surveys and Mapping Branch of the Ministry of Lands and Forests. The instruments used were a Wild T2 theodolite for measuring angles and a M100 Tellurometer for measuring distances. Wright would receive his commission BCLS 467 in 1970.
RICHARD WRIGHT

of the EDM was "the start of a process that would quickly lead to the abandonment of the steel tape as a measurement standard, and to the introduction of competitive instruments," he said. Also in 1969, however, 174 miles of linen and paper were used by the government to produce maps and plans. There was not yet any indication that any other more easily mass-produced medium might be available as an alternative. What was really starting to change life back in the office was the introduction of calculators and computers.

"The computation of traverses was a time-consuming and error-prone task when I entered the first year of the survey technology course at Calgary Tech in 1952," wrote Duffy. Laborious hours were spent turning the pages of books of logarithm tables to resolve field data. Mechanical calculators were available, but it was the Curta field calculator, with its crank handle, that started to make a real difference when it was introduced in 1955. Duffy's Curta cost him $125, the equivalent of one hundred hours' work as a survey technician, "but worth every penny." Ten years later the Olivetti 101 desk calculator took over as the first electronic calculator with trigonometric capability, able to calculate traverses and store coordinates, as well as print the results. "Surveyors," said Duffy, "at last could retire their Chambers trigonometric function tables." Not everyone could afford one immediately: in 1969, when Peter Thomson,

A topographical survey to determine the flood elevation of Williston Lake, which was to be formed by the Bennett Dam near Hudson's Hope. Setting up camp are Dick Wright, with axe, and Peter Liedtke. RICHARD WRIGHT

Helicopter landing at Station "Klay" during the same survey project, 1964. RICHARD WRIGHT

Dick Wright setting up target over control station "Cail," during topographical surveys near Hudson's Hope, 1964. RICHARD WRIGHT

BCLS 472, bought his first calculator, it cost him $650 and "was glued to a counter. That was a month's wages for an eight-function calculator that wouldn't do the square root!"

If calculators were nonetheless a boon, the advantages of computers were embraced with more cautious enthusiasm. In 1957 the use of computers was still a dream, but one that seemed it might become reality in the not too distant future: Gerry Andrews was already "anticipating future use of electronic computing-machines for high-speed processing of...survey control data." The first provincial government IBM 650 computer was installed in December 1960 and Michael Perks, BCLS 338, was assigned to work with it. A mathematical genius as well as a qualified land surveyor, Perks immediately started designing programs for the IBM 650 for such computations as the reduction of distances to sea level and the adjustment of traverses. Perks reported that "card punching and printing results at times become bottle necks and sometimes delays for a day or two have occurred." This didn't matter, said Perks, because the department wasn't doing computations for anyone "who would require results quickly. Most of the work done on the computer has been routine office work not required in a great hurry." Andrews referred to the new government computer semi-affectionately as a "tireless, agile, obedient, and infallible moron."

Within two years a newer model, the IBM 1620, replaced the original. A special program dealing with control survey data, called GROOM (*general reduction of observed material*), was acquired from the Geodetic Survey of Canada, who had developed it in 1961. The GROOM program had its limitations, however, being "somewhat cumbersome, involved, and not very efficient." After analyzing GROOM, Perks developed a companion program, which he promptly dubbed BRIDE: *balanced reduction of interlocking data elements*. The BRIDE program, stated Andrews in his 1964 government report, "appears to reduce machine time by about one-third, a worth-while saving." Carried away by his own wit, Andrews continued: "The combination of BRIDE and GROOM will be prolific of valuable results in the propagation of survey control." By 1965, however, as is the nature of things, while BRIDE was still in active service, GROOM was no longer of any great use.

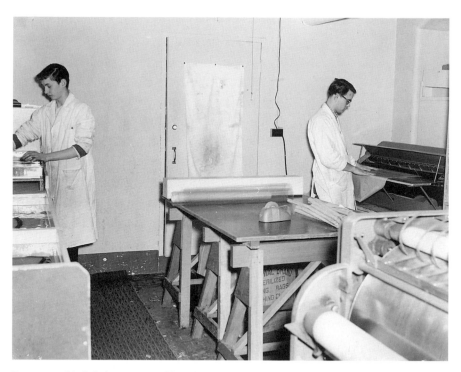

Reprographic lab, basement of legislative buildings, circa early 1960s. OFFICE OF THE
SURVEYOR GENERAL

In 1968, Gerry Andrews retired as surveyor general after seventeen
years in the position, and the annual reports of the surveys and mapping
branch immediately became much shorter and a lot less colourful. By
that time computers in general were still not necessarily regarded as time
savers and were relatively scarce. Arthur Holmes, BCLS 256, presenting
a paper on the use of electronic computers in survey practice at the 1965
annual BCLS meeting, wrote: "The best criterion that I have as to whether
a computation should be done on the electronic computer is, 'Can I get
it to the computer and back by the time that I need it?' Unfortunately
quite a lot of the surveyor's work does not stand up to this question."
Few private businesses had their own computers, but Gordon Thomson recalled in 2005 that in private practice during the 1960s "we did
have some electronic computer ability, although I did not run the system.
Burnetts had purchased a used Royal McBee LGP-30 computer and had
trained an operator. The machinery and its readers, typing system, and

the box, a container of tubes, took up a wall of a small office and required at least a half hour to warm up."

By the mid-1970s, computers in one form or another had more or less become an accepted part of daily life in the surveying profession. In 1974, Surveyor General Arthur "Bert" Ralfs reported that "recent decreases in cost and increases in versatility have also led to the increased use of hand and desk-top calculators which now, particularly in the area of legal surveys, are able to provide on-the-spot solutions to most of the survey-ors' problems." The members of the BCLS were seriously concerned with the ethics of students using calculators in examinations, especially since some students could not afford them. Many hours of debate over several annual general meetings swayed back and forth in favour of requiring traditional methods of calculation versus accepting the inevitability of electronic assistance. The latter would ultimately prevail from necessity, as it became increasingly difficult to conform to technical, administrative, and regulatory requirements without using a computer. The electronic processing and storage of data, if still unsophisticated, was considered the standard way of the future; even more so was the use of EDMs, which were almost universally employed by that point. A provincial standard calibration base for EDMs was installed in 1975 on the highway leading north out of Victoria. That same year, the lands department reported that "in preparation for metrication, two 75 metre tape calibration bases were established—in the City of Kelowna and in Penticton."

The change in Canada in the 1970s to a broad use of the metric system of measurement naturally had significant consequences for people whose business was the measurement of the surface of the earth. A metric system was nothing new, in fact: its use in Canada had been permitted by dominion law since 1871 and statutory standards under the 1951 Weights and Measures Act converted yards to metres and pounds to kilograms. But in 1971 the federal government upped the ante by establishing a formal metric commission with a view to rolling out metric conversion across the board. Everything from product labelling to weather forecasts to vehicle speedometers was considered and, within the space of a decade, these areas changed over to metric equivalents. Some standard changes were compulsory; others, such as the standards for house measurements,

Robert Allen on the
survey of the Beaver River
pipeline right-of-way
north of Fort Nelson,
circa 1972. Allen received
his commission BCLS 487
that year. ROBERT ALLEN

were voluntary. Confusion reigned in many minds, most famously in that
of the commercial pilot on a flight from Ottawa to Edmonton in July 1983
. He calculated his fuel in pounds instead of kilograms and ran out of fuel
just past the Ontario–Manitoba border. The pilot managed to glide to a
safe landing near the tiny village of Gimli, Manitoba, and the simple but
fundamental error made national headlines.

Surveyors in British Columbia had seen the conversion coming for
some time. As early as 1959 they had been instructed by the surveyor
general to adapt measurements in feet and decimals rather than the
outdated chains and links, and at the 1966 annual general meeting of the
Corporation Jorgen Embreus, BCLS 398, discussing chains as a unit of
measurement, stated: "If a second unit of measurement is required then
let us slowly break into the metre unit as it will probably be the accepted
practice in the future." Following the establishment of the federal metric
commission, a provincial government metric system conversion committee was established to liaise with it, and Bert Ralfs was appointed as a
member. Ralfs's view was that "surveys and mapping is an area in which
metric conversion presents relatively few problems and may therefore be
expected to be among the first to make the change."

It took almost another six years, however, before the transition would
even start in the province, at least as far as surveyors were concerned. On
May 21, 1976, Surveyor General Bill Taylor sent out a circular letter to all
surveyors advising them that January 1, 1977, had been set as the target
date for a changeover in land measurement. The conversion would not

be exact: it was thought better to adopt near-equivalent metric measurements in whole units for long-term ease of reference. A three-foot post would become a one-metre post, for example; road allowances would change from sixty-six feet to twenty metres even. While there was no intention to re-survey existing lots, the coordination implications between those lots and ones measured in metric were also immense. "One can foresee that a tremendous amount of work must be done for everything to be timed perfectly and it is beyond comprehension to believe that someone will not fall behind," Taylor wrote in his notice. He advocated a generous transition period: "The various units of chains, feet and metres will be with us for generations so there is little point in insisting on a hard and fast date for change."

Nonetheless, the target date was nearly met: the Land Act amendment bringing in the new standard metric measurements came into force on January 3, 1977. The provincial Metric Conversion Act would take a little longer; it was passed on August 31 that year. The debate on the draft bill in the legislature revealed little opposition to the change. Education Minister Patrick McGeer, who was sponsoring the bill, introduced it with his tongue firmly in his cheek, reviling the "gloriously illogical mingle mangle" of the old measurement system: "The mile originally was a thousand double steps by the legionary until good Queen Bess added 280 feet so that it would be eight furrows long, or eight furlongs. We have all kinds of other measures we use which are similarly logical: the barrel, which is anywhere from 31 to 42 gallons, quarts, pints, ounces, fifths and mickeys, hands, cords, drams, pecks, carats, grains, points, firkins, hogsheads, cubits, lengths and chains." McGeer pointed out that the Canadian construction industry was to go metric on January 1, 1978, and that four sample metric construction projects were underway in British Columbia. The speed limit had already been converted to one hundred kilometres per hour on the highway. The opposition poked equally light-hearted fun at the bill, protesting the impact on "six furlong" horse racing and, more seriously, demanding assurance that no taxation consequences would occur. Despite these reservations, the bill passed with ease.

Less comfort was associated with the way in which surveyors

responded to the call for change. In June 1977, Bill Taylor complained about the lack of enthusiasm greeting the changes. Only five surveyors out of about 250 had lodged any plan using metric measurements since the beginning of the year. On the most recent BCLS examination, "one lad gave the diameter of his bearing trees as 4, 5 and 6 centimetres—smaller than a ball bat! He either has no conception of equivalents or something has happened to the trees in British Columbia! How many surveyors are in the same position as this student?" cried Taylor. "I urge you," he wrote to his colleagues in the profession and taking on a more serious tone, "to support this form and have a good metric year."

The surveys and mapping branch of the provincial government had been working for some time on another initiative aimed at improving efficiency and the coordination of measurement in land surveys—the concept of integrated survey areas, or ISAs. The notion of a system of province-wide, accessible, and accurate reference points by which all surveys could be connected had been touted for years, and since at least as early as 1940. ISAs were to have survey control monuments established at key locations, each visible to two other control monuments. Any surveys to be undertaken in the ISA would have to be referenced to at least two such control monuments. In 1962, Gerry Andrews enthusiastically advocated adopting the new system: "Both relocation and restoration of lost points, as well as detection and equitable reconciliation of errors accruing from the past, right back to the earliest colonial times, [can] be effected with confidence, simplicity, accuracy, and economy. This ideal conception is the real solution to the problem of lost monuments and contentious confusion arising from survey anomalies of the past." At that stage, in an attempt for consistency, most surveyors were tying in their surveys to what was known as the geodetic North American Datum of 1927, or the NAD27, a series of control points or coordinates for the United States using Meades Ranch in Kansas as its starting point.

In 1962, the British Columbia minister of lands authorized a trial ISA project to begin. An ad hoc integrated system already existed in northeastern British Columbia, as a result of the coordinated location of well sites and leases which had then been used for mapping control. The field

The unveiling of the centennial monument on June 21, 1967, at the new provincial museum in Victoria, with Attorney General Robert Bonner speaking, Surveyor General Gerry Andrews seated at left. OFFICE OF THE SURVEYOR GENERAL

trial, which took place in the lower Fraser Valley, was to be entirely dedicated to the establishment of the first ISA. The objective was to "establish an array of survey control monuments accurately coordinated on the NAD27 of sufficient density for public authorities such as cities, municipalities, harbour and power commission, boards, federal and provincial agencies, private surveyors and engineers, to integrate all surveys…on the same universal co-ordinate datum." The Official Surveys Act was duly amended in 1964, using the District of Surrey as a guinea pig for the establishment of the first ISA, which took place in July 1967. Thereafter, all new legal surveys in that ISA had to be coordinated to the control monuments in that area. Integrated Survey Area No. 2 was gazetted at Dawson Creek on May 9, 1968. Eventually, fifty-one ISAs would be scattered over the province in a comprehensive network of control. From what Kenneth Bridge, BCLS 350, called a "faltering start" in 1964, the outcome was all that had been hoped for.

Land surveyors in British Columbia also had much to occupy their minds regarding various administrative and professional matters, ranging from the peripheral to the serious. In 1963 the members of the Corporation firmly resolved that land surveyors' names should be printed in the yellow pages of the telephone directory only in small print. The Land Act was amended in 1970, removing rights of pre-emption and along with them a certain amount of surveying work. Work was also declining in the Peace River region as oil exploration slackened off in the early 1970s. On the other hand, the Air Space Titles Act of 1971 provided for new forms of title in airspace predicated on surface cadastral surveys. The surveying and development of airspace became another source of work for surveyors. The mapping of northern British Columbia had also begun the year before, requiring considerable resources to be applied over a period of five years.

In 1974, the issue of competition with engineers briefly raised its head once more, and as rapidly it vanished again. An equally brief discussion on breach of process and whether a new election would be required ensued when it was discovered that the presidential spats would not fit the oversized feet of the incoming president, Don Duffy. The question of the ability to incorporate in private practice and the tax implications was under discussion by 1976. The same year, a revolution took place in plan draughting. Ernie McMinn, by then director of the surveys and mapping branch housed within the Ministry of the Environment, reported that "the opportunity was seized to introduce long-anticipated basic changes, such as the allowance of a Mylar film material for the original drawing as an alternative to the tried and true Imperial linen." No longer would the annual government reports contain a faithful recital of how many hundreds of miles of linen had been used that year.

Educational requirements for surveyors were an increasingly press-

A former survey control tower in northeastern British Columbia, north of Fort St. John, circa 1969. ROBERT ALLEN

A survey control tower, no longer in use but still standing, circa 1971. ROBERT ALLEN

ing concern as the years progressed. While many surveyors of the past had worked their way into a commission with only a secondary school education, increasingly students were seeking university qualifications in order to keep up with technological and scientific advances. By 1963 the Corporation membership had already begun turning their minds to the need to influence, if not control, the establishment of a degree program in surveying and preferably one that could be undertaken in British Columbia. Whether that was to be located at the British Columbia Institute of Technology (BCIT) in Burnaby, near Vancouver, Simon Fraser University, or the University of British Columbia was uncertain.

There were two schools of thought on the necessity for university standard qualifications. A traditional group prioritized the ability to work hard, technical ability, professionalism, field experience, and common sense over academic qualifications. Ernie McMinn urged his colleagues not to be obsessive. Doug Roy was not opposed to a college education: he had one himself. "It's not necessarily a bad thing," said Roy, "but I am opposed to the idea that we should eliminate the other route to a status as

A survey control tower north of Fort St. John, circa 1968. ROBERT ALLEN

a land surveyor...it takes a lot of courage, a lot of conviction, and one hell of a lot of determination to pass those examinations without going the university route." Others felt that for the profession to maintain its standing in public, members needed the credibility of academic qualifications. John "Jack" Anderson, BCLS 389, thought that the then-current two-year BCIT diploma would not suffice: "As far as maintaining our position, our status in society...we have to have a degree after our name." In 1972 outgoing Corporation president William "Bill" Robinson, BCLS 328, decried the fact that the error rate in BCLS examinations was accepted to be as high as 30 percent: "The moment we obtain our commissions we must always be 100% correct—not 70%—not 99%—but 100% correct....Gentlemen," he continued, "our future depends on ourselves." By 1973 the Corporation had resolved to pursue the establishment of a degree program "with all vigour." A committee was formed to work on an appropriate syllabus, and both Simon Fraser University and BCIT were under consideration. By 1978, however, discussions were in limbo, with an apparent impasse as to how to solve administrative difficulties in coordinating the degree courses. For the time being, those who wished to pursue a degree would have to attend the University of Calgary in Alberta.

In 1977, Cornelis "Case" Wagenaar, BCLS 416, proposed to his colleagues that a magazine be established, as a means of communications between members and to host book reviews, equipment appraisals, and other such matters. Most important, emphasized Wagenaar, was that the new magazine have editorial independence from the management of the Corporation. The idea was well received. Bryan Berting, BCLS 349, hoped there would be "a few good jokes in there." The scheme was endorsed by the members, provided that Wagenaar put his money where his mouth was and volunteer as editor. "I'm willing to give it a try," he replied gamely. The first issue of the as yet unnamed magazine appeared in June 1977, announcing a "name the magazine" and logo design contest. The prize: a lifetime subscription and a bottle of a beverage of the winner's choice. The winner was Alexander "Sandy" Watts, BCLS 497, an accomplished artist who came up with the name *The Link* and a design that incorporated the BCLS seal hanging from a chain. Rye whisky was his choice of beverage, but Ernie McMinn had the last laugh on the younger man in presenting him the bottle: he pulled out three glasses, one each for himself, Watts, and Corporation president John Matthews, and proposed a toast to the newly named magazine.

Various reports and articles on subjects such as metric conversion were included in the new magazine, as was a section entitled "Women's Page (?)." The very first column, written by Nerine Berting, was addressed "to all wives and girl-friends of surveyors." It too offered a prize: for the best bannock recipe to be submitted before the next issue. Berting also invited suggestions on a better name for the column than "Women's Page" (hence the "?" in the title). Even in 1977, it was generally accepted that the role of women as regards surveyors was to marry them. Women like Kittie Cotton had taken brief forays into the world of field work, and certainly many women had taken on similar support roles for decades, often as clerical staff in both private and government offices and assisting their spouses on close-to-home surveys which didn't require the difficulty of travel and overnight accommodation. But more or less, in terms of having a professional role as a surveyor, that barely seemed conceivable even in the 1970s. Despite the burgeoning women's liberation movement of the 1960s, the general assumption prevailed that men were surveyors and women were their wives. In 1966 Gerry Andrews, reporting on a conference, wrote: "In the daytime, while the men were engrossed in official business, the ladies were agreeably occupied with teas and tours." It was not an unusual perception for the time or circumstances. In 1973, Donna Goudal was named "Survey Queen" at the annual conference of the Canadian Institute of Surveying in Ottawa. It was a source of great pride for the British Columbia delegation: "This makes her the first Survey Queen from Western Canada." Once again, "the ladies were kept busy with a variety of tours and luncheons."

Nonetheless, women were starting to make themselves known in the halls of surveying offices, despite the challenge of having to fight perceptions that were steeped in decades, if not centuries, of tradition. Heather West started work draughting in the government legal surveys division in 1970, using linen and pens that had to be dipped into inkwells. "When I was interviewed for the position," she recalled thirty-five years later, "the prospect of bringing a woman into the office was not viewed very favourably. In fact I was told that they did not hire women." West was also told not to expect to pass her promotional exams on the first try. "That was enough incentive for me to prove the boss wrong." West succeeded on both counts.

In 1973 Lynda Longair signed on to article with David Burnett, but dropped out of sight before completing her articles. An obituary of William Kerr, BCLS 442, boasts that Kerr was "very proud of the fact that in the early '70s, he was one of the first to have an all female crew." Nonetheless, at the 1979 annual general meeting of the Corporation, held in Prince George, Keith Errington, BCLS 498, remarked: "We're getting a fair amount of young women in the survey technology at BCIT who, when they're looking for summer work and for permanent employment on graduation, are being told things such as—I don't hire women, things like that, which I believe is illegal." Errington suggested ensuring that all members be reminded of that fact. Adam Burhoe protested that the Corporation itself "was not against a female serving articles," but another member reminded his colleagues that a BCLS had recently been charged with refusing employment to a woman. "The important thing, I think," said the member, "regardless of how you feel about it, don't deny her a job for that particular reason." In the meantime, no name had been found for the "Women's Page" by the second issue of *The Link* in September 1977, and only one bannock recipe had been submitted. "Men were still doing most of the survey camp cooking, even in those days," remarked Robert Allen. "Perhaps if they had asked men for a bannock recipe, they might have received more." The prize was held over in the hope of further contributions. Not until March 1979 would the page rejoice in a new name: "Ladies Link."

Some things never change for surveyors in British Columbia: their prosperity, for instance, depends on the economic fortunes of the province at any given time. When times are busy, surveyors worry about things such as whether sufficient numbers of new surveyors are coming up the ranks, and how to get paid more for the work they do. When times are lean, they concern themselves with how to improve public understanding of the work that land surveyors do, how to guard their turf against infiltrators such as engineers and the like, and how to get paid more for the work they do. And, when in doubt, they form a committee; by 1979, the Corporation had no less than thirty-seven committees.

Another reliable constant during the latter half of the twentieth century was government restructuring. In the 1960s and 1970s, restructuring took place again and again. In 1978, reminisced Heather West, "I was tempted to answer the telephone as 'Lands, Parks, and Housing, and Anything Else That Is Left Over!'" Governments themselves, of course, also changed. In 1952, W.A.C. Bennett took over as premier of the province, with a Social Credit government, and held his seat for an unprecedented twenty years. Dave Barrett's NDP government took power in 1972, to be replaced after only three years by Bennett's son Bill. But political imperatives changed little, despite the changes in administration.

All three governments pushed for improved economic performance, efficient land use planning, and better mapping and registration systems. All aspects of surveying had become more and more complex, with more sophisticated field technology married to administrative systems that required an in-depth knowledge of dozens of statutes and regulations, the application of hundreds of court case decisions, and increasing familiarity with electronic methods of drawing and disseminating plans and maps. On top of everything else, the rapidly expanding base of scientific knowledge was adding information that required surveyors to think differently and to adjust their entire approach to measurement. In the late 1960s, for example, geoscientists accepted the concepts of plate tectonics and continental drift, which affected existing perceptions regarding the stability of land and its location.

As the 1970s drew to a close, it seemed hard to imagine that things could become more complex, either on the technological front or in terms of British Columbia's political direction. But both continued to evolve, and they did so with direct implications for the surveying fraternity in the province.

A topographic control survey with the first camp set up at Kluskus Lake, near the Nazko Indian Reserve, 1963. An audience had gathered to see the helicopter, still not a very common sight at that time. RICHARD WRIGHT

18

God Gave Us a Good Survey

A typical mining camp "tent" adorned with caribou antlers picked up on the mountainside east of Dease Lake, circa 1980. ROBERT ALLEN

Outgoing Corporation president John Matthews told his fellow members in 1978: "Society is changing. We must change to keep pace."

Matthews was referring to the electronic route on which surveyors as a profession were well and truly embarked, even if they had not all yet found their sea legs. After hearing a presentation on the operation of a new surveying tool called an "inertial survey system"—which included not only a measuring unit but two gyroscopes, a computer, a cassette recorder, a power system, and a display and command unit—Rodney Power, BCLS 478, asked plaintively: "Is this thing ever going to come down to where you can carry it in a backpack?" But social changes were also occurring in other fundamental ways that, especially in British Columbia, were integrally linked to the work of surveyors—even if at the beginning they were for the most part unaware of that fact.

The lengthy 1975 report of the provincial lands service states tersely on page 41: "Increased activity in the Indian land question and cut-off land disposition generated considerable map-making, and description." Behind that simple sentence lay a history of tension between aboriginal people and government that had been accumulating over the previous hundred years, to the point where it had finally spilled over into action. First Nations around British Columbia had been slowly gathering strength in the battle to reclaim lost lands; assisted by a belated recognition on the part of both government and the courts of their rights not only as Canadian citizens, but as aboriginal people of Canada.

In 1949 British Columbia had enfranchised aboriginal, Mennonite, and Japanese Canadians in provincial elections, and Frank Calder, from the Nisga'a community in the Nass Valley, was almost immediately afterward elected to the provincial legislature. Two years later, the bar to pursuing land claims was removed from the federal Indian Act. By 1955, the Nisga'a had put together a tribal council with the specific goal of dealing with the land issue, and 1960 saw two extraordinary federal initiatives—extraordinary, that is, in the sense that they took so long. On March 10 of that year, status Indian people under the Indian Act received the right to vote in federal elections alongside their fellow Canadian citizens. Five months later, the Canadian Bill of Rights affirmed the right to equality before the law for all Canadians—including aboriginal people.

Len Marchand, a member of the Okanagan Indian band from central British Columbia, made history in 1976 when he became the first federal aboriginal Canadian cabinet minister, in Pierre Trudeau's Liberal government. Both Trudeau and Marchand agreed that the appointment was based on merit rather than symbolism. It nonetheless represented an accord of political thought that had not existed seven years previously, when Trudeau's government had issued a White Paper disclaiming the existence of aboriginal rights and title to traditional lands. In 1968, the same year Marchand was first elected, the Nisga'a had finally taken their land claims to court in Frank Calder's name; the White Paper had been produced shortly afterwards. But in 1973, the decision of the Supreme Court of Canada in the Calder case established unequivocally for the first time that aboriginal title to land exists in Canada.

It was an overwhelming victory in the push to engage government in the issue, notwithstanding that the court did not rule on the specific existence of title on Nisga'a lands. By 1975, the federal government had embarked on a comprehensive claims process with the goal of dealing with "the Indian land question" at last, and discussions commenced with the Nisga'a in 1976. By 1982, aboriginal rights in Canada were entrenched in the constitution. Court case followed upon court case, refining and strengthening aboriginal rights and title to land. In a province such as British Columbia, where very few treaties had been concluded, the scope for litigation on land claims was massive. By 1992 the provincial government recognized the inevitable and agreed to participate in a process of land claims negotiations with First Nations alongside the federal government. A modern treaty-making process was under way. Within a year, British Columbia land surveyors were discussing how their services could best be used by government to support the process, and a committee was formed to monitor aboriginal land issues.

As the 1975 provincial lands report had indicated, this was not the first time that the question of title to lands had arisen within the provincial government. "Cut-off" claims, which dealt with portions of Indian reserves that had been unfairly removed in the early part of the twentieth century, and disputes over reserve boundaries required the services of surveyors in two respects: in the field location of legal property boundaries, and research. Much of the historic information required to establish what had occurred decades earlier was contained in correspondence and field notes of the land surveyors given the task of laying out reserves in the latter half of the nineteenth century. Mapping of the claims was also a critical requirement; hence the reported level of "increased activity."

However, as is typical of governments, while one hand was giving the other was taking away. By 1982, British Columbia had launched a massive campaign to market and sell interests in Crown lands to meet the growing demand for forestry and mining initiatives, farming, parklands, and recreational uses, especially ski resorts. The deputy minister of lands, John Johnston, remarked on the need to make difficult land use decisions to balance competing demands: "Consideration of recreational, environmental, agricultural, forestry, and mining priorities produced a complex and competitive situation with innumerable interests in direct opposition." Johnston made no mention of where native land claims fit into that equation.

This did not mean that no progress was being made on settling some outstanding issues. Settlements on reserve cut-off claims were reached that year with several Indian bands, with more following over subsequent years. In 1987 the lands branch reported that "research and documentation was provided on native land claims in support of provincial and federal negotiations." In 1988, the surveyor general's branch spent more than 1500 hours of research time on "matters relating to aboriginal rights and title." But no Crown land was being held against future possible land claims based on aboriginal title.

This more or less remained the status quo until after 1992; if anything, the provincial government simply became more aggressive in its campaign to dispose of Crown lands as a major source of revenue. In August 1995, this situation contributed to an infamous standoff at Gustafsen Lake in the interior of the province. A dispute arose between a cattle rancher leasing Crown lands adjacent to his property for grazing, and members of the Secwepemc Nation endeavouring to hold Sundance ceremonies at a sacred site on the same lands. The Secwepemc occupied the site; dozens of police officers were deployed to end the occupation, using firearms and land mines, and an ugly standoff ensued. After the occupation ended a few weeks later, several people were charged with mischief and trespass. Nigel Hemingway, BCLS 671, was employed to survey and map the standoff area for the purposes of the forthcoming court case. "When the trial started I was called as an expert witness to give evidence as to the exact locations of the private and Crown land properties," recalled Hemingway ten years later. "This involved re-establishing early-1900 surveys based on evidence located on the ground." The survey evidence, however, did nothing to help the Secwepemc in their quest for the return of their sacred land.

But at much the same time, farther to the west in the Nass Valley, government negotiators were about to reach a preliminary deal on the Nisga'a land claims, nearly a century after the Nisga'a people had first started to protest the loss of their lands. As part of the agreement in principle that would be signed in 1996, negotiators were starting to hammer out the process for surveying the boundaries of the new Nisga'a lands. Like the Gustafsen Lake survey, part of the job would require the re-establishment of long-lost corner posts on the old Indian reserves. But these surveys, supporting the first contemporary treaty to be signed in British Columbia, would also pose a complexity and challenges unlike any previously considered in the province.

The size and location of the area alone required careful consideration: more than two thousand square kilometres of land was involved, for the most part in remote and rugged terrain. Decades of distrust lent the Nisga'a negotiators a strong sense of caution in agreeing to detailed technical matters concerning the location of their borders. The province, which would be paying for the surveys, wanted to keep costs down by maximizing the use of satellite technology and minimizing on-the-ground work. The Nisga'a, keen not only to ensure that their boundaries would be properly surveyed but also to take advantage of any employment opportunities that might ensue from the work, were determined that extensive line-cutting, or clearing of brush, would take place along the boundaries, necessitating considerable expense. (In the end a combination of both techniques was used.) The surveyor general of British Columbia was guiding the government negotiators; the Nisga'a promptly hired former surveyor general Patrick Ringwood, BCLS 491, to help protect their interests.

The final treaty agreement between the Nisga'a, Canada, and British Columbia was signed in December 1999. On October 11, 2000, the *Terrace Standard* newspaper reported: "Surveyors have had a busy summer taking measurements in the Nass Valley." This was a historic step, the newspaper pronounced: "The very first surveyors who tried to enter the valley in 1887 were turned away by the Nisga'a, who then embarked on protests to Victoria, demanding a settlement of the land question." This time, surveyors were welcomed into the valley; and this time, although still employed by the government, they were working for aboriginal people, not against them. David Bazett, BCLS 576, was one of the surveyors who spent two years under contract working on the Nisga'a surveys. "It was a long time coming," said Bazett in 2005. "I was up there at the start of it, looking for evidence of some of the early surveys."

From a surveying perspective the job had unique aspects, apart from the size and location of the area under scrutiny. When the survey crews found discrepancies between the negotiated agreement and what existed on the ground, they could not simply use their best judgment to deal with the error: those discrepancies had to go back to the parties for the negotiation of a solution. A new bronze cap was designed to be used for the boundary monuments, incorporating both the traditional provincial government crown and the Nisga'a Lisims government logo. "Those bronze caps were pretty popular as paperweights," said Bazett ruefully. "They had to make new ones eventually that couldn't be so easily cut off the monuments."

To mark an official beginning to the surveys in 2000, a ceremony was held at the site of one of the original corner posts on what was soon to become a former Indian reserve. "The post had to be removed and a new one set in," recalled Bazett. "So we had asked the Nisga'a if they wanted to mark the event some way, perhaps to elevate the awareness generally in the community about the surveys taking place. But it became much more than that. It became a very big deal." For the Nisga'a, replacing that old post had a significance going far beyond the insertion of a new bronze monument in the ground with their government logo on it. "That old

The ceremony marking the placing of the first survey post on Nisga'a territory, October 12, 2000. Pictured are (on left) Sim'oogit Minee'eskw (Rod Robinson) of the Nisga'a Lisims government; and on right, Sim'oogit Baxk'ap (Jacob Nyce). DAVID BAZETT

Setting the first survey post on Nisga'a territory, near New Aiyansh, October 12, 2000. Pictured is Herbert Morven, chairperson of the Nisga'a Lisims government in 2000. DAVID BAZETT

The survey crew at the Nisga'a ceremony marking the placing of the first survey post on Nisga'a territory, October 12, 2000. Pictured are (left to right): (back row) Myrna Wright, Vern Evans; (front row) Medrick Azak, Ken Azak, Bruce Azak. DAVID BAZETT

post represented the Indian Act, it represented control and domination; it was a symbol of the old ways. So the Nisga'a really took ownership of the new monument. It was their symbol of the future." The elders blessed the new post; each of the hereditary chiefs present "took a turn to pound it in." For the Nisga'a, a new day had begun.

The year 2000 was also a good year for workers in the oil patch of northeastern British Columbia. From Fort St. John, Wayne Brown, BCLS 758, reported in *The Link* in July that year: "Everybody up this way is forecasting a busy summer and a hold onto your pants kind of winter." Land surveyors were flocking to the northern city to take advantage of the work opportunities, notwithstanding the rigours of working the oil patch in the depths of northern winters—an easier time to get around on the frozen ground than in summer, when the muskeg softens and the mosquitoes zero in. "Being in the field, in the oil patch, is unlike any other kind of surveying, I think," said Brown. Brown, who had received

Dave Bazett operating a WM 101 GPS receiver during a control survey in northwestern British Columbia, July 1987. DAVID BAZETT

his commission in 1996, loved the excitement: "The camaraderie of [being] in the patch with several other crews, helping each other with the inevitable logistical, technical, and mechanical difficulties that always appear...each day is never like the last." Comparing the detailed survey work required in engineering projects, Brown also observed: "The actual amount of surveying done in most oil patch jobs is minimal. You tend to spend most of your day in just trying to find a way into your job site, and locating control in a new area can always be an exciting, time-consuming task. After that everything just seems to fall into place and it's just a matter of surveying your well site, pipeline or whatever."

Things hadn't been so rosy in the oil patch in the early 1980s, when it sank into a major "bust" cycle as the province struggled through yet

Allan Hardie, BCLS 475, left, and Peter Thomson, BCLS 472, at the base station for the survey of Nisga'a lands, near New Aiyansh, October 2000. DAVID BAZETT

Dave Bazett observing control, using a Wild T2 theodolite and D13000 EDM, near Squamish, December 1994. DAVID BAZETT

another recession. Earl Little and Kenneth Longstaff, BCLS 410, who had formed a partnership in Fort St. John in 1965, found themselves forced to dissolve it in 1983 as work slackened so much that it was no longer sustainable. The recession was hitting hard everywhere: Gordon "Bert" Hol, BCLS 646, found himself repeatedly laid off as he searched for and found odd jobs ranging from house building in the southern Gulf Islands to the survey of the new SkyTrain line in Vancouver. Hol was still undertaking his articles, a significant challenge when there was "so little development work at the time." He should have been able to write his final exams in April 1983, but it took another whole year to meet the field work requirements. Still unable to find a surveying job anywhere, he—like many of his colleagues—borrowed money and hung out his own shingle, working out of his house for the next few years. "During those early years," said Hol, "I worked in the field with my wife during the day—often dragging our infant son along—and calculated and draughted at night."

Things would eventually improve for surveyors like Hol. By the 1990s he was employing several other surveyors as development in southern British Columbia eventually took off once again, spurred on by the election of a business-oriented Liberal government in 2001. By 2004, Hol had merged his partnership into the McElhanney Group.

In 1986, the director general of the federal government's surveys and mapping branch, Ray Moore, addressed the BCLS annual general meeting. Moore reminisced about being part of the "fortunate generation"—those who had had a hand in starting the mapping of much of British Columbia. "We started with a blank sheet of paper, and the challenge was there, with the minimum resources we had, to do something about it." Given the amount of information that was available by the mid-1980s, thanks largely to the massive leaps forward in technological capability that had taken place in the last two or three decades, said Moore, "we're going to get out of the data gathering business and start to manage the data we now have." The surveyor general of British Columbia, Don Duffy, concurred on the need for effective data management. "We've seen in about 30 years more change, I would suggest, in technology than were seen in the previous three thousand years in our

Robert Allen, BCLS 487, on a mineral claim survey east of Dease Lake, 1980. ROBERT
ALLEN

profession." If that much change was possible, Duffy speculated, what
was achievable in the next thirty years?

Global positioning system (GPS), the use of satellite technology to
accurately identify the coordinates of any location on earth to within
ten centimetres, had been developed first by the U.S. Department of
Defence and launched in 1978. GPS was made available by the Americans for general use free of charge, and it had been used for the first time
in surveying applications in 1985. The same year, the Geodetic Survey of
Canada phased out field astronomy completely in favour of GPS. Within
a few years, GPS would be so broadly applied that even heavy equipment operators on construction sites would be using it to shift earth,
rather than looking for the surveyor's wooden stakes. But such breadth
of utility was still almost inconceivable in 1986. "We're trying to develop
systems that will work," noted Duffy with a tinge of wonder, "without
really knowing what technological changes we're going to see in the next
few years."

The objective of effective data management was simple: arrange and manage all the information that had been gathered by surveyors over the years, and which was continually being updated and augmented with the help of new technology such as GPS, so as to make it as accessible to the general public as possible and in any form required. Both businesses and individuals needed detailed legal information about land delivered quickly and efficiently. Maps, plans, and geographic information about flood plains, parks, Indian reserves, new subdivisions, condominiums and ski hills, provincial and international boundaries—if it was there, the correct data should be readily available, ideally in an electronic format accessible through a computer as well as in paper form. But by 1986 technology had not yet caught up with ambition. "We can now communicate between computers by carrying tapes and that sort of thing from building to building," said Duffy. "But," he continued hopefully, "we do anticipate that the information systems [of government] will be integrated. We are making great strides, I think."

While things might have been slow initially, the digital age started to move more and more rapidly as the 1980s progressed. The automation of Crown land information was well under way by 1983, with a significant amount of data already stored on computer files. There was still no easy way, however, to transmit that information around the province. Then, in 1985, the Ministry of Lands reported:

> A computerized Land Inventory System (LIS) which records all available titled and appraised Crown land parcels, as well as lands with development potential, was introduced as a way to improve Crown land marketing. A Crown land marketing catalogue, to be published semi-annually, will provide the real estate industry and the general public with descriptions and process of Crown land parcels.

The push for systems management in the 1980s also brought with it an unfortunate proliferation of acronyms that gave the original BRIDE and GROOM computer programs an aura of old-fashioned sentimentality, and those charming acronyms would be recalled somewhat wistfully for the ease with which the programs they stood for could be remembered. In 1986 the government launched TRIM. The goal of the *terrain resource information management* program was to digitally map all of British Columbia at a scale of 1:20,000, a very high level of accuracy. The TRIM program would be completed by 1996 and would include more than seven thousand map sheets.

TRIM utilized the universal transverse mercator (UTM) coordinate system, based on the 1983 North American Datum (NAD83). The NAD83 had been adopted in British Columbia in 1990 to replace the outdated NAD27, and was implemented from 1990 to 1992. By 1987, the feasibility of "geo-referencing"—creating an electronic link between textual and graphic information systems to support LIS—was the latest thing to be studying. In 1988, the surveyor general's branch released a systems development update. If nothing else was clear, it was that another whole new raft of acronyms had been launched. Projects under way included reference map automation ("the spatial cornerstone of LIS," stated the report loftily), *automated official plans* (AOPs) whereby surveyors could transfer digital survey information directly to the *Crown land registry information system* (CLRIS); and updating digital reference maps, whereby the SGB could utilize information in the CLRIS to update both the MUL and the IGDS design files. There was GIS, or *geographic information system*, which was relatively self-explanatory; MAPS-BC, for *maps and air photo sales*, which was rather clever and certainly easy to remember; and the completely inexplicable MASCOT, a survey control data processing system. There was even an acronym for the management strategy itself: CLISP (*corporate land information strategic plan*). "There is now a need for the profession to be information consultants rather than producers," wrote Deputy Surveyor General Rob McQuaig with no trace of irony, "because information will be the new wealth of the future." Once one had got past all the acronyms.

Women, in the meantime, were continuing to make inroads into the profession. One of the keynote speakers at the 1993 annual meeting of the Corporation was Suzanne Jacques, president of the Canadian Council of Land Surveyors. The 1997 speaker was Valerie George, from Nova Scotia, the first female president of a provincial survey association in Canada. It remained an uphill battle for some in British Columbia, however, and those who were undertaking articles for one reason or another were not completing their final exams in British Columbia. Nigel Hemingway's wife, Susan Harding, graduated from the BCIT survey program just a few years after he did, articled with Stan Nickel, BCLS 665, in 1989, and went to work with Blair Smith, BCLS 569, in the federal government department managing Indian reserve surveys. "We met on a survey job in Ashcroft. Pretty romantic, eh?" chuckled Hemingway. Susan left the government and moved to the town of 100 Mile House to join her husband's business. "We've worked together ever since," said Hemingway in 2005. "She comes in the field, does some draughting, and takes care of the books, or in other words does just about everything." Devoting herself to her family, Harding decided to home school one of her children and did not complete her BCLS. "I had plans for being the first female BCLS," she recalled in 2005. "I was halfway there." Harding did not regret her choice, hard as it was to give up her dream. "I have a wonderful life. I get out surveying most of the interesting jobs, and I still love doing it."

Connie Rae Petersen, who articled in the province in 1981, did not complete her BCLS commission either. Petersen's reason was straightforward: she moved to Alberta for family reasons and simply completed her commission in that province instead, where she is now a project manager for Midwest Surveys Inc. in Medicine Hat. Petersen said in 2005 that she felt "fortunate," having worked with "some exceptional land surveyors who treated me as they would any articled student, male or female. I faced the same challenges as any man in this profession, as far as obtaining my commission as a land surveyor, and I never felt that my gender held me back in any way." Women in the surveying profession are naturally reluctant to admit to any hardship in this regard: they are, after all, part of a small and tightly knit group of colleagues who rely to a great extent on each other's integrity and support. Nonetheless, surveying is steeped in tradition. As in many other professions, the business of surveying did not often familiarize men with the concept of working alongside women as fellow professionals.

Written reports from annual general meetings at the beginning of the 1980s are revealing of pervasive but generally benign chauvinism. It must have been difficult for some of the young women involved to swallow, all the same. In 1981 outgoing president Kenneth Bridge announced with evident pleasure that the Corporation had awarded its annual bursary of three hundred dollars to Deborah Tressider, a second-year student at BCIT. By the following year Tressider was articled to Blair Smith, and another woman named Kathy Mather was articled to Robert Brown, BCLS 365. Tressider attended the annual BCLS meeting, perhaps the first woman to do so in that role. Ernie McMinn, ever one to try to raise a laugh, brought up a legitimate policy issue with a straight face: "I believe that some changes are indicated in the way we conduct our meetings and one of these is, would this lady surveyor come to the men's stag? Will her husband, should she have one or acquire one, attend the ladies' tour?" The response, called out from the floor, was no doubt intended to be funny, and it attracted a round of appreciative applause. But unless Tressider had nerves of steel it must have made her cringe, at least inwardly: "Ernie, Debbie has already been invited to the stag, provided she's prepared to come out of the cake!"

But things did change, and rapidly. The last "Ladies Link" page appeared in March 1985, written by Dorothy Fenning and thanking Anne Berting for her huge contribution to the page. Outgoing president Rich-ard Wright, BCLS 467, commented in his 1996 address: "Gentlemen, and I dwell on that word somewhat, as I hope soon we'll be able to say 'Ladies and Gentlemen,' for I truly believe that without the input from women professionals in our organization, we run the risk of being declared inbred and not taken too seriously." The same year, a student at the University of Calgary named Teresa Myrfield received the BCLS annual scholarship, telling Jon Magwood, BCLS 504, that she was going to become a British Columbia land surveyor. "She may be our first," remarked Magwood.

She was indeed the first. In 1999, Teresa Myrfield and Julia MacRory received their BCLS commissions, 773 and 775 respectively. Outgoing president O'Brian Blackall, BCLS 564, simply but eloquently noted: "It is my pleasure and my honour to address this assembly as 'Ladies and Gentlemen.' The gender mix of our Corporation has finally changed, and our profession will most certainly be the better for it." Myrfield's take on the situation was that chauvinism was the least of the barriers that women have faced. Surveying can require long periods of time away from home and family. It also demands considerable physical strength and mechanical ability. While these are characteristics that Myrfield emphasized are not attributable wholly to either men or women—"How many male or female graduates of the geomatics program do you think come out knowing how to wield an axe properly? Not many!"—neither has the education system, until very recently, directed young women at surveying as a career choice.

"Being a woman in a male-dominated occupation has certainly been an interesting experience," said Myrfield. "But there really isn't any black-and-white way to characterize it." She had been warned before graduation in the late 1990s that she might have trouble getting work. "And it was hard to get a job. It was. There's no getting around that." In part, there was little hiring going on in general during that period of economic volatility in the province. But Myrfield said she could also understand why she experienced reluctance from potential employers in the beginning. It was not unreasonable, in context: "If you had no experience of a capable female surveyor before, why would you think otherwise?" Just before receiving her degree, she did land a job, with Jim Christie, BCLS 692, at McElhanney Associates in Vancouver. Christie had a summer camp job he thought Myrfield could cope with and hired her straight away as a junior field assistant. "I was very lucky to work for Jim. He simply wanted the work done well, it didn't matter who you were." On the whole, said Myrfield, her main experience with male land surveyors has been a "genuine pleasure in seeing that [women] are here at last."

MacRory left for California soon after receiving her commission. In January 2005, exactly one hundred years after the incorporation of the land surveyors of British Columbia, Shauna Goertzen joined Myrfield and MacRory as BCLS 798. Goertzen, who was working with McElhanney in Fort St. John in 2005, made history in a different way, as the first BCLS who is a daughter of another BCLS, 557 John Henderson. By the end of the year, a fourth woman, Shannon Onderwater, had also joined the ranks as BCLS 802. Perceptions, assumptions, and viewpoints were changing across the board. It seemed unlikely that things would ever be the same again.

Teresa Myrfield, BCLS 773, was the first woman in the province to receive a commission, in 1999. TERESA MYRFIELD

West Coast Salal and Chilcotin Mosquitoes

Some on-site field calculations are still required, regardless of the availability of electronic equipment and GPS technology. Party chief Jason Playtor, "Helmet" area north of Fort Nelson, 2000. WAYNE BROWN

The *Encyclopedia of British Columbia,* first published in 2000, has no entry under "land surveying" or "Surveyors General of British Columbia." A handful of surveyors are mentioned by name—Pemberton, Moody, even Walter Colquhoun Grant—but the entries tend to focus on the other things for which those people are known, rather than on their roles as surveyors.

It is a surprising omission, given how integrally linked land surveying is, and has been, to so many aspects of life in British Columbia. "Without land surveyors, there would be no widespread prosperity," commented Surveyor General Richard "Rick" Hargraves in 2005. The "custodians of the cadastre," as former Corporation president Dave Bazett referred to surveyors, have laid out the province's townsites, private lands, and parks. Their names are liberally scattered over many of the province's geographic features. Surveyors drew the lines marking the boundaries between British Columbia and its neighbouring jurisdictions. Arthur Wheeler started the Alpine Club of Canada. Gerry Andrews helped bully British Columbia into becoming a world leader in the development of aerial survey photography.

British Columbia's land surveyors provide expert evidence in court cases. They certify lengths of swimming pools and race tracks for international competitions. A land surveyor measured exactly where the puck should drop on centre ice at the Vancouver Canucks' home stadium, BC Place. Hughes & Taylor certified the velodrome track, the rifle range, and the swimming pool built for the 1994 Commonwealth Games, held in Victoria. The swimming pool was initially found to be fifteen millimetres too short, related Brent Taylor, BCLS 642. A last-minute panicked rearrangement of moveable bulkheads saw it successfully certified at 11 p.m. the evening before the championships were scheduled to start. The technology developed to support surveying is now used in everything from sports events to archaeological digs to laser eye surgery. Yet in 2005, the perennial question came up at the 2005 annual general meeting: how can we make the public understand who we are, and what we do?

A lot of water has passed under the proverbial bridge since those early days when a Scottish settler named Walter Grant—with no surveying qualifications—was hired as a surveyor simply because he happened to

337

Equipment may have become more sophisticated over the years, but it hasn't become any less bulky. Temporary accommodation, on the other hand, has become relatively luxurious. This camp is north of Fort Nelson, 2003. WAYNE BROWN

Helicopters have proven to be one of the greatest boons to surveyors over the years. Even in the twenty-first century when road access is almost universal, in the northeastern region of the province it is still often necessary to drop four-wheelers into sites by helicopter. Here party chief Gary Manley is waiting for the helicopter to pick up the slack, in July 2000. WAYNE BROWN

Survey assistant Wes Dynna, next to a trig monument and rock cairn northwest of Fort Nelson, near the Liard River, summer 2003. WAYNE BROWN

Joseph Despard Pemberton was effectively the first official surveyor in Fort Victoria, in the new colony of Vancouver Island. His great-grandson, Philip "Pip" Holmes, still lived in Victoria in 2005, working as an aide-de-camp to the lieutenant-governor. Holmes is pictured with former BCLS president David Bazett in 2005, at Government House. B. JERRITT

be on Vancouver Island. The "practice of land surveying" was formally defined for the first time in the provincial Land Surveyors Act in 2004, following decades of disputes about non-surveyors undertaking cadastral work. In 2005, the Corporation kept a cautious eye on the professional engineers of the province to ensure that they made no further inroads on surveyors' traditional turf. Although many surveyors continued to hold engineering degrees, the increasing technical complexity and specialization of the work meant that fewer of them worked as both engineers and surveyors. New land surveyors in British Columbia no longer had to swear to maintain sobriety, although they might be expelled from membership for offences involving "moral turpitude." In January 2005, the one-hundredth anniversary of the Corporation of Land Surveyors of the Province of British Columbia, the membership formally approved a change of name to the Association of British Columbia Land Surveyors.

Would-be surveyors can now study not just for engineering qualifications but to receive university degrees in geomatics and surveying sciences from the British Columbia Institute of Technology in Vancouver. Technical diplomas remain an alternative. Students Spencer Hagen and Steve Fraser, studying at BCIT in 2005, said they spent a lot of time in front of the computer and only a fraction of it in the field. Fraser said he liked the outdoor aspect as much as the interesting technological progress: "I love playing with the toys; at the same time I love the fact that no matter what fancy toy you've got you can still get out in the bush, in the mountains, it all comes down to the same thing: you're doing the same thing they were doing a hundred years ago, measuring and mapping." But the days are now gone of seventeen-year-old boys starting to study mathematics and astronomy in tents and sitting preliminary exams after a summer working as axemen on survey crews in the mountains. Now advertisements in contemporary trade magazines emphasize the necessity of "good communication skills" and "client relationship accountabilities," rather than a strong arm—even though that is still required. Companies tout themselves as "equal opportunity employers," calling for "draughtspersons" and "instrumentpersons." A positive attitude and team spirit remain prerequisites of the job.

On May 26, 1982, the A-176 chronometer once used by Captain

The tools of the trade have changed over the decades, some a great deal and some less so. Here some latest versions of various surveyors' equipment are laid out at a 2005 trade show. B. JERRITT

Vancouver as he charted the waters of coastal British Columbia returned to the west coast from Britain, this time aboard a modern aircraft. It now resides in the Vancouver Maritime Museum. Five years later, a bronze bust of former Royal Engineer Henry Spencer Palmer was unveiled in his memory in Japan, Palmer's adopted homeland, and the place where he had died of typhoid in 1893. By then, the Royal Engineers had been in the business of military surveying for 240 years. Also in 1987, another unveiling ceremony was held in September to re-establish boundary cairn 1A marking the British Columbia–Alberta boundary at the site of the continental divide in Kicking Horse Pass. Arthur Wheeler's grandson John, a research geologist, attended the ceremony. With an eye to the country's southern neighbour, perhaps, Surveyor General of Canada Gerard Raymond commented in his address to the gathered crowd that "good fences make good neighbours."

International boundary disputes between Canada and the United States are not a thing of the past. In 2005, at least seven disputes remained unresolved on Canada's borders, including the maritime boundaries in

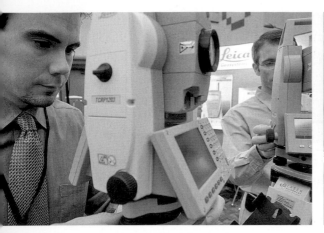

The invention of electronics changed the technology of measuring fundamentally. Today an EDM, or electronic distance measurer, weighs no less than the theodolites that preceeded it but costs significantly more—as much as $50,000 for some models. This equipment, including the antique models shown below, was on show for the benefit of browsing surveyors at a 2005 trade show in Victoria. B. JERRITT

Juan de Fuca Strait and the Dixon Entrance south of the Alaska Panhandle. The International Boundary Commission (IBC) has become a permanent institution, responsible for maintaining the border in an "effective state of demarcation." That means keeping clear of all obstructions a six-metre-wide strip of land that runs for nearly nine thousand kilometres across North America—although admittedly most of it does not cross forested land. Power saws and bulldozers have replaced axes, as has an extensive chemical spraying program to control weeds. The herbicides used, the IBC states, have been "approved by the environmental regulatory agencies of both countries."

In a 1998 article in the *Vancouver Sun* newspaper, journalist Larry Pynn poked holes in the international boundary along the 49th parallel. Modern technology, claimed Pynn, was revealing that the border did not match up: "The border is, in fact, a line of bronze monuments that weave back and forth across the true 49th parallel like a swaggering drunk." Pynn blamed it squarely on surveyors using "less-than-accurate" methods. Tallying up the discrepancies, he reckoned Canada had come out ahead by about seventy square kilometres. Rick Hargraves immediately lashed back in a stinging letter to the editor that condemned Pynn for failing to recognize "the enormous task that pioneer surveyors undertook....One can only marvel at [their] determination and workmanship." The most important consideration, said Hargraves, is the fact that the boundary is physically marked out on the ground. Whether it is an international boundary or a fence between neighbours, Hargraves reminded readers that the monument or post is always right, regardless of whether it was originally put in the correct place: "With the never-ending march of technology, there will be tremendous pressure to accept boundaries defined by coordinate values rather than monuments placed in the ground. Don't buy it. You may find your newly constructed garage is half on your neighbour's property."

Technology had indeed marched on, and continues to do so at a blistering pace. By 1997 the practice and ethics committee of the Corporation had to recommend an amendment to the bylaws to include the right to advertise not only fax telephone numbers, but Internet addresses—and indeed, to advertise on the World Wide Web. Another perennially thorny issue was relevant to the discussion: the need for solidarity in the profession. Ethical requirements of BCLS membership had always sought to prohibit showmanship or gaudy advertising intended to gain an advantage over one's peers. Bold print in the yellow pages was still discouraged. The Internet, with its search engines that could be manipulated to highlight certain companies over others through the use of banner advertising, threw a wrench in the works. All the same, the committee favoured the use of the Internet. Michael Taylor, BCLS 640, reported his views: "The media is often painting the Internet as being somewhat sinister, with all sorts of things on there that are inappropriate in today's society. And that's true. But I think that far outshadows the valuable nature that the Internet poses today. It's really an incredible communications tool." One year later, in 1998, Taylor proudly reported that it was the first anniversary of the launch of the Corporation's home page on the World Wide Web.

Electronics and the digital age had taken over virtually every aspect of surveying work by the turn of the twenty-first century. Lands, resources, and geographic information were almost universally accessible through computer programs with endearing names like DIM (*digital image management*); GNU Gama (a GPS coordination program), and Tantalis GATOR, a Crown land database. Land Information British Columbia, supported by its base mapping and geomatic services branch, "is one of several components of the government's overall e-BC strategy and will be delivered through the government portal," announced manager Brad Hlasny importantly in *The Link* in December 2003. GPS satellite technology that permitted accuracy of measurement to within ten centimetres was authorized in 2000 for use in geo-referencing legal surveys in the province.

The use of conventional survey ties continued to be an alternative. By the turn of the twenty-first century more than fifty thousand physical survey control monuments across the province had been logged in the government's database. But GPS was undeniably attractive, especially when it was linked into the government's electronic control system. "The service will provide users with the ability to survey and lay out points, accurate to a few centimetres, instantaneously," said Hlasny. "[It] will substantially improve the efficiency of engineers and surveyors as they will not need to transfer precise coordinate information over long distances from control monuments to perform their duties; the [system] will give them the accuracy they need to complete the required tasks in real time." Even users in other countries could access the data they needed over the Internet. The Canadian government also had numerous Internet databases available. Local government dived into the action. In 2005 the Greater Vancouver Regional District launched its real-time GPS service to the public. At the same time, the Integrated Cadastral Information Society, a partnership between local governments, utilities, and the provincial government, was endeavouring to pull together a consolidated database of land information held by each of those entities.

The name and location within government of the provincial surveyor general's branch has changed countless times since its inception in the mid-nineteenth century. Its latest incarnation in 2005 was the "Surveyor General Division" of a new independent authority called the "Land Title and Survey Authority of British Columbia." Rick Hargraves became the province's twentieth surveyor general on June 10, 2002. "I never thought in my wildest dreams I would be surveyor general one day," admitted Hargraves in 2005. "It's such a revered position in this profession and I just thought of myself as a guy who's done a lot of surveying. I have a great deal of respect for all the surveyors general who have gone before me. Each and every one of those gentlemen is a very tough act to follow. But now I'm here I'm comfortable with it." Surveyors, Hargraves believes, must remain steadfast in being ethical and non-judgmental in maintaining the cadastre: "We're really working for the land, that's the thing."

Under Hargraves's tenure, the "full digital future" was launched for land surveyors in British Columbia. By 2005, the phase-out of hard-copy Mylar or paper plan copies in favour of the submission of digitally signed electronically filed plans was under way. The goal of the "e-survey" system, said BCLS Association president Jeff Beddoes in 2005, is simple: to avoid the risks of errors that used to arise out of multiple transcriptions from digital data to hard copy and back again before a final version was available on computer. The digital file is entirely prepared and submitted electronically, without any intermediate "paper step." The version in the ether has become the original plan; any printout of it is merely a copy. Spilling coffee on plans is no longer any cause for concern, although spilling it on computer keyboards remains a problem. Beddoes, who received BCLS commission 660 in 1985, can perhaps be characterized as a child of the digital era. "Soon there will be a paperless and efficient submission of statutory survey plans," he said happily in 2004. Some of his colleagues have struggled with the concept, however. Hargraves noted: "After about 140 years of preparing plans on various mediums, such as linen and Mylar, the switch to electronic PDF plans as the official record will be hard for many folks to adjust to."

Electronic distance measuring had also taken a massive leap forward during the 1980s, with the introduction onto the mass market of the "total station." A total station not only measures angles and distances but it will also calculate coordinates, accept text, and is capable of remote control. In 1990, a fully robotic total station was introduced. By 1999, total stations could transmit the data directly back to the office—wherever it was. "They even come now in handy backpacks custom-designed for carrying them," said Brett Findlater of Spatial Technologies Inc. When a total station fails to work, however, filament from a spider web will no longer suffice to fix it. "Electronics are more complicated than the old optical technology," admitted Findlater. "When something does go wrong, it's harder to solve."

Shauna Goertzen used to chain for her father, John Henderson, when she was a teenager. "So I can use the older equipment if I need to. And you might need to, sometimes. You certainly need to know when your [electronic] equipment isn't working. You need to be able to recognize when what's on the screen doesn't make sense." Working out of Fort St. John in northeastern British Columbia, Goertzen occasionally has had to revert to the old-fashioned method. "You have to know what to do when the battery runs out on you in the field. In Vancouver you can just run back to the office for another one, but in Fort St. John you might have driven three hours to get to the site. You don't want to have to come back the next day."

Total stations remain items of wonder and excitement all the same, especially for those who once laboured under older, slower technology.

"These are marvellous toys!" enthused Neil Bennett, BCLS 527, in 2005 in the exhibitors' hall at the BCLS annual general meeting. Bennett had received his commission thirty years previously, in 1975. "We just plunked down $80,000 on GPS equipment!" he exclaimed. Donald Highe, BCLS 461, who received his commission in 1969, overheard Bennett's comment. "I started off with $200 for equipment and $140 for supplies!" he growled, wandering off toward an exhibitor's stand hawking what almost seemed to be relics of the past, even though they remain in use: field notebooks, coloured flagging tape, and plumb bobs.

The little company named Okanagan Helicopters Ltd. that was started in Penticton by three friends in 1947 had become the largest commercial helicopter operator in the world by 1954. By 2005, absorbed into Richmond, British Columbia–based helicopter repair and mainte- nance company ACROHelipro Global Services, it still formed part of the third-largest operation of its kind globally. Megalithic British Colum- bia surveying companies Underhills and McElhanney had grown yet again. Now anchored by Underhill Geomatics Ltd., the Underhill group in 2005 provided its services not only in the province where it had its humble origins in 1912, but worldwide. In Canada, a significant portion of its work has consisted of aboriginal land claims surveys, including the delineation of the boundaries of the new territory of Nunavut. The McEl- hanney group, of the same vintage and reach, has provided its expertise in support of such projects as surveying and mapping the Trans-Canada Trail in the late 1990s and helping war-torn Cambodians set up a secure land title system in 2003. Together with Victoria company Geospatial International Inc., McElhanney sent a surveying team to Cambodia to initiate the project and train a group of Cambodian men and women to take over the process at the end. It was a remarkable project: the chal- lenges included the unique requirement to develop a safe system to survey in landmine-infested terrain. The team's efforts were recognized with the Lieutenant-Governor's Award for best project at the annual awards gala, ironically, of British Columbia's professional engineers—a poetic recognition, perhaps, going beyond the project itself to the value now attributed to surveying work by consulting engineers.

Dominion land surveyors had become known as Canada lands

surveyors in 1979. In 1985, a new Association of Canada Lands Surveyors (ACLS) was formed to promote the interests of its members. Many
British Columbia land surveyors are also qualified as CLS. By 2005, that
just made both practical and economic sense, and the tension between
home-grown surveyors and the "intruders" from Ottawa had been greatly
mitigated. CLS members were now required to "study native government issues as a prerequisite for qualification." The ACLS also awarded a
number of scholarships to aboriginal students wishing to pursue geomatics as a career, in coordination with Indian and Northern Affairs Canada,
which provided similar financial support. Natural Resources Canada
had created a "Geomatics for Aboriginal Property Rights Infrastructure"
program, to support treaty negotiations in British Columbia and northern Canada. Nevertheless, 120-year-old scribbled field notes remained
compelling evidence of the history of the land issues under negotiation.

In 1951, room had run out on the presidential spats to write any more
names on them, and a new pair had to be purchased for the incoming
president. By 1996, room was running out on the second pair. But trying
to purchase new spats in 1996 was almost an impossible task. Donald
Whyte stepped into the breach, donating not just one but two pairs,
which he found in his mother-in-law's possession and which had originally been purchased in Whitehorse, Yukon Territory, in 1926. "At the
rate of use of one pair every thirty or so years, these spats will ensure
our tradition lasts until the year 2060, more or less," Whyte proclaimed.
When the spats will be fitted on female feet for the first time remains to
be seen.

Bute Inlet, in many places, looks not unlike it did when surveyor
George Hargreaves described its wonders in 1875, gazing at "peak after
peak until they were lost in the distance, those on the east side like
burnished gold from the setting sun, those on the west side in dark
shade but all covered in deep snow." Other things haven't changed: in
2005, Russell Shortt, BCLS 454, was still bringing boxes of Okanagan
apples to the annual general meeting, as he had done for the past twenty
years. Members still complained that there weren't enough surveyors for
all the work coming up: transmission rights-of-way, new recreational
developments, increasing urbanization, the Olympic Games facilities to

Dalby Brooks Morkill, BCLS 57, pictured, started the tradition in 1928 of passing on a pair of spats to each incoming president. The Association of British Columbia Land Surveyors is now onto its third pair of spats, because the previous ones were filled up with presidential signatures. OFFICE OF THE SURVEYOR GENERAL

Here soon-to-be past president Dave Bazett, BCLS 576, places the spats on the feet of new 2005–2006 president Jeff Beddoes, BCLS 660. B. JERRITT

be completed in Vancouver and Whistler by February 2010. Not enough young blood coming up the ranks, said some; others said there were more than enough new recruits: just wait for the next economic recession to hit. Regardless of such gloomy speculation, Surveyor General Rick Hargraves believed emphatically that in British Columbia "the future is bright for land surveyors."

Chapman Land Surveying Ltd. in West Vancouver celebrated its ninetieth anniversary as a family firm on May 23, 1996. The date was also the fiftieth anniversary of the day Ray Edward Chapman, BCLS 270, received his commission. His son William "Bill" Chapman, also a BCLS, told his colleagues: "As most of you know, Dad's eighty-seven now. This is his fiftieth year of active practice. He was designing a $120 million subdivision last year for us, so I think that qualifies as active practice." In 2005, Ray Chapman attended the BCLS annual meeting in Victoria. The frail but indomitable ninety-six-year-old still went into the office almost every day.

Another doughty surveyor received the Order of British Columbia on June 21, 1990. Gerry Andrews, then in his eighties, was pictured in *The Link* wearing "his ice cream suit" and a broad smile while standing next to fellow OBC recipient, rock musician Bryan Adams. In 2005, along with Doug Roy and others, Andrews was given a BCLS Association Lifetime Achievement Award. "That's very good," remarked the centenarian amiably from his residence in Victoria. On December 5, 2005, Gerry Andrews died in Victoria. He was one week short of turning 102.

Exactly fifty years earlier, Andrews had stood up in front of his fellow surveyors and remarked: "There will always be plenty to do." On January 19, 2005, his former colleagues and past presidents of the Association raised a glass in toast to Andrews and to that philosophy in the Captain J. Herrick McGregor lounge at the Union Club of British Columbia in Victoria. Named in tribute to the former land surveyor who had been killed in the First World War, the room displays sombre portraits of other august members of the provincial surveying fraternity. On that day they looked down on a roomful of men aged from forty-something to ninety-six as they speculated about the future and reminisced about their past and friends and colleagues long gone. Energy leapt from table

Ray Chapman's company Chapman Land Surveying Ltd., in North
Vancouver, is one of the oldest in the province—and at ninety-six
years of age in 2005, Ray, BCLS 270, still went into the office on a
regular basis. He is pictured here with his partner and son, William
"Bill" Chapman, BCLS 526. B. JERRITT

to table as lively conversations erupted, charged with humour, pride,
and wistfulness. All in business suits, with, for the most part, grey heads
alongside silver, and silent gazers sitting alongside animated chatterers.
A camaraderie and ease of presence with each other in the space they
occupied was patent. Blunt, gnarled hands, scarred and worn, gripped
soup spoons and beer glasses. The memory of those gone before rever-
berated in the room. The strength of the foundation these men had built
for those following them into the future was almost tangible.

"It's been a hard life," mused 1985 president Patrick Joseph "Paddy"
Brennan, BCLS 396. "But it's the life I chose. I'm not a bit unhappy about it."

I am proud to have been a land surveyor. It is a good profession and I have thoroughly enjoyed my career, including working with pack horses, away from home three months at a time, no helicopters and sitting around the campfire trying to outdo each other with survey stories.

We have done a good job. Be proud of yourselves. Be proud of our early surveyors, they have set a good path for us to follow. Be proud of what you have done, and also feel pride in where surveying is going now. Our new surveyors are advancing with the latest technology and are proving that B.C. land surveyors can not only work here in B.C., but all over the world.

You are a unique group of professionals, good on you. Keep up the good work for the next 100 years. I am thinking of you, until we meet again.

John Matthews, BCLS 356, January 2005: letter to Association of British Columbia Land Surveyors.

Technology may have improved over the decades, but outdoor working conditions remain unchanged. In 1963 Ron Scobbie (who would receive his BCLS commission 447 in 1966) was working as instrument man at the new microwave site in the Moyie area. GORD THOMSON

Surveyors and their crews would find all kinds of oddities in the bush. Here, in 1953 near Atlin, an unusual sign was found in the middle of the bush. STIRLING KNUDSEN

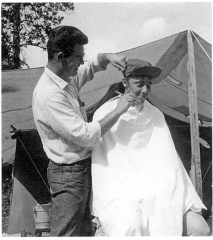

A typical bush camp outhouse, constructed from poles cut from the bush and lined with sheeting. "The outhouse was my specialty," reminisced Dick Wright of camp days in the north during the 1960s. RICHARD WRIGHT

Northeast of Stewart, at a survey camp at Surprises Creek, circa 1967. Dick Wright is the barber. "The hat fit better than a bowl," he said in 2005. RICHARD WRIGHT

NOTES ON THE CHAPTER HEADINGS

Each chapter heading in this book is a salute to the surveying profession. The words are taken largely from writings of various land surveyors and from related reports and documents. Notes on their sources are set out below.

Acknowledgements: From the mouths of many land surveyors, and some non-surveyors. The latter ask: "What are those guys doing on the side of the road, anyway?" The former groan, clap hands to foreheads, and exclaim: "Why don't people understand we are more than just **the guys on the side of the road!**"

Introduction: In an interview in January 2005, Surveyor General Rick Hargraves spoke of the passion of surveyors for their work: their ethics, their diligence in being non-judgmental, and the strength of their adherence to the integrity of the cadastre: "We're **working for the land**: that's the thing."

Chapter 1: In 1972, Gerald Smedley Andrews published a commemorative tribute to Sir Joseph William Trutch. In his introduction, Andrews confesses a predilection for dates, calling them "indispensable calibrations of the time scale." Describing them in surveying terms, Andrews states: "Dates are the fixed points in **the traverse of history** to which its colour and pattern must be coordinated."

Chapter 2: At the southwest corner of Hamilton and Hastings streets in Vancouver, a bronze plaque commemorates Lauchlan Alexander Hamilton: "Here stood HAMILTON, First Land Commissioner, Canadian Pacific Railway, 1885. In the silent solitude of the primeval forest, he drove a wooden stake in the earth and commenced **to measure an empty land** into the streets of VANCOUVER."

Chapter 3: Writer John D. Spittle wrote a technical but interesting article in the June 1980 issue of *The Link* magazine regarding the precision of Royal Engineers who were determining longitude from their observatory in New Westminster in 1859. Longitude determinations were made using sidereal (star-based) observations. "However," notes Spittle, "since the transit of the moon's centre cannot be observed directly, observations are made on **the moon's bright limb**."

Chapter 4: In his annual report for 1930, Surveyor General F.C. Green noted: "Owing to its high relief, British Columbia requires **more than the average ground control** before the full value for mapping can be got from aerial photographs."

Chapter 5: New Westminster mayor Beth Woods was the invited speaker at the 1964 annual general meeting of the Corporation of British Columbia Land Surveyors. Recalling the past, she said: "Today, with modern speedboats, the automobile, helicopters and with sea and ski planes, your ability to get to your jobs and do them, certainly is much less a hardship than it was in the days gone by...My father... knew different kinds of hardship—there wasn't always running water nor was there always electric light. That was **no push-button era** nor were things comfortable and warm. There was hardship and deprivation and people did without to get ahead and build this country of ours..."

Chapter 6: When Henry Spencer Palmer explored North Bentinck Arm in 1862, he was very admiring of many of the aboriginal people he met, if he expressed his admiration in distressingly colonial terms: "The villages...remain in their purely savage originality, unmodified by **the touch of civilization**."

Chapter 7: In his history of the Nisga'a land claims, *Without Surrender, Without Consent*, Daniel Raunet quotes Chief Frank Calder talking about the arrival of the first survey party in his people's territory: "This particular day, a beautiful day, somebody reported to the chiefs that there's five people across, over Gitlakdamix. And they're looking through **some strange instrument**."

Chapter 8: In 1909, Walter Moberly took the time to write—or perhaps rewrite—his own version of events regarding the history of the CPR in British Columbia. In *Early History of the CPR*, Moberly recalls: "The rough experiences I had...gone through when exploring in British Columbia's '**Sea of Mountains**,' led me to think that it was possible that Captain Palliser might be mistaken in reporting so unfavourably regarding a feasible line for a railway..."

Chapter 9: A handout brochure of the Corporation of British Columbia Land Surveyors in 1981 noted: "The term legal surveying covers...a wide range of individual areas in which the BCLS is considered a prime source of information. Establishment of original property corners, redefinition of existing property corners, site planning, descriptions for deeds and...property law are all areas in which the British Columbia Land Surveyor must obtain and maintain **an exacting level** of knowledge."

Chapter 10: Alfred Slocomb, BCLS 267, headed the Topographic Division of the provincial government's Surveys and Mapping Branch for many years. In his 1955 report to the Deputy Minister of Lands, Slocomb wrote: "When it was realized that most of [northeastern British Columbia] was relatively flat, and, to a large extent, covered by muskeg with hardly a prominent feature in the whole area, [topographical surveying there] was labelled impossible...but like most things apparently impossible, there is usually an answer if you have **the wit to see and the will to do.** Tower-building was the magic solution, the helicopter was the magic carpet, and a group of agile, fearless young men, most certainly akin to squirrels, were the magicians." This was the sentiment and attitude that predominated in British Columbia's settlement history—never more so, perhaps, than during the optimistic 1890s.

Chapter 11: In the 1913 report of the Survey Branch of the Department of Lands to Minister of Lands William R. Ross, W.S. Drewry waxes lyrical about the beauty of the Cariboo country: "To the west is the great basin of Bridge Creek, some 600 square miles in area, containing innumerable lakes set like inlays of polished silver in broad valleys rimmed by fir-crowned hills; **a great silent country waiting** for the advent of road and rail to bear the population whose footsteps are even now approaching it."

Chapter 12: In his report to the Corporation's annual general meeting of 1918, President Townsend stated: "It is doubtful that there will ever be the same demand for our services as there was five or six years ago, still I can see no reason why our profession should not share in the bright future which lies before this Province, and which will most assuredly come when **this present titanic struggle** is ended."

Chapter 13: In September 1987, boundary cairn A1 on the British Columbia–Alberta border at Kicking Horse Pass was re-established and an interpretative sign unveiled. This cairn is located at the point where the Kicking Horse divides into two streams, one flowing west to the Pacific Ocean and the other east to the Atlantic. The Surveyor General of Canada Lands, Gerald Raymond, noted in his speech (reprinted in the January 1988 issue of *The Link*): "It is said that **good fences make good neighbours**. Likewise, good neighbours maintain their common fences. This also applies to provincial and park boundaries...The survey of this boundary is a credit to the skill, professionalism, and dedication of the original Boundary Commissioners and their staff."

Chapter 14: In the president's address given at the 1924 annual general meeting of the Corporation, Mr. S.S. McDiarmid reflected at length on the distressing economic situation in the province. "Many will find it difficult," he noted sombrely, "**to hold on for the brighter day**, and it is incumbent upon all of us to remain loyal to the other members of the profession."

Chapter 15: The 1943 president's address by A.J. Campbell was sombre, reflecting on the impact of the war: "The why of it, or the need of it, is not apparent to earthbound peoples, but surely it can be hoped that we will come out of it **as steel from the furnace**, purified and strong, and imbued with the idea of making, not only our own beloved country, but the whole world, a better place in which to live."

Chapter 16: Gord Thomson, who articled from 1959 to 1963 and became BCLS 425 in 1963, remarked in 2005: "Becoming a 'Surveyor' was an accident, but **a most fortunate twist** or turn in my life."

Chapter 17: Milton Denny, discussing surveying in the 1950s and prior decades: "If the rodmen were the arms and legs of the crew, **the instrument was the heart**" (from "The Golden Age of Surveying," *Georgia Land Surveyor*, May/June 2001).

Chapter 18: In *Without Surrender, Without Consent*, Daniel Raunet quotes Chief Skadeen of the Gitlakdamix, speaking of the dismay of his people at the notion that their land could be arbitrarily divided by white men who had not signed any treaty with them: "**God gave us a good survey** when he gave us the land, and we do not want [Reserves Allotment Commissioner] Mr. O'Reilly to survey the land unless the government make a treaty with us..."

Chapter 19: "The only things that haven't changed in a hundred years," said Dave Bazett in the Winter 2004 issue of *The Scrivener* magazine, "are **West Coast salal and Chilcotin mosquitoes**."

BIBLIOGRAPHY

The technical and academic literature on surveying is abundant, but this does not pretend to be a technical or academic book. Accordingly, the sources listed here are intended to provide further material of general historical interest as a background to British Columbia's surveying and settlement history.

Remarkable efforts have been made by many surveyors, doubling as historians, to document the lives and achievements of their profession. In recent years they include among their ranks such dedicated individuals as Messrs. P.J. Brennan, H.B. Cotton, and R. Allen, whose written efforts are frequently recorded in *The Link* magazine. Moreover, British Columbian surveyors have been accomplished wordsmiths from the earliest days of the province. The many government reports and papers available in archival collections contain a wealth of comprehensive and entertaining information that has proved invaluable in my research for this book. Last but not least, the Internet is simply a part of literary life in the twenty-first century: websites of interest are also listed for further reference.

Akrigg, G.P.V., and Helen B. Akrigg. *1001 British Columbia Place Names* (3rd ed.). Vancouver: Discovery Press, 1975.

————. *British Columbia Chronicle 1778–1846: Adventurers by Sea and Land.* Vancouver: Discovery Press, 1975.

————. *British Columbia Chronicle 1847–1871: Gold and Colonists.* Vancouver: Discovery Press, 1977.

Andrews, G.S. *Sir Joseph William Trutch.* Victoria: British Columbia Lands Service, 1972.

————. *The Land Surveying Profession in British Columbia.* Victoria: Corporation of the Land Surveyors of British Columbia, 1955.

Barman, Jean. *The West Beyond the West: A History of British Columbia.* Toronto: University of Toronto Press, 1991.

Berton, Pierre. *The National Dream.* Toronto: McClelland & Stewart, 1970.

Birrell, Andrew. "Survey Photography in British Columbia." *B.C. Studies*, no. 52, winter 1981–1982.

Bowering, George. *Bowering's BC: A Swashbuckling History.* Toronto: Viking, 1996.

Brody, Hugh. *Maps and Dreams: Indians and the British Columbia Frontier.* Vancouver/Toronto: Douglas & McIntyre, 1981.

Bryson, Bill. *A Short History of Nearly Everything.* Toronto: Anchor Canada, 2004.

Cail, Robert E. *Land, Man, and the Law: the Disposal of Crown Lands in British Columbia, 1871–1913.* Vancouver: UBC Press, 1974.

Christensen, Bev. *Too Good to be True: Alcan's Kemano Completion Project.* Vancouver: Talonbooks, 1995.

Coates, Ken. *North to Alaska!* Toronto: McClelland & Stewart, 1992.

Cole, Douglas, and Bradley Lockner, eds. *To the Charlottes: George Dawson's 1878 Survey of the Queen Charlotte Islands.* Vancouver: UBC Press, 1993.

Corley-Smith, Peter, and David N. Parker. *Helicopters: The British Columbia Story.* Victoria: Sono Nis Press, 1998.

Cotton, Barry. *First in the Field.* Saltspring Island: Cranberry Eclectics, 1995.

Coull, Cheryl. *A Traveller's Guide to Aboriginal BC.* Vancouver: Whitecap Books, 1996.

Fisher, Robin. *Contact & Conflict: Indian–European Relations in British Columbia, 1774–1890.* Vancouver: UBC Press, 1990.

Forward, Charles, ed. *British Columbia: Its Resources and People.* Victoria: University of Victoria, Western Geographical Series, vol. 22, 1987.

Francis, Daniel, ed. *Encyclopedia of British Columbia.* Madeira Park, BC: Harbour Publishing, 2000.

Gough, Barry. "The Character of the British Columbia Frontier." *B.C. Studies*, no. 32, 1976–1977.

Grant, Rev. George. *Ocean to Ocean: Sandford Fleming's Expedition Through Canada in 1872.* Rutland, VT: Charles E. Tuttle, 1967. (Full text of original 1873 edition available online at www.canadiana.org/ECO)

Green, Lewis. *The Boundary Hunters: Surveying the 141st Meridian and the Alaska Panhandle.* Vancouver: UBC Press, 1982.

Hamilton, A.C., and L.M. Sebert. *Significant Dates in Surveying Mapping and Charting.* Ottawa: Geomatica Press, 1996.

Harris, Cole. *Making Native Space.* Vancouver: UBC Press, 2002.

Hill, Beth. *Sappers: The Royal Engineers in British Columbia.* Ganges, BC: Horsdal & Schubart, 1987.

Johnston, Hugh J.M., ed. *The Pacific Province: A History of British Columbia.* Vancouver: Douglas & McIntyre, 1996.

Kissam, Philip. *Surveying Practice: The Fundamentals of Surveying.* Toronto: McGraw-Hill, 1971.

Koroscil, Paul. *British Columbia: A Settlement History.* Vancouver: Simon Fraser University, 2000.

Leonard, Frank. *A Thousand Blunders: The Grand Trunk Pacific Railway and Northern British Columbia.* Vancouver: UBC Press, 1996.

Lillard, Charles. *Seven Shillings a Year: The History of Vancouver Island.* Ganges, BC: Horsdal & Schubart, 1986.

Linklater, Andro. *Measuring America: How the United States Was Shaped by the Greatest Land Sale in History.* London: HarperCollins, 2002.

MacGregor, James G. *Vision of an Ordered Land: The Story of the Dominion Land Surveyors.* Saskatoon: Western Producer Prairie Books, 1981.

Mackie, Richard. *The Wilderness Profound.* Victoria: Sono Nis Press, 1995.

Moberly, W. *The Rocks and Rivers of British Columbia.* London: H. Blacklock & Co., 1885 (available at British Columbia Archives).

Neering, Rosemary. *Continental Dash: The Russian-American Telegraph.* Ganges, BC: Horsdal & Schubert, 1989.

North, M., et al. "A Brief Guide to the Use of Land Surveyors' Notebooks in the Lower Fraser Valley, B.C., 1859–1890." *B.C. Studies*, no. 34, summer 1977.

Ormsby, Margaret A. *British Columbia: A History.* Toronto: Macmillan Canada, 1959.

Peters, Helen Bergen. *Painting during the Colonial Period in B.C., 1845–1871.* Reproduced courtesy of the Maltwood Museum, Victoria.

Raunet, Daniel. *Without Surrender, Without Consent: A History of the Nishga Land Claims.* Vancouver/Toronto: Douglas & McIntyre, 1984.

Reksten, Terry. *"More English than the English": A Very Social History of Victoria.* Victoria: Orca, 1986.

Robin, Martin. *The Rush for Spoils: The Company Province, 1871–1933.* Toronto: McClelland & Stewart, 1972.

Robinson, Noel. *Blazing the Trail Through the Rockies: The Story of Walter Moberly and His Share in the Making of Vancouver.* Vancouver: 1914 (available at British Columbia Archives).

Rylatt, R.M. *Surveying the Canadian Pacific Railway.* Salt Lake City: University of Utah Press, 1991.

Sanford, Barrie. *McCulloch's Wonder: The Story of the Kettle Valley Railway.* Vancouver/Toronto: Whitecap Books, 1978.

Schwartz, Joan M. "The Past in Focus: Photography and British Columbia, 1858–1914." *B.C. Studies*, no. 52, winter 1981–1982.

Shaw, C. *Tales of a Pioneer Surveyor.* Don Mills, ON: Longman Canada, 1970.

Sherwood, Jay. *Surveying Northern British Columbia.* Prince George: Caitlin Press, 2004.

Sleigh, Daphne. *Walter Moberly and the Northwest Passage by Rail.* Surrey, BC: Hancock House, 2003.

Taylor, Geoffrey W. *The Railway Contractors.* Victoria: Morriss, 1988.

Taylor, W.A. *Crown Lands: A History of Survey Systems.* Victoria: Surveys and Land Records Branch, Ministry of Lands, Parks and Housing, 1981.

Thomson, Don. *Men and Meridians,* Volume 1. Ottawa: Queen's Printer, 1966.

————. *Men and Meridians,* Volume 2. Ottawa: Queen's Printer, 1967.

————. *Men and Meridians,* Volume 3. Ottawa: Queen's Printer, 1969.

Turner, Robert D. *West of the Great Divide: The Canadian Pacific Railway in British Columbia, 1880–1986.* Victoria: Sono Nis Press, 1987.

Twichell, Heath. *Northwest Epic: The Building of the Alaska Highway.* New York: St. Martin's Press, 1992.

Vogel, Aynsley, and Dana Wyse. *Vancouver: A History in Photographs.* Banff: Altitude, 1993.

Walbran, Captain John T. *British Columbia Coast Names: Their Origin and History.* Vancouver/Toronto: Douglas & McIntyre, 1971.

Wheeler, Arthur. *The Selkirk Range.* Ottawa: Government Printing Bureau, 1905.

Whittaker, John, ed. *Early Land Surveyors of British Columbia.* Victoria: Corporation of Land Surveyors of the Province of British Columbia, 1990.

Woodcock, George. *British Columbia: A History of the Province.* Vancouver: Douglas & McIntyre, 1990.

Zaslow, Morris. *Reading the Rocks.* Toronto: Macmillan Canada, 1995.

Zuehlke, Mark. *Scoundrels, Dreamers & Second Sons: British Remittance Men in the Canadian West.* Toronto: Dundurn, 2001.

GENERAL SOURCES

Annual reports of the Corporation of Land Surveyors of the Province of British
    Columbia, 1905–2005
Annual reports to ministers by government officials
BC Historical News (Journal of the British Columbia Historical Federation)
British Columbia Provincial Archives, Victoria (government correspondence, field
    notes, and private manuscripts and collections)
BC Studies Magazine (University of British Columbia)
The Beaver (journal of Canada's National History Society)
The Canadian Surveyor, CISM journal ACSGC 1988–92, and *Geomatica:* journal of the
    Canadian Institute of Geomatics, 1993–present
The Link (journal of the Association of British Columbia Land Surveyors)
National Archives of Canada

USEFUL AND INTERESTING WEBSITES

Association of British Columbia Land Surveyors: www.bclandsurveyors.bc.ca
Association of Canada Lands Surveyors: www.acls-aatc.ca
B.C. Archives: www.bcarchives.gov.bc.ca (includes manuscripts, texts, photographs,
    maps, and guides to land records, pre-emption and homestead claims, and Crown
    grants)
B.C. Geographic Names Information System: http://srmwww.gov.bc.ca/bcnames
B.C. Land Title & Survey and Surveyor General of British Columbia: www.ltsa.ca
British Columbia Government mapping sites: http://maps.gov.bc.ca
Canadian Council on Geomatics: www.geobase.ca
Canadian Institute of Geomatics: www.cig-acsg.ca
Canadian Spatial Reference System, Natural Resources Canada: www.geod.nrcan.gc.ca
Collins Overland Telegraph: www.telegraphtrail.org
CPR Archives: www.cprheritage.com
Fort Steele: www.fortsteele.bc.ca
Geological Survey of Canada: http://gsc.nrcan.gc.ca
Integrated Cadastral Information Society: www.icisociety.ca
International Boundary Commission: www.internationalboundarycommission.org
Royal Engineers: www.royalengineers.ca
Union of British Columbia Indian Chiefs manual of Researching the Indian Land
    Question in B.C.: www.ubcic.bc.ca

INDEX

References to illustrations are in *italic type*.

RESEARCHER HEATHER WEST

Certain things are meant to be. When the opportunity arose to do this book, I knew I wanted the help of an experienced and knowledgeable researcher. And really, at the time, there was only one person that would do. I called Heather West immediately. Heather had worked in the Legal Surveys Division of the government of British Columbia from 1970 until 1998. "We were always facing change. They were challenging times, but exciting! The opportunity also provided me with a very unusual skill set; one that continues to be sought out even though I left the public service."

Heather is quite right in that last statement. Late as it was on a Sunday evening in the fall of 2004 when I called her with the scintillating invitation to undertake the research for this book for a paltry sum, knowing I was competing against many other contenders for her valuable time and knowledge, Heather responded with overwhelming enthusiasm. That enthusiasm was maintained throughout the process. Her diligence, willingness to pursue obscure but fascinating odds and ends, and look over the manuscript to check the details, has been invaluable.